A Modern Eve

The Typist

in T.S. Eliot's

The Waste Land

W. K. Brannigan

ālep press

ISBN 978-1-738-5265-0-5

Published by

 ālep press

aleppress.com

Cover typography: Caslon Old Face
(typeface of 1ˢᵗ edition of *The Waste Land*)

Book typography: Garamond Premier Pro

Back Cover: Detail from *Sappho and Alcaeus* by Lawrence Alma-Tadema (1881)

With thanks to The Walters Art Museum, Baltimore,
and the Friends of City Churches.

Photos and plates: Thanks to John Salmon,
the Church of St. Magnus the Martyr, London Metropolitan Archive.

For D, mighty mother.

and for Anna, Bona, Dawn and Deborah

Kritan women once danced supplely
around a beautiful altar with light feet
crushing the soft flowers of grass.

(Sappho *Dancers at a Kritan Altar*)

Anyone who is acquainted with these works will immediately recognise in the poem certain references to vegetation ceremonies.

(T.S. Eliot *Notes on the Waste Land*)

Animism ... ascends, deeply modified in its transmission, but from first to last preserving an unbroken continuity, into the midst of high modern culture ... Animism is, in fact, the groundwork of the Philosophy of Religion ... for where the root is, the branches will generally be produced. (Edward Tylor *Primitive Culture*)

I found, not only the final link that completed the chain of evolution from Pagan Mystery to Christian Ceremonial ... The problem involved was not one of Folk-lore, not even one of Literature, but of comparative religion in its widest sense ... I here set forth elements that may prove of real value in the study of the evolution of religious belief.

(Jessie L. Weston *From Ritual to Romance*)

I should like to ask these genuine musicians whether they can imagine a man who could perceive the third act of Tristan and Isolde ... without expiring at the convulsive spreading of their souls' wings? ... How can he bear, in the wretched bell jar of human individuality, to hear the innumerable cries of delight and woe from a 'wide space of the world's night', without inexorably fleeing to his primal home amidst the piping of the pastoral metaphysical dance?

(Friedrich Nietzsche *The Birth of Tragedy*)

It is at the outset one and the same impulse that sends a man to church and to the theatre.

(Jane Harrison *Ancient Art and Ritual*)

In using the myth, in manipulating a continuous parallel between contemporaneity and antiquity, Mr. Joyce is pursuing a method which others must pursue after him. They will not be imitators, any more than the scientist who uses the discoveries of an Einstein in pursuing his own, independent, further investigations. It is simply a way of controlling, of ordering, of giving a shape and a significance to the immense panorama of futility and anarchy which is contemporary history. It is a method already adumbrated by Mr. Yeats, and of the need for which I believe Mr. Yeats to have been the first contemporary to be conscious. It is a method for which the horoscope is auspicious. Psychology (such as it is, and whether our reaction to it be comic or serious), ethnology, and *The Golden Bough* have concurred to make possible what was impossible even a few years ago. Instead of narrative method, we may now use the mythical method. It is, I seriously believe, a step toward making the modern world possible for art, toward that order and form which Mr. Aldington so earnestly desires. And only those who have won their own discipline in secret and without aid, in a world which offers very little assistance to that end, can be of any use in furthering this advance.

(T.S. Eliot *Ulysses, Order, and Myth*, 1923)

Spring is new, spring is now full of song, in spring the world
    was born.
In spring lovers come together, in spring the birds wed,
And the wood lets down her hair under nuptial downpours
(The *Vigil of Venus*, circa 250-450 CE. *Notes on the Waste Land* 428)

Contents

Part II
The Classical Order of the Mythic Layer

Preface

This is the story of the imagery and history T.S. Eliot found in the Church of St. Magnus the Martyr in London, and how he used it to extraordinary effect in his masterpiece, *The Waste Land*. The church becomes a portal into the unifying mythic layer in the poem.

This new reading of the poem shows it to be of the same modernist ambition and cohesive classical discipline as James Joyce's *Ulysses*. Eliot so ardently admired Joyce's contemporary prose work at the time that he wrote of its mythic method with the commitment of a literary manifesto. Because of that complexity, this book is the first of a series. It looks at the character of the typist and her relationship to the biblical Eve, and to Sappho and her evening star. Sappho, representing the classical world, plays an important role in the mythic layer, which runs from first to last, from April to Shantih, unifying the poem. Since Eliot tells us that all the women of the poem are one woman, she is Eliot's forlorn modern typist in another place and time.

The next book holds supporting essays. The third book will look in detail at the typist's romantic partner. In presenting this clerk's assault on the typist, Eliot inverts Milton's *Paradise Lost*. In Part III of *The Waste Land*, a dark Adam assaults Eve, representing a profound criticism of misogyny and scribal egoism since the creation of the biblical genesis myth.

At the same time, the poem is not anti-Christian. As you will see, an aspect of Part III of the poem is a ruthless criticism of the vehemently anti-Christian philosopher Friedrich Nietzsche. In that context, it should be said that I am not a Christian, nor a believer in any creed.

The Waste Land is a profound literary masterpiece, which also makes it challenging. For that reason, these books aim to be short and written in plain English. Each chapter is divided into subheadings dealing with separate themes, seeming the best way to survey the depth of the poem. The subheadings are listed in detail on the contents page and, with the Themes, Characters and Motifs pages, give you something of a map of this book as you set out on the journey within the poem. That said, reading is, like a fingerprint, unique to each person. The only advice is that you might take your time. What is described in this book is only part of the import of Part III of the poem, one of the greatest achievements in world literature. I hope I have done it some justice.

THEMES, CHARACTERS, AND MOTIFS

Notation in this book: As this is a new reading of the poem, some of the imagery is set out here. Square brackets are a direct reference to the poem, marked 'n' when referring to the set of notes attached to the poem. So, [100] is line one hundred of the poem, and [100n] refers to the corresponding note. For short, the *Notes on the Waste Land* are referred to as Notes. The book holds many quotes from Eliot and the excellent scholars who have studied his work, signified with single quotation marks to minimise textual clutter.

Characters

The Typist: The embodiment of the experience of woman in the 1920s. Isolated, alienated, lonely, and shocked into muteness by her brute modern environment. She serves as an intense rebuke to a continuum of misogyny with significant roots in the myth of Eve, the seditious first woman of the Judeo-Christian Book of Genesis.

Sappho: The ancient Greek poet-songstress who is the embodiment of classical guidance and art in the poem, and a positive representation of women. Sappho is the repository of the ancient oral poetic meters of the primeval sacred wood, and her classical musical influence underlies vespers in the Church of St. Magnus the Martyr.

Aphrodite: Sappho's ally in love, who opens the poem in 'April'. Of Phoenician origins, she is the Roman Venus.

Aaron: The first Judeo-Christian high priest. He represents the Christian Church and its connections to Rome and Jerusalem. In the poem, he is the fellow guide of Sappho.

The Young Man Carbuncular: One of the most multifaceted characters in literature. A dark version of Milton's Adam, among other aspects he represents a lineage of male scribes from the Old Testament to Max Stirner and his 'desiring man' and Friedrich Nietzsche and his overman, who see a need for power over women.

The Overman / *Übermensch*: The title used by Nietzsche in his 1883 work of philosophical fiction *Thus Spoke Zarathustra* to name his proposed man of the future. He is the new secular Adam who has evolved from the lineage of the male cult of the individual embodied in Eliot's carbuncular clerk. Eliot views the overman as a destructive iconoclast descended from the Satanic hero of Romanticism, and the enemy of culture and order. The overman, carrying the message of his creator, is also the misogynistic enemy of women and a neo-puritan scribe of Old Testament and Reformation provenance. As powerful a fictional character as Milton's Satan, he also transcends the work of his creation to become mythopoetic and culturally formative.

Satan: A literary character of extraordinary power who appears with glowing 'carbuncle eyes' in *Paradise Lost* as he stalks Eve. He is the proto-egoist of early modernity unleashed by Milton and the new supremacy of Lutheran self-belief, the 'inner voice' of the Reformation. He evolves through many forms, including the Satanic hero of Romanticism, to terminate in modernity in the overman of Nietzsche.

Places, Themes and Motifs

The Church of St. Magnus the Martyr: The London temple that is the modern embodiment of the Temple of Solomon, serving as a portal to the ancient world.

The Carbuncle Gem: Worn on the breastplate of the high priest Aaron in a portrait in the Church of St. Magnus the Martyr. In this book, the gem is linked to the young man carbuncular, the carbuncle eyes of Milton's Satan, the boils afflicting biblical figures such as Hezekiah and Job, and the boils of Johann Wolfgang von Goethe's Mephistopheles.

The Evening Star: The planet Venus in the night sky, introduced to the poem by Sappho [221n]. Named Hesperus in ancient Greece, it is a visible representation in the ancient night sky of Aphrodite, Venus, and their antecedents in cultures across the ancient world. As the morning star, its classical name is Lucifer. The church music of vespers at the close of day is suggested, among other allusions, through Vesper, the Roman name for Hesperus.

Hebraism and Hellenism: Named by those such as the critic and poet Matthew Arnold as the entwined cultural lodes of Western society, and seen in the 'Jewgreek is greekjew' of James Joyce's *Ulysses*. In Eliot's poem, represented by the combined guidance of Sappho and Aaron.

The Eternal Feminine: In Goethe's epic poem *Faust*, Mephistopheles breaks out in boils as the Eternal Feminine — a composite of predominantly Christian heavenly figures — rescues Faust from his Devil's bargain. Later, Friedrich Nietzsche uses the term to contemptuously insult independent women as barren and 'abortive', repeating Old Testament slurs. In the twentieth century, Simone de Beauvoir uses the term to encapsulate misogynistic perspectives on women, illuminating one of the numerous dualities of the poem. Since Eliot states in the Notes that 'all the women are one woman', the Eternal Feminine is embodied in forlorn form in his typist.

Animism and the Continuum of Ritual: Animism (originally termed 'spiritualism') represents humankind's first spiritual awakening in which all humans, animals and things were felt to hold some form of spirit. The 'vegetation ceremonies' of Eliot's preamble to the Notes are an expression of animism. At the time, James Frazer postulated primal foundation myths; Jane Harrison traced the evolution of the primeval cry of such rituals into religions; and Edward Tylor saw animism become modern religion, 'from first to last preserving an unbroken continuity'.

Classicism opposed to Romanticism: In Eliot's words, 'the difference between the complete and the fragmentary, the adult and the immature, the orderly and the chaotic'. In Eliot's view, the egoist lode of Romanticism discards accumulated cultural heritage in favour of anarchic individualism. That culminates in the extreme iconoclastic egoisms of modernity such as those of Max Stirner and Friedrich Nietzsche.

Pandemonium: The city of Hell in Milton's *Paradise Lost*, inspired in part by the biblical city of Babel, from which Satan builds a bridge to the upper world.

Londinium: The Roman city that underlies the City of London, as it does in the poem, representing the world of Classicism.

The Via Media and Zealotry: The moderation and restraint of the middle way opposed to the certitudes of zealotry.

The Golden Bough: James Frazer's influential work of cultural anthropology, tracing continuums between humankind's earliest rituals and those of the modern world including Christianity. Termed a 'counter-bible' for its depiction of all such belief as arising from superstition, he explores widespread representations of the yearly dying god in successive cultures. Eliot greatly admired this work, while disagreeing with aspects, including by suggesting the possibility of a genuine spiritual essence.

From Ritual to Romance: The second book named in Eliot's preamble to his Notes. Jessie Weston was much influenced by the work of Frazer and the esteemed classicist Jane Harrison. She looks at the progression from pagan to Christian life in Britain, and argues that aspects of Arthurian legend, particularly the Fisher King, are ultimately of very old eastern provenance.

The Waste Land
III. *The Fire Sermon*

At the violet hour, when the eyes and back   215
Turn upward from the desk, when the human engine waits
Like a taxi throbbing waiting,
I Tiresias, though blind, throbbing between two lives,
Old man with wrinkled female breasts, can see
At the violet hour, the evening hour that strives   220
Homeward, and brings the sailor home from sea,
The typist home at teatime, clears her breakfast, lights
Her stove, and lays out food in tins.
Out of the window perilously spread
Her drying combinations touched by the sun's last rays,   225
On the divan are piled (at night her bed)
Stockings, slippers, camisoles, and stays.
I Tiresias, old man with wrinkled dugs
Perceived the scene, and foretold the rest—
I too awaited the expected guest.   230
He, the young man carbuncular, arrives,
A small house agent's clerk, with one bold stare,
One of the low on whom assurance sits
As a silk hat on a Bradford millionaire.
The time is now propitious, as he guesses,   235
The meal is ended, she is bored and tired,
Endeavours to engage her in caresses
Which still are unreproved, if undesired.
Flushed and decided, he assaults at once;
Exploring hands encounter no defence;   240
His vanity requires no response,
And makes a welcome of indifference.

(And I Tiresias have foresuffered all
Enacted on this same divan or bed;
I who have sat by Thebes below the wall   245
And walked among the lowest of the dead.)
Bestows one final patronising kiss,
And gropes his way, finding the stairs unlit ...

She turns and looks a moment in the glass,
Hardly aware of her departed lover;   250
Her brain allows one half-formed thought to pass:
'Well now that's done: and I'm glad it's over'.
When lovely woman stoops to folly and
Paces about her room again, alone,
She smooths her hair with automatic hand,   255
And puts a record on the gramophone.

'This music crept by me upon the waters'
And along the Strand, up Queen Victoria Street.
O City city, I can sometimes hear
Beside a public bar in Lower Thames Street,   260
The pleasant whining of a mandoline
And a clatter and a chatter from within
Where fishmen lounge at noon: where the walls
Of Magnus Martyr hold
Inexplicable splendour of Ionian white and gold.   265

Introduction

I find, in reading *Paradise Lost*, that I am happiest where there is least to visualize. The eye is not shocked in his twilit Hell as it is in the Garden of Eden, where I for one can get pleasure from the verse only by the deliberate effort not to visualize Adam and Eve and their surroundings ... So far as I perceive anything, it is a glimpse of a theology that I find in large part repellent, expressed through a mythology that would have better been left in the Book of Genesis, upon which Milton has not improved.

(T.S. Eliot on John Milton)

The bleak modern scene enacted in Part III of *The Waste Land* would be remarkable if written in poetry today. A self-absorbed young man pursues selfish lust with no regard for the object of his attentions, a struggling typist shocked into muteness by her impoverished social, romantic and spiritual modern environment. This book explores the link between this modern woman and Sappho, Aphrodite, and the mythic creation of male scribes, the seditious Eve of the Judeo-Christian Bible.

To know the typist, we should know something of her romantic partner in the poem, the 'young man carbuncular.' His carbuncle affliction forms part of the symbolism that has accumulated around the carbuncle gem across millennia. One ancient representation is the gem worn on the Breastplate of Judgement by the first Judeo-Christian high priest, Aaron of the Old Testament. In London, he wears this breastplate in a portrait on the sacred wood of the altar-piece of Magnus Martyr, the modern temple at the centre of Eliot's poem. One hundred years since publication, the presence of the carbuncle gem on that portrait has not been recognised, and so its implications for *The Waste Land* have not been considered.

Aaron is joined in portraiture by his brother Moses, said to be the author of the biblical creation story. Three mythic characters arise in the poem from the association with those portraits in Magnus Martyr and the link between the young man carbuncular and the glowing carbuncle eyes of John Milton's Satan. They are the first woman Eve, the first man Adam, and Satan. A significant aspect of the typist scene of Eliot's poem is then revealed to be an inversion of Milton's *Paradise Lost* in which the typist as Eve, and as all women, is assaulted by the dark Adam of egoist modernity.

Accompanying Aaron and his sacred gem is the church music of vespers, brought to the poem through a number of allusions. At its centre is Sappho, the preeminent poet-songstress of ancient Greek culture. Her evening star Hesperus, to which Eliot guides the reader in the Notes, is the heavenly guide whose Roman name is Vesper, giving the church music at the violet hour of dusk its name. That the primary introduction to vespers is through the classical Sappho rather than a Judeo-Christian reference is of fundamental importance to the poem. These core entwined strands of Western culture are the Hebraism and Hellenism of Matthew Arnold's *Culture and Anarchy* and the 'Jewgreek is greekjew' of James Joyce's *Ulysses*.

Eliot later termed this period his 'pre-Christian state of mind'. His position was creedless but not atheist, spirituality being entwined with culture in the poem. Universal in intent and scope, it extends far beyond the Judeo-Christian. An aspect of the poem is a chronicle of humanity from its primeval beginnings, showing the need for community, the central role of culture in that, and the place of the individual. The consequences of the iconoclastic destruction of accumulated cultural heritage in pursuit of extreme ideals — the classical wisdom of the ages fragmented in the interests of a new version of man — is embodied in the brute clerk. The tensions between the ego and society, and between the *via media* and zealotry, between the middle way and extremism, are important themes in the poem.

Beneath its anarchic action the poem is firmly of classical principles. The fragmented layer of the poem deliberately sits at the border with Romanticism, with which there is a deep dialogue. Two perspectives are contrasted, the world views of Eliot, and of those such as the poet Lord Byron and the philosopher he influenced, Friedrich Nietzsche. The question asked is whether modern egoism frees humans to achieve greater things, or damages society. Nietzsche has had such a pervasive impact that he is part of the cultural air we breathe, and in that the fragmented layer of the poem serves as a caution. The drive to limitless gratification of the ego at the expense of the communal leads not to personal satisfaction and happiness, but to the clangourous world of alienating babel in the poem.

Since Eliot valued individualism, it is how individualism is engendered and expressed that is in question. It is not man himself who is criticised, but a certain type: the egoist who, on the errant advice of certain scribes, sacrifices community and those around him for selfish gain. This is particularly so in the typist and clerk scene, in which the egoist thought systems of modernity are darkly personified. In that, the clerk is not only fortified by modern egoist thought; he is also the progeny of one of the original sins of theological egoism, the elevation of Adam at the expense of Eve.

In this exploration of humanity, Eliot returns to the prebiblical times of the Phoenicians and before, to emergent human civilisation. In his preamble to the Notes, he writes that anyone who is acquainted with James Frazer's *The Golden Bough* and Jessie Weston's *From Ritual to Romance* 'will immediately recognise in the poem certain references to vegetation ceremonies'. These books of anthropology and comparative religion are interested in primeval origins, such as foundation myths that inform the divergent mythos of subsequent divergent cultures. In Eliot's poem, such ritual represents the first spark of the combined spiritual and artistic drives of humankind that continues into modernity. The Cambridge classicist Jane Harrison observed that it is 'at the outset one and the same impulse that sends a man to church and to the theatre'.

Through the heritage of the aeolic meter of her poetry, which was ancient even in her own time, Sappho and her evening star as the Roman Vesper are again central, carrying forward a rhythmic inheritance from preceding oral cultures. Her Greek music underpinned the music of the Roman Empire, which transported it to the Levant where it fused with the Syriac and Hebraic elements of early Christianity. This fusion informs all subsequent Christian music, including vespers. Through Sappho, the vegetation ceremonies of Eliot's Notes and the opening of his poem are connected to Part III and the 'music upon the waters' of the Thames, one aspect of which is the sound of vespers flowing from the temple of Magnus Martyr in 1920s London. Sappho's poetics in *The Waste Land* also represent a continuum, linking the most ancient of incantations with the poetics of T.S. Eliot in 1922. In that, both in the poem and in culture, Sappho represents the fusion of ritual and art, of spirituality and culture, from their primeval genesis.

In those musical and poetic continuums the unifying mythic layer of the poem begins to reveal itself. Akin to a poetic fugue, the Hebraic and Hellenic guides Aaron and Sappho create an underlying harmony contrapuntal to the clangourous anarchy of the fragmented layer. The mythic layer is itself layered, composed of a series of interwoven mythic, poetic, visual, literary and spiritual continuums arising from humankind's first primal recognition of itself. The themes of Eliot's Classicism, such as guidance, community, and ennobling art and culture, flow through this mellifluous layer. It contrasts to the discordant babel of a fragmented society of egoist iconoclasts such as the degenerate clerk of the poem.

The Waste Land is considered to be one of the most important works of literary modernism. It is said to represent the same achievement in poetry as James Joyce's *Ulysses* in prose. Yet, unlike the understanding of Joyce's novel as a disciplined masterpiece of classical control, form, and universal import, many see Eliot's poem as intentionally and irredeemably fragmented, without a unifying narrative or scheme. It is often read in a romantic way, as a personal complaint poem. Others see it as an expression of unpleasant, unsuccessfully disguised aspects of his personality central to which is misogyny, a charge that weighs heavily on both the poem and Eliot. Some agree with all these characterisations. Poetic fragmentation and what Matthew Arnold saw as a disabling subjectivism are among the hallmarks of romantic poetry, held in low regard by the firmly classical Eliot. In this light, fragmentation and misogyny exist in his poem not as expressions of despair or gender animus, but to serve as representations of an anarchic, alienating world of selfish individualists.

Science is also important to *The Waste Land*. The poem sits at the cultural meeting place of spirituality, Darwin's theory of evolution, and the rise of anthropology and comparative religion as they investigated the origins of myth, including the biblical origin myth. The literal belief that had underpinned Judeo-Christian perspectives for over two millennia, that a primal couple called Adam and Eve were the first humans of a world created in seven days, was no longer credible to an increasingly scientific world. The scholars of comparative religion were relatively genteel participants in religion's existential struggle, the most lethal and effective heresiarch of which, because of his genius and writerly bravura, was the vehemently anti-Christian Nietzsche. His ruthless polemical attacks were continued by those such as Eliot's transatlantic contemporary H. L. Mencken. Among the first to translate works such as Nietzsche's *The Antichrist*, he advocated an American society shaped by egoism and the political principles of anarchy and minimalist government, persistent themes in American politics up to that time and now.

Eliot's attitude to the focus on origins at the time was complex, a mix of scholarly interest, spiritual concern and literary possibility. He did not study comparative religion with the same motives as those who would debunk religion, but nor did he deny science. In his view, the brute intelligent ape of evolution is ennobled over time by the evolution and accumulation of culture from primeval to modern humanity. The egoist who discards such heritage and tradition for the claimed improvements of such romantic fictions as Nietzsche's overman becomes regressive, iconoclastic and even dangerous, engendering types such as Eliot's degenerate clerk.

We have glimpsed Eliot's clerk. Who is the typist? Eliot writes in the Notes that 'all the women are one woman'. Through Eliot's allusion to Sappho's evening star, the planet Venus in the night sky, the typist as Eve is also Venus and her Greek counterpart Aphrodite. She is Isis and the Christian Mary, both titled *Stella Maris*, 'Star of the Sea'. It is this woman, the typist of Part III of *The Waste Land*, who is the focus of much of this book, exploring how she transcends her stark modern circumstances to embody the universal. Through such links, an exploration of mankind's often erroneous and often misogynistic understanding of women throughout history is engendered. With other venerated and traduced females in the poem, the typist represents the depleted modern embodiment of the Eternal Feminine, slandered throughout history by a lineage of male scribes from the Old Testament to Cleopatra and modernity. The typist is mute in the poem so that she might be forlornly eloquent on behalf of all women across time.

Through that, the accusation of misogyny directed at the poem and its author is reversed. Rather than an expression of authorial misogyny, the poem reads as an intense critique of grave scribal error since the creation of the myth of a seditious Eve, the first woman and primal mother said to be in need of male control. Since the rape of Philomela from classical mythology and the cutting out of her tongue are also depicted in the poem, the misogyny addressed is not only Judeo-Christian. It is universal, from ancient wellsprings of male vanity and the lust for power of the intelligent ape.

Following this introduction, we visit the typist on the streets of her 1920s London, and look at why she has sometimes been termed a slut. We view a snapshot of the typist's romantic partner, the young man carbuncular, in light of the fractious world politics of the time. Part I visits the Church of St. Magnus the Martyr. Following a review of the carbuncle gem in literature and Christian symbolism, we explore the Temple of Solomon. The colours of that fabled temple were 'white and gold', the colours of the Church of St. Magnus the Martyr and the colours of the Magnus Martyr altarpiece itself in previous times.

Our first visit to Sappho explores how she connects primeval animist ceremonies to the temple of Magnus Martyr through music. We visit the festival of Venus through a poem Eliot explicitly directs the reader to in the Notes, sitting as it does at the cultural crossroads of late-classical and Christian Europe. An exclusively female festival welcoming bounteous spring, the *Vigil of Venus* undermines ideas of *The Waste Land* as a miserabilist poem.

The link between the young man carbuncular and the carbuncle eyes of Milton's Satan shows that Satan to have escaped his creator to become a founding father of modern egoism. We also meet the Satans of Coleridge and Baudelaire, Goethe's carbuncular Mephistopheles, and the Satanic hero of the romantics. In the poem, all cross the bridge connecting Milton's infernal city of Pandemonium to the pandemonium of London in 1922. The chapter *Broken Images* explores iconoclasm in the broken imagery of the relentless battle of creeds in the Church of St. Magnus the Martyr at the time. The facet of the pustular clerk which represents the puritan church clerks in that battle of creeds also represents the puritan iconoclast and extremist of any creed, religious or secular, who would destroy culture in the pursuit of zealotry. The battle in Magnus Martyr is one version of an intense battle of scribes that reverberates across millennia, from the Old Testament and before to Milton, Nietzsche and Eliot. Many of the resulting new Adams accompany the pustular clerk of *The Waste Land*. All these visions, including the Adam of the Old Testament, elevate a new type of man. Among the risks, as each attempts to reshape the world to his liking, are zealotry, iconoclasm, puritanism, vanity, and anarchy.

Part II turns to the contrasting order of Eliot's Classicism. It explores the mythic layer in the poem, holding a poetic argument for the universal value of cultural heritage. The mythic layer enwraps all human cultures as valued continuums emerging from humankind's first primeval cultural and spiritual consciousness of itself. Revisiting Sappho, the classical aspects of those continuums are further developed through her guiding star Hesperus as the planet Venus in the night sky. The extraordinary mythic riches the star brings to the poem include the array of female divine figures it has represented in history. Sappho's presence in the poem and insights from his life show Eliot to be interested only in the ennobling value of love, regardless of a person's sexuality. We close with a further look at Eliot's guidance in the Notes that all women are one woman, and how that enwraps ideas of women from Eve, Sappho, and their respective divine female entities to the circumscribed typists of modernity.

Between Moses and Aaron within the Church of St. Magnus the Martyr, the inner Corinthian pillars of the altarpiece enclose the Ten Commandments of the Bible. These pillars represent a figurative entrance into the Holy of Holies and the Temple of Solomon, built, if it existed, by the Phoenician master builders of 'Phlebas' of Part IV of the poem. Through the imagery of the Church of St. Magnus the Martyr, Eliot invites you to step through that portal and step into the mythic layer of *The Waste Land*, where you will see wonderful things: the rituals, temples, ancient cultures and origin stories of the poem.

Since the classical Sappho is so fundamental to the story, the import of the poem is literary, cultural and universal rather than Judeo-Christian. However, the Church of St. Magnus the Martyr, the temple at the centre of the poem, holds the carbuncle gem. To understand the mythic layer of the poem, you should know the visual language of the church. For those who are not believers, Eliot does not ask you, at the creedless moment of his poem, to believe any creed, religious or secular. You are invited to see the Church and its history as a repository of culture, myth and spirituality from humankind's primeval beginnings, now further enriched through its visual and mythic conversation with his poem. To think, then, on the human spirit, and the society we create.

I deny, in short, that the reader must share the beliefs of the poet in order to enjoy the poetry fully ... But the next step after reading Dante again and again should be to read some of the books that he read, rather than modern books about his work and life and times, however good.

(T.S. Eliot *Dante* 1929)

1. Context
London, Europe and New York

Genesis

> She turns and looks a moment in the glass,
> Hardly aware of her departed lover;   [250]
> Her brain allows one half-formed thought to pass:
> 'Well now that's done: and I'm glad it's over.'

Eliot's typist is a forlorn character, struggling for a dignified existence in a remorseless urban environment. Is she solely a woman of 1920s London? Understood only as a modern woman, she has been characterised as disreputable. She has been termed a slut, with an accompanying reading that Eliot intended to convey such a censorious and misogynistic perspective. This perspective is said to be informed by Eliot's underlying fear and horror of the female, repeated throughout the poem: a poison pen letter to women.

Viewed through a mythic lens incorporating Eve and her part in the biblical genesis story, the typist becomes a different literary character. Michael North comments on the prevalent sense of the genesis of a new world following the First World War.

> According to Ezra Pound, the Christian era ended on October 30, 1921, when James Joyce wrote the final words of *Ulysses*. Actually, Pound had proclaimed the end of the Christian era at least once before, but this time he was

serious enough also to propose a new calendar, in which 1922 became year 1 of a new era ... Although the Christian era did not quite come to an end in 1922, a considerable number of observers besides Ezra Pound felt the world breaking in two that year, and the changes they sensed seemed to go well beyond stylistic innovation in poetry and the novel ... Virginia Woolf dated the definitive break to 1910, though it is worth mentioning in this context that she first started writing about this break in 1922. And according to D.H. Lawrence, "It was in 1915 the old world ended"; but he also wrote that in 1922.[1]

James Joyce's *Ulysses* was published in the same year as *The Waste Land*. Judged obscene by many, it had been available in serial form since 1918 to Eliot and Ezra Pound, who became ardent advocates. In March 1922 Pound declared it a work of such importance that it would split the literary history of the world in two. He wrote to H.L. Mencken that 'the Christian era ended at midnight on Oct. 29.30 of last year. You are now in the year 1 p.s.U' — post-scriptum *Ulysses*.[2] He may have had in mind Leopold Bloom's grandiose hallucination while drinking absinthe in the sordid Nighttown of *Ulysses*. As 'emperor-president' and 'king-chairman', Bloom builds a new 'Bloomusalem' in 'our loyal city of Dublin in year 1 of the Paradisical Era'.[3]

Both Pound and Bloom imagine the genesis of new worlds. Friedrich Nietzsche also does so in his *dies nefastus*, the classical Roman term for an inauspicious day on which no important decisions should be made. Nietzsche saw the arrival of Jesus as splitting history, seen in the calendar markings of his time: B.C. (Before Christ) and A.D. (Anno Domini — Year of Our Lord). He also aimed to divide history through his famous assertion that God is dead. 'I call Christianity the *one* great curse, the *one* great intrinsic depravity, the *one* great instinct for revenge for which no expedient is sufficiently poisonous, secret, subterranean, *petty* — I call it the *one* immortal blemish of mankind ... And one calculates time from the *dies nefastus* on which this fatality arose — from the first day of Christianity! *Why not rather from its last? From today?* Revaluation of all values!'[4]

We will soon meet Nietzsche's new man who is to lead this revaluation of all values, his secular Adam of the future known in German as the *übermensch*, and in English as the overman. Eliot's pustular clerk embodies a profound criticism of this fictional philosophical character.[5] The elevated romantic ideas of self-exceptionalism the overman embodies degenerate, in the scheme of the poem, into the clerk's street creed of brute selfishness.

Eliot is not excluded from this new genesis. Of the line 'Like a patient etherised upon a table' in his *The Love Song of J. Alfred Prufrock*, Mathew Hollis comments that it 'has been said of this third line that upon reaching the word *etherised* the history of modern literature began, so surprising and juxtaposed and electrifying was its introduction'.[6] The consternation it caused can be seen in the reaction of Louis Untermeyer in 1915. 'I confess that his "Love Song" is the first piece of the English language that utterly stumped me. As a post-impression, the effect was that of the Muse in a psychopathic ward'.[7]

A Panorama of Anarchy
The New York Times of 8th March 1921

> In using the myth, in manipulating a continuous parallel between contemporaneity and antiquity, Mr. Joyce is

pursuing a method which others must pursue after him. They will not be imitators, any more than the scientist who uses the discoveries of an Einstein in pursuing his own, independent, further investigations. It is simply a way of controlling, of ordering, of giving a shape and a significance to the immense panorama of futility and anarchy which is contemporary history.

(Eliot, '*Ulysses,* Order, and Myth', 1923)[8]

Eliot completed and published Prufrock's love song in London, the new cultural home he was absorbing up to the time of *The Waste Land*. Robert Crawford introduces him as a 'young, London-based, St. Louis born, Harvard educated poet'.[9] The Eliot family originated in Boston, Massachusetts, the city founded by separatist Puritans fleeing England, and had links to such important cultural figures as Ralph Waldo Emerson. Before his university philosophy studies, Eliot was schooled in St. Louis, Missouri, including in 'Latin and Greek, together with Greek and Roman history, English and American history, elementary mathematics, French and German'. He termed this 'the most important part of my education'.[10] That during his first year at Harvard the infamous outlaws Butch Cassidy and the Sundance Kid were finally corralled and shot to death in South America offers a glimpse into that evolving culture. In a later interview, Eliot said that America always remained part of him, informing his poetry.

Eliot: I'd say my poetry has obviously more in common with my distinguished contemporaries in America than with anything written in my generation in England. That I'm sure of.

Interviewer: Do you think there's a connection with the American past?

Eliot: Yes, but I couldn't put it any more definitely than that, you see. It wouldn't be what it is, and I imagine it wouldn't be so good; putting it as modestly as I can, it wouldn't be what it is if I'd be born in England, and it wouldn't be what it is if I'd stayed in America. It's a combination of things. But in its sources, in its emotional springs, it comes from America.[11]

Visit the London of the early 1920s and you will experience the world of Eliot and his typist. In the restaurants and cafes where Eliot might have breakfasted there are newspaper racks. One holds *The New York Times* of Tuesday the 8th of March 1921. It is not a particularly notable date in the turbulence of the time, in the creation of *The Waste Land*, or in the life of T.S. Eliot. Similar eventful days are recorded in English, European and American newspapers following the First World War. For the people on their daily journeys here, it is another day in the life of London and news from elsewhere. It is a snapshot of the world of T.S. Eliot, of the English, European, American and other nations, and of the typists of the 1920s in their struggle for independence, shelter and food.

On that day, Eliot decided to write to his mother Charlotte to encourage her to move her trip to London forwards. During her walks with Eliot's brother Henry, she will visit the Church of St. Magnus the Martyr. They will meet the newly appointed rector, as we will also meet him in the chapter *Broken Images* during the intense battle of creeds over his restoration of forbidden imagery to the church. She wrote of the beauty of the carved wood of the altarpiece. 'Close to the foot of the steps leading down to the water from the bridge, is the Church of Magnus Martyr. It is small but exquisite, having some beautiful Grinling Gibbons carving on the altarpiece and the doors. While we were in the church the Rector entered and made his devotions ... He told us that Saint Magnus was one of the 19 churches selected for demolition, but he thought it would be spared, as it was used on weekdays by men employed on the waterfront'.[12]

Before the appointment of the new rector the church had been kept free of imagery. It was described by John Betjeman as 'low church, locked, box-pewed, dead and dusty'.[13] In a 1933 book dedicated to 'T.S. Eliot with affection and respect', Geoffrey Faber noted a 'depressing condition' of decrepitude in such churches resulting from the preferment of sermon over ceremony, including 'the mean table with a moth-eaten red cloth upon it in the chancel ... the dirt ... the indescribable smell of decay', and the 'mean and dirty appearance of the font and altars'.[14]

The Eliot's visit to the church is not likely to be chance. Ralph Waldo Emerson's list of notable treasures he visited while in England includes 'the temples and pleasure-houses which Inigo Jones and Christopher Wren built; the wood that Gibbon carved'.[15] A renowned orator and essayist of the first half of the nineteenth century who was of formative influence on the emerging American individualist psyche, Emerson was close to the wider Eliot family. Since they would have thoroughly read his works, there is a slim possibility that Eliot and his family were not aware of his writings about his travels to England. It is likely that Charlotte, Henry and T.S. Eliot also visited those temples and carvings in part motivated by New England scribal history.

On that day Eliot might be glimpsed walking to his banking job in the city, perhaps crossing paths with the typist on her way to work, while he thinks on the immense challenge of matching James Joyce's *Ulysses* in poetry. Within the flowing crowds the pustular clerk roams these streets, the young man carbuncular who will, in the year following, climb the stairs to take advantage of the typist. Lawrence Rainey notes what a striking presence she is. 'It is difficult today to appreciate just how innovative Eliot was in making the typist a protagonist in a serious poem. Their ever-increasing presence in offices after 1885 was registered instead in fiction and early film ... often they were shown being tempted by unscrupulous bosses or fellow workers'.[16] It was a society of great change, in which women's struggle for freedom in society met opposition of deeply conservative temperament.

> In fact, it was still to be determined in the United States whether a woman could legally hold office or not, it having been argued in state court in Michigan that a married woman could not serve because she was "chattel and not a person." The passage of the Cable Act in 1922 established for the first time in the United States that a woman's citizenship was not contingent on that of her husband ... Entry into the workforce, however, seemed a different matter, and it was still widely believed at this time that women worked only to supplement the income provided by husbands. The vanguard of change in this respect seems to have been made up of typists, who appear in a number of works beside *The Waste Land*. In *The Fruit of the Tree*, Tanstead's godfather, a bishop, is first scandalised merely that Margaret comes to his office to type, not inappropriately considering what this arrangement ultimately leads to. In Arnold Bennett's *Lilian*, a typist also becomes her employer's mistress, though with happier results in this case, since he marries her and then obligingly dies. Elinor Glyn's *Man and Maid* is also about an affair between a man and his typist, though in this case the fairy-tale ending is supposed to resolve rather more than the plot.[17]

Hamilton Fyfe's 1922 *The Fruit of the Tree* is a reference to the biblical Eve. Edith Wharton's 1907 novel was also titled *The Fruit of the Tree*. In 1914, the prolific popular novelist May Edginton published *A Modern Eve*, setting the action in her native London. The story of a young woman who pains her 'fiery English clergyman' father with her successful determination to become a suffragist was not well received in New York, where a review described her as a 'monster of selfishness — no less'. He goes on, 'we are expected to give our allegiance to Ellen, though it would be hard to find a girl with so many unlovely traits ... both she and her creator are strangely dense in failing to perceive that her course would be impossible to what used to be called "a decent female." The scene is laid in London, and yet there is not any hint that a young women should not go again and again to teas and dinners alone with an actor in his bachelor apartments. If we remember aright one such error in free and easy New York was the ruin of the heroine of "The House of Mirth".[18]

When Eliot engages with Satan, he is also engaging with the culture of his time. In 1895 Marie Corelli released *The Sorrows of Satan*, often called the first bestseller. It is described as a Faustian novel in which a young author makes a bargain for earthly success with the devil in human form, a deal from which he eventually escapes. Such was its popularity that it was brought to the cinema screen three times: in 1917 as *The Sorrows of Satan*, in 1921 as *Leaves from Satan's Book*, and again in 1926 as *The Sorrows of Satan*. As they strove to explain the modern moment, the popular literature and cinema of the time deployed biblical and other mythic types to represent the universal in their characters. The title of this book is *A Modern Eve* because Eliot's typist, like the Molly Bloom of James Joyce, is one version of that mythic first woman.

Front page news on *The New York Times* is the punitive Treaty of Versailles that has burdened Germany with vast reparations debt.

Pleas for a reduction in the burden of 'the Diktat' are ignored, and German postwar social unrest and political extremism are intense. An uprising by the communist Spartacists in 1919 combines a general strike with armed insurrection and is in part put down by a *Freikorps*. In 1920 there follows the Kapp Putsch, organised by Wolfgang Kapp and executed through a *Freikorps*. There are more than fifty such Free Corps, militias of conservative, nationalistic, anti-communist politics most often led by ex-officers and manned by unemployed youths and demobbed soldiers. At the same time, the Bavarian government is socialist, and the Kapp Putsch is prevented by a general strike of workers in Berlin organised by communist and socialist elements.

The headline states that the armies of General Foch, the Allied Commander during the First World War, are now advancing into Germany itself. Other headlines and articles in the paper add detail.

Foch's Armies Advance to Seize More German Towns as London Reparations Conference Ends in Failure; No Peace Until Germany Makes Definite Settlement.
LONDON, March 7. Orders were this evening dispatched to the allied military commanders on the Rhine to put into immediate operation the plans drawn up for enforcement of the penalties outlined in the four-day ultimatum delivered to Germany last Thursday.

Majority Count on Pressure to Bring Change of Mind to German People. Daily News and The Express, Dissenting, See Only Calamity in British Participation.
FRENCH REJOICE AT INVASION ORDER. Sentiment Is General That Germany Requires the Chastisement Decreed. PATRIOTIC SPIRIT IS HIGH. Even Re-enlistment of the Discharged Classes Would Be Welcomed if Called For.

Troops Already On The Way
French Contingent Occupies Two Towns on Way to
Duesseldorf. GERMANS ARE RECONCILED. "Better
End With Horror Than Horror Without End," Is Rhine
Feeling.

COLOGNE, March. 7 (9 P.M.) — The French have
been moving up to the Rhine all day — horse, foot and
guns. They occupied Langenfeld and Wiesdorf tonight,
right on the frontier ready to cross into Dusseldorf.[19]

The front page also reports war between a number of factions in
Russia, as Royalists attempting to retake control instigate anti-
Soviet risings and rebellions.

Hot Bombardment Between Petrograd And Rebel Forces
Kronstadt Shells the City, While Some Soviet Batteries
Maintain the Defense. PART OF PETROGRAD TAKEN
... Anti-Soviet Rising in Far East.
Russian Diplomats Admit That Czarist Forces Are at Work.

On page three, the United States exercises its influence in South
America. 'WASHINGTON, March 7. — The Costa Rican Government has met the objections of the United States Government in the
Panama-Costa Rica boundary dispute by ordering the withdrawal
of the Costa Rican forces, which had advanced across the Sixaola
River'. The brutal war of independence in Ireland is also front page,
reporting the killing of the mayor of Limerick in his bed by anonymous assassins.

Mayor Of Limerick Is Shot Dead In Bed
Ex-Mayor Is Also Killed in Residence, and Another Citizen
Is Killed in Field. MAYOR'S WIFE SHOT IN ARM. She
Makes Heroic Effort to Protect Her Husband, as Does Also
Wife of the Ex-Mayor.

DUBLIN, March 7. — These tragedies throw a lurid
light on the state of Ireland today. The long-awaited manifesto by Eamon de Valera, the Irish Republican Leader, was
issued this evening through the Sinn Fein publicity depart-
ment ... "This is a legitimate application" it declares, "of the
principle of national self-determination."

"This was met by the British government with immediate
and murderous exercise of brutal force. The terror failed: the
regulars could not be relied on to carry it out. Ex-convicts and
degenerates from the trenches could be depended on to have
few qualms in dealing with the victims, and a special force of
these fiends was accordingly embodied. Allured by the pros-
pect of easy prey and unlimited loot, with the whole British
army as a cover in the rear, they let loose on the unarmed
and defenceless population. An orgy of murder and robbery
began: neither age, sex nor profession was respected."

It was announced today at the headquarters of the Irish-
American Labor league that a meeting will be held tomorrow
night at Bryant's Hall, at which resolutions will be drawn
and presented to President Harding protesting against the
killing of Mayor Clancy.

Socialism is as strong a force in Ireland as it is throughout the fraught
European landscape. Page six of the newspaper shows similar activity in the domestic politics of America.

White house again will be picketed
BOSTON, March 7. — The White House will be picketed by Socialists, in connection with the campaign to be conducted at Washington in the interest of amnesty for Eugene V. Debs and others whom they designate as "political prisoners" ... and resubmission of a formal constitutional provision that Socialists in public office should be instructed not to vote for military or naval appropriations were placed on the convention program ... "no elected member of the Socialist Party should be allowed to vote for military expenditures except in cases where the arms go directly to the workers."

The fear of a collapse into anarchy is global, so that Eliot's concern for order is not only literary. *The Second Coming* of W.B. Yeats had already expressed contemporary anxieties regarding anarchy and cultural degeneration in 1919.

> Things fall apart; the centre cannot hold;
> Mere anarchy is loosed upon the world,
> The blood-dimmed tide is loosed, and everywhere
> The ceremony of innocence is drowned;
> The best lack all conviction, while the worst
> Are full of passionate intensity
> ...
> And what rough beast, its hour come round at last,
> Slouches towards Bethlehem to be born?[20]

That rough beast might be kept in mind when meeting similar dark presences in Eliot's poem. The 'preoccupation with the beginnings and endings of history is omnipresent in the work of Yeats, Pound, Joyce and Eliot', and Jewel Spears Brooker sees *The Second Coming* as a powerful companion poem to *The Waste Land* because it gives 'an immediate sense of the early twentieth-century crisis in western culture'.[21]

In the previous century, Matthew Arnold wrote *Culture and Anarchy* as an examination of cultural anxieties in an industrialising, rapidly evolving, increasingly secular and democratising modernity. Arnold had a formative effect on Eliot, who described *Culture and Anarchy* as the bedside book of his youth. 'My livre de chevet of long ago'.[22] Arnold wrote of 'Hebraism and Hellenism, — between these two points of influence moves our world'.[23] We will see that Eliot reconfigures Arnold's Hebraism and Hellenism through Aaron and Sappho. Some fifteen years after Arnold's book, Nietzsche introduced the overman, his secular egoist as the 'guarantee of the future', who we will meet shortly. An important theme of the poem is the way such extreme egoisms, as a response to modernity, fragment society.

The Slut

It is impossible to glance through any newspaper, no matter what the day, the month or the year, without finding on every line the most frightful traces of human perversity, together with the most astonishing boasts of probity, charity, and benevolence and the most brazen statements regarding the progress of civilisation. Every Journal, from the first line to the last, is nothing but a tissue of horrors. Wars, crimes, thefts, lecheries, tortures, the evil deeds of princes, nations, of private individuals. And it is with this loathsome appetiser that civilised man daily washes down his morning repast. Everything in this world oozes crime: the newspaper, the street wall, and the human countenance.

(Charles Baudelaire *Intimate journals* 1821-1867)[24]

Not all agree with Virginia Woolf and Ezra Pound that modern literature started in the 1900s. Peter Nicholls traces it to the rise of a new urban sensibility in work such as that of the poet Charles Baudelaire. That was 'Paris in the early 1840s and a moment when visitors to the Champs-Élysées were entertained by the music of two young girls who begged their way between cafes, singing and playing the guitar. The striking beauty of one of them fascinated the writers and artists who frequented this part of the city. Théodore de Banville wrote a poem about her, and Emile Deroy, a friend of Charles Baudelaire, painted her portrait. Baudelaire himself devised his own poetic tribute, 'To a Red-haired Beggar Girl' ... this early work already shows traces of what we might think of as a distinctly 'modern' style.' This new modern style is both 'an effect of the glimpses the poem gives of the new urban scene' and 'a certain complexity of *tone*'.[25] That urban realism loses its traces of romantic and pastoral sensibilities and is sharpened to photographic intensity in Eliot's poem, particularly in the rendezvous between the typist and the clerk. Dana Gioia's understanding of Baudelaire's importance to modern literature casts light on his presence in Eliot's poem.

> Charles Baudelaire was the first modern poet. In both style and content, his provocative, alluring, and shockingly original work shaped and enlarged the imagination of later poets, not only in his native France but across Europe and the Americas. His work guided the symbolist movement, which became the dominant school of Modernist poetry, and inspired the Decadent and Aesthetic movements. Half a century later, his presence still haunted Surrealism. Nor was Baudelaire's impact restricted to literature. His ideas on the autonomy of art, the alienation of the artist, the

irrationality of human behaviour, the intellectualisation of poetry, the cult of beauty (and the beauty of evil), and the frank depiction of sexuality became central to Modernist aesthetics. He also popularized less exalted cultural trends such as Satanism, sexual degradation, and the use of drugs for artistic inspiration. Not all of these ideas originated with Baudelaire, but his distinctive articulation of these principles became the lingua franca of international Modernism.[26]

Turning to matters outside the political, page three of *The New York Times* reports a tragedy averted in Paris: the attempted suicide of two destitute young women.

Plight Of Two Girls Stirs Pity Of Paris
Out of Work and Penniless, They Tried to Drown Themselves Together.

PARIS, March 7. — Two girls, Marie Guy and Yvonne Gesupret, both 17 years old, yesterday threw themselves into the St. Martin Canal in Paris. One was an orphan, and the other had been turned out of doors by her stepfather. Both were out of work and penniless and had for several nights been compelled to sleep in the streets because they could not pay rent for the little room in which they had lived together ... "Life isn't so hard to bear when one isn't alone," said one of them yesterday to the magistrate. Three months ago both girls fell ill and went to a hospital. When they left it they tried to return to the factory where they had worked, but their places had been filled, and there was no work for them. Soon the last of their savings was spent, and when they could no longer pay the rent of their room they were turned into the street. For four days before they decided to throw themselves into the canal they had had nothing to eat and had slept in the street.

"What else was there to do?" they asked the magistrate when he demanded why they had attempted suicide. "We didn't know how or where to beg."

"And will you throw yourselves in the water again if I let you go free now?" the Magistrate asked.

"What else can we do," was the answer, "since we have no work, no money and no place to live?"

Until some definite future can be arranged for the girls they are being kept at the police station.

It is to be hoped that the young women found work, shelter and a bearable life. But for the meagre benefits of her job, such could be the fate of Eliot's typist, her small lodgings similar to those of her unfortunate French contemporaries. In Rainey's sympathetic understanding of this character, he also lists novels of the time featuring typists, noting that in 'four of these novels the heroine engages in what would now be termed consensual premarital sex'. The personal choice and independence of women were themes in such risqué fictional representations, countered in contemporaneous criticism by male critics with the term 'slut'. Since it is likely that the more elevated of such critics availed of typists within their publication establishments, those women would have encountered that slanderous label during their workday of silently transcribing the words of those scribes. Rainey observes that in 'this tableau, the typist vanishes entirely as an autonomous agent'.

From perspectives such as those of Rainey, the typist is not a slut. Vulnerable as she is in such a brute male world, she is even valiant in adversity, mutely exhausted and depressed as she is by the relentless challenge and hardship of her life. The position of typist granted some independence and dignity compared to other work available to women of the time, though her position is voiceless, reiterating as she does the scripts of men. She is the modern 'Philomel' [99], her tongue brutally excised. Rainey also notes that overtime work for typists was paid with bread, jam and tea for one hour, and scrambled eggs, scones and tea for two hours, and that it was 'not unknown for a girl to faint at her work from lack of adequate nourishment'.[27]

Other work available to women in London is listed in such publications as the *Church Times*, which prints one or more pages of advertisements for 'Christian young women 'from respectable families' to act as housekeepers and maids'.[28] An examination of the 'Help Wanted — Female' section on page eighteen of *The New York Times* reveals that positions for stenographers and typists represent roughly half of the advertisements, the others being for maids, governesses, models and shop assistants. While some suggest testing attitudes, asking the applicant to state their 'religion etc.', others suggest the possibility, at least in New York, of achieving positions of responsibility extra to stenographer and typist duties. It does seem that, if a woman is of independent mind either from choice or through circumstance, and does not wish to serve the matrons and men of the city in menial roles, these office positions are incrementally better in the context of the restrictive social climate of the time. A typist's job provides the means to independently secure food and shelter and so offers an alternative, such as it is, to the waters of the canal.

In that light, John Hayward's characterisation of the typist as a 'slut, as much by force of circumstances as by nature' seems unkind, even if said in different times.[29] The reading of wantonness is not unique either to Hayward or to stern readings of the character of the typist. An early critic wrote of the woman wishing 'goonight' [170] in the pub that we 'have a passage seemingly spoken by a slut'.[30] The ease with which such judgements were made, and the censorious power of those critical expressions, have contributed to those subsequent readings of the poem as an expression of direct misogyny by Eliot. Rather than a fierce critique of the misogyny inherited from the pen of Adamic scribes since the creation of the Eve myth that continues into modernity.

Behold the Man
The Typist's Romantic Partner

> Let woman be a plaything, pure and fine, like a precious stone, illumined by the virtues of a world that is not yet here. Let the light of a star shine in your love! Let your hope be: 'May I give birth to the Overhuman!'
>
> (Fredrich Nietzsche *Thus spoke Zarathustra*)[31]

In the late nineteenth century, an extraordinary fictional character arose in philosophical polemical writing as an expression of extreme egoism. He is Nietzsche's *übermensch*, variously translated as superman, overhuman, and overman. 'Nietzsche is arguably the greatest German prose stylist of the nineteenth century', and his overman is as powerful and seductive a figure as the Satan of *Paradise Lost*, who we meet later.[32] He is also surprisingly close to him through later manifestations such as the Byronic Satanic hero of Romanticism. Nietzsche formed a deep connection with the work of Lord Byron, particularly his tortured, contemptuous poetic character Manfred: 'to Byron's Manfred I must be profoundly related: I found all these abysses in myself — at thirteen, I was ripe for this work'. The young Nietzsche first applied the term overman 'to Byron's Manfred ... Nietzsche calls Manfred an *'overmanen* who controls spirits".[33]

The translation of *übermensch* has evolved over time. The term superman, seen in George Bernard Shaw's *Man and Superman* of 1905, has fallen out of favour, not least due to the later Superman comic character. The term overhuman is a subsequent translation, in significant part intended as a gender gesture. It implies that it is only as a product of his time that Nietzsche's concept is exclusively male, and therefore modernity should include women in Nietzsche's schema by default. To the contrary, it was never Nietzsche's intention to include women in this exalted status. An insistent misogyny is one of the most reliable themes in his work, in which his new Adam seeks to continue to diminish and enchain Eve.

A parallel theme is his increasingly relentless insistence on reformation of a society that in his view has become decadent and degenerate, principally because of Christian morality. Decadence and degeneracy have troubled civilisation from its earliest roots. A glance at any page of the *Satyricon*, which provides the epigraph of his poem, shows that Eliot is aware of this. It is not, then, those aspects of Nietzsche's claim that are questioned. What Eliot disputes is both the cause of such decadence and the solution offered by Nietzsche, seeing the overman and the perspectives he embodies as atavistic, puritan and misogynist. Eliot inverts the charge of degeneracy through the brute pustular clerk, in turn directing it at Nietzsche, his overman, and the romantic lineage of vainglorious, iconoclastic scribes that precedes them. Nietzsche frames his accusations of decadence in feminising tropes that echo the polemical imagery of Old Testament and Puritan scribes who also insisted on reformation. He often expresses his cultural ideas through the imagery of emasculation and potency, and accuses independent women of being barren and abortive, Old Testament slurs. Since this book argues that Eliot regards misogyny as Nietzsche's Achilles heel, the term overman is used.

In the young man carbuncular, Eliot's transfigures Nietzsche's new first man of the future into the dark Adam of egoist modernity. In his licentiously insistent assignation with the typist the clerk also resonates with a near contemporary of Nietzsche and an earlier advocate of extreme individualism, Max Stirner. He champions another version of new man, his *unique one* or 'desirous man', lamenting that the state 'stigmatises as an 'egoistic man' the man who breathes out unbridled desire'.[34]

In Genesis III of the Bible, Satan advises the first couple, 'ye shall be as gods'. A lineage of scribes has ensured that it is Eve who carries the burden of this false promise. The multifaceted carbuncular clerk then becomes the embodiment of this lineage, from the Old Testament to Milton, Max Stirner, and Nietzsche. The secular puritanism of the latter two is surprisingly close to the preceding two: an evangelical preaching of similar histrionic voice, similarly insistent on reformation. They rail against social idolatries such as community and shared morality in favour of the genesis of a new Adam of extreme individualist creed who is to be freed, through their pens, from such false beliefs. Eliot's multifaceted clerk is the egoist in whom that continuum of male scribal vainglory since the creation of the Eve myth terminates. In this book, that lineage is embodied in the overman who represents, as one facet, the history of the universal brute will to power.

In examining these facets of man, *The Waste Land* is involved in the intense struggle of the time over the soul of humankind: over the new Eve and Adam who might arise from a Europe reborn from the destruction of the First World War. What scribes will inform them and their frenetic modernity? Do they abandon the desire for unity and order and accept the alienation and chaos of a fragmented society? Will they discard religion as superstition on the advice of cultural anthropologists and scribes such as Nietzsche? Will they retain any spirituality? Other questions are asked of this new first man. Does he see himself as merely Darwin's intelligent ape? Is he to be a decultured individualist disdainful of heritage, or part of a cohesive community at least in part informed by tradition and classical culture? Since the poem uses the particulars of this modern moment on the streets of London to explore timeless, universal aspects of humanity, the same questions are asked of us.

Eliot sees the modern man who prioritises individualism above all else as an unintended consequence of Luther and the Reformation. He recognises 'the extreme importance of Luther for anyone who would understand the modern world', and that 'Luther was an initiator of individualism'. This new individualism soon escaped Luther's intentions, so that the 'ultimate progress of Lutheran Protestantism was not wholly such as Luther foresaw, or such as he could have approved'.[35] The new Protestant Adam of Luther was carried to England by the Revd. Miles Coverdale as he returned from exile in Europe. A pivotal proto-Puritan of the English Reformation, his body is interred in the Church of St. Magnus the Martyr.

We will see that Coverdale's Reformation Adam underlies Milton's Adam of *Paradise Lost*, who then undertook a trans-Atlantic return journey. Ralph Waldo Emerson explicitly recognises Milton's Adam as part of the foundation of his new American man. 'I call our system a system of despair ... Let us wait and see what is this new creation ... A new Adam in the garden'. Further, Emerson's Adam is for the most part Milton. 'Was there not a fitness in the undertaking of such a person to write a poem on the subject of Adam, the first man? ... when we are fairly in Eden, Adam and Milton are often difficult to be separated'.[36] Like Nietzsche's overman, Emerson's new American is to rid himself of the past. 'Can we never extract this tape-worm of Europe from the brain of our countrymen? ... One day we shall cast out the passion for Europe by the passion for America'.[37]

Nietzsche was a keen reader of Emerson, whose idea of a new man unencumbered by Old World culture journeys back to Europe to influence the overman, the extreme egoist who heralds his creator's famous declaration of the death of God. Through Emerson, the Lutheran Adam of Coverdale and Milton returns to become Nietzsche's iconoclastic Adam of modernity. He turns with secular reformist zeal to destroy churches such as Magnus Martyr and the heritage, culture and spirituality they represent. 'What then are these churches now if not the tombs and sepulchres of God?'[38]

A Romantic Rendezvous

I have grown weary of the poets, the old ones and the new ones: superficial are they all to me, and shallow seas. They have never taken their thought deep enough: therefore their feeling never sank down to the grounds. A little lust and a little boredom: that has so far been their best reflection.

(Friedrich Nietzsche *Thus Spoke Zarathustra*)

The Waste Land has always been understood as a disjointed masterpiece: 'the famous inconsequence or discontinuity was there from the beginning'.[39] Yet Eliot always advocated order and completeness in literature, seeing the difference between his preferred Classicism and Romanticism as 'the difference between the complete and the fragmentary, the adult and the immature, the orderly and the chaotic'.[40] A significant part of his rejection of Romanticism is its glorification of the opinionated self over the wisdom of the ages accumulated within Classicism. This perspective is evident in *The Sacred Wood*, his 1920 book of essays in which, as Northrop Frye notes, Romanticism is 'already in the intellectual doghouse'.[41] In the introduction to the book, Eliot agrees with Mathew Arnold's opinion of the Romantics.

> In other words, the English poetry of the first quarter of this century, with plenty of energy, plenty of creative force, did not know enough. This makes Byron so empty of matter, Shelley so incoherent, Wordsworth even, profound as he is, yet so wanting in completeness and variety.

> This judgment of the Romantic Generation has not, so far as I know, ever been successfully controverted; and it has not, so far as I know, ever made very much impression on popular opinion.[42]

In his critical work, Eliot agrees with Bertrand Russell and other philosophers of the time that Nietzsche is a late-romantic whose overman arises from the cult of the individual within ardent Romanticism. In his poem, the rendezvous between the typist and the clerk, such as it is, is a romantic encounter in which there is a marked difference between the promise and reality. So too with the philosophical promise of Nietzsche's reformation. In Eliot's view, the pustular clerk as the typist's romantic companion who assaults her for brute sexual gratification is the most likely street-level, misguided manifestation of Nietzsche's elevated romantic character the overman, and that extends to society. For citizens, represented in their vulnerability by the typist, the clerk marks the difference between the society promised by the overman to a very few, and the feudalist actuality for the many. Through self-evaluated exceptionalism, the overman releases himself and his fellows from the constraints of common morality and society. So, that Eliot's central male character in this twilit scene is a lowly clerk should not misguide. He is surrounded in the poem by the scribes who advise him in modernity, and the long lineage of scribes who have over time created the cultural conditions for his existence.

Like Milton's Satan, Nietzsche's overman is of such literary power that he breaches the confines of the work of his genesis to become mythopoetic. Both fictional characters not only reflect aspects of the male version of the evolving modern Western human: they have, with characters like Goethe's Faust, the Byronic antihero, and Emerson's American individualist, become constituent parts of the cultural amniotic fluid in which this human is engendered. As Eliot's adversarial portrait of such overreaching 'vanity' [241], the pustular clerk of *The Waste Land* enters and contests the same mythopoetic space.

To support his poetic critique of Nietzsche, Eliot ruthlessly exposes a deeply troubling flaw in Nietzsche's work: his failure to examine his own attitude towards women. How can the self-declared revaluer of all values be what he claims if he cannot revalue his own misogyny? The 'problem of the old faith and the new, the challenge of Darwin, and the sanction and derivation of moral values: these are the themes of most of Nietzsche's later works'.[43] Yet Nietzsche's insistent enjoyment of misogyny is catastrophic, both in social terms and in terms of the thoroughness of his philosophical claims. It undermines his vision of a new secular genesis through his overman. Eliot suggests that to find Nietzsche's Eve is to see his Adam. Bertrand Russell held the same opinion.

He is never tired of inveighing against women. In his pseudoprophetical book, *Thus Spake Zarathustra*, he says that women are not, as yet, capable of friendship; they are still cats, or birds, or at best cows. "Man shall be trained for war and woman for the recreation of the warrior. All else is folly." The recreation of the warrior is to be of a peculiar sort if one may trust his most emphatic aphorism on this subject: "Thou goest to woman? Do not forget thy whip." He is not always quite so fierce, though always equally contemptuous. In the *Will to Power* he says: "We take pleasure in woman as in a perhaps daintier, more delicate, and more ethereal kind of creature. What a treat it is to meet creatures who have only dancing and nonsense and finery in their minds! They have always been the delight of every tense and profound male soul." However, even these graces are only to be found in women so long as they are kept in order by manly men; as soon as they achieve any independence they become intolerable. "Woman has so much cause for shame; in woman there is so much pedantry, superficiality, schoolmasterliness, petty presumption, unbridledness, and indiscretion concealed ... which has really been best restrained and dominated hitherto by the fear of man." So he says in *Beyond Good and Evil*, where he adds that we should think of women as property, as Orientals do. The whole of his abuse of women is offered as self-evident truth; it is not backed up by evidence from history or from his own experience, which, so far as women were concerned, was almost confined to his sister.[44]

Russell was one of the preeminent British philosophers of the first half of the twentieth century. He is not minded to be reserved in his criticism of Nietzsche and that is only reciprocal, since Nietzsche is renowned as a ruthless attack philosopher. Leiter writes that opinions such as those of Russell 'are now routinely held up for ridicule by Nietzsche scholars'.[45] This is often accompanied by a silence regarding Nietzsche's misogyny since Walter Kaufmann declared it irrelevant in his 1950 rehabilitation of Nietzsche. 'Nietzsche's writings contain many all-too-human judgements — especially about women — but these are philosophically irrelevant; and *ad hominem* arguments against any philosopher on the basis of such statements seem trivial and hardly pertinent'.[46] Women and misogyny are almost entirely absent from otherwise excellent books on Nietzsche since Kaufmann, including that of Kaufmann.

Notably, Kaufmann expresses sustained dislike of Eliot and a distain for his poetry, forcing literalist readings on it so that he can portray Eliot as a totem of Christian self-pity.[47] This allows him to confirm the Nietzschean theme that no good art can come from a Christian. Whereas, when Nietzsche follows his observation that 'Europe was dominated by the single will to turn humanity into a *sublime abortion*' with the claim that 'Christianity has been the most disastrous form of arrogance so far. People who were not high and hard enough to give *human beings* artistic form', Eliot might point to his pustular clerk.[48]

Writing in 1945, Russell reflects the more adverse opinions on Nietzsche prevalent during the first half of the century also seen in the work of Josiah Royce and George Santayana, Eliot's philosophy professors at Harvard. Russell states his purpose is not to show the 'isolated speculations of remarkable individuals' but to 'exhibit philosophy as an integral part of social and political life', and this is a significant part of Eliot's poetic intention with the young man carbuncular.[49] Despite the complications of their personal relationship, including over a speculated affair between Russell and Vivienne Eliot, there is much evidence in Eliot's critical writings that he and Bertrand Russell — who he termed a 'very powerful mind' — always remained intellectually engaged, and that included on Nietzsche from an early stage.[50] Eliot wrote to Russell in June 1916 on his recently published book review, 'I am glad to hear you like the Nietzsche review.'[51]

Postmodern opinions of Nietzsche did not exist for Eliot, nor any such opinions following what Leiter describes as Kaufmann's 1950 'whitewash' of Nietzsche's views.[52] That does not mean that Eliot was under-informed, since he had read the published works of Nietzsche in the original German. He wrote to his mother in November 1915 of his preparations for both that book review and his Harvard philosophy exams, which included translating works of German philosophy. 'As for the book on Nietzsche, I have finished it, and now am reading some of Nietzsche's works which I had not read before, and which I ought to read anyhow before my examinations. The book I am to review is rather sight and unsatisfactory — it is neither a guide to Nietzsche's works for beginners, nor a commentary for advanced students.'[53]

For women, the elevated romantic promise of the overman becomes in reality a rendezvous with the pustular clerk. Not even retreat to the kitchen grants refuge from the scorn of Nietzsche, and in that an aspect of the typist's futurist 'food in tins' [223] seems a black joke. Even more than Christian society, it is the atrocious cooking of women that has inhibited the evolution of man.

Stupidity in the kitchen; woman as cook; the dreadful thoughtlessness with which the nourishment of the family and the master of the house is provided for! Woman does not understand what food *means*: and she wants to be the cook! If woman were a thinking creature she would, having been the cook for thousands of years, surely have had to discover the major facts of physiology, and likewise gain possession of the art of healing. It is through bad female cooks — through the complete absence of reason in the kitchen, that the evolution of man has been longest retarded and most harmed: even today things are hardly better. A lecture for high-school girls.[54]

For Eliot, Nietzsche's promises are empty save for iconoclasm, disorder, misogyny, and a society fragmented by extreme individualism. Part III of *The Waste Land* holds a 'glass' [249] to that, as does the poem's structural anarchy. The response in the poem is a deeper order, the harmony of the mythic layer.

Of the poem, Frank Kermode observes that most people who know poetry 'will still admit that it is a very difficult poem, though it invites glib or simplified interpretation. As I said, one can think of it as a mere arbitrary sequence upon which we have been persuaded to impose an order. But the true order, I think, is there to be found, unique, unrepeated, resistant to synthesis'. Rachel Potter writes that 'Eliot insists that femaleness produces a significant unity of being in the poem'. Mark Ford sees Eliot's note on Tiresias imply 'a coherent overall plan and a way of understanding the various characters the poem presents ... This seems to encourage us to view *The Waste Land* not as a 'heap of broken images' or a series of sprawling, disconnected 'fragments' shored against the poet's ruins, but as a skilfully orchestrated jeremiad by a prophet-like creator'.[55]

The moment of the poem was unique, both in literature and in Eliot's life. It was the white-hot moment of modernist literature that saw the emergence of writers and poets such as Virginia Woolf, Wyndham Lewis, Marianne Moore, H.D., and Mina Loy, and the emergence of a high modernism of the mythic method in James Joyce's *Ulysses* and, until recently, the lamentably neglected masterpiece *Paris: A Poem,* by Hope Mirrlees. That moment is of great intellectual and literary challenge for Eliot, driven in part by his intense admiration for *Ulysses*. It is also a time of personal and spiritual challenge, from which he emerges on a path to Anglo-Catholicism. In all that, Eliot's preference was always for order. This book argues that the unified order of Kermode, Potter and Ford does exist in the poem in the mythic layer. It is much embodied in women, and is of the same cohesive classical discipline and scope as *Ulysses*, with which it is in deep conversation.

The Bold Stare, The Setting Sun, and The Rose

This is a time of philosophies which lend themselves, or at least offer themselves, with great facility to emotional consequences. A time of what a pragmatist friend of mine has called lyric philosophies ... The present, furthermore, is a time of lively agitation of political theory. Radicalism is become conventional. Socialism has settled down on Beacon Street ... all our millionaires are socialistic theorists who will dispose of their incomes — later — according to their own theories. And there are of course books and books with theories to account for the present misery — biological, sociological, economic ... and to hymn the coming liberation and the fundamental goodness of man. All this is natural enough. What interests me is not the uncritical character of this cerebration, but its uncritical attempt to be critical, its feeling of the need for law at the same that it denies law; its demand for a philosophy of the lawless, an intellectual justification for anti-intellectualism, a metaphysical justification of its blind enthusiasm. Whole theories of knowledge are directed into political platforms, and biological theory is diverted into ethics.

(Eliot, address to Harvard Philosophical Club, 1914)[56]

Opinion on what Nietzsche intended with the overman is not uniform. It ranges from advocacy of a pseudo-aristocracy of a few men who pitilessly accumulate power through the enforced servitude of the contemptable human herd, to a sage dispensing advice to do no harm and improve yourself through art and study. The latter, it might be remarked, more T.S. Eliot than Napoleon or Caesar, Nietzsche's heroes. Nietzsche approved a description of his work as 'aristocratic radicalism', and makes similar pseudo-aristocratic claims of himself in his works, though he was of middle-class origins. His 'philosophical standpoint is a deeply *illiberal* one: what matters are *great* human beings, not the "herd"'.[57] Russell wrote in 1945 of Nietzsche, 'I will not deny that, partly as a result of his teaching, the real world has become very like his nightmare, but that does not make it any the less horrible'.[58]

In 1916, Eliot wrote that 'Nietzsche is one of those philosophers whose philosophy evaporates when separated from its literary qualities'.[59] In his 1914 address to the Harvard Philosophical Club, of which he was president, he spoke of Nietzsche in a notably direct attack. Eliot's use of the word 'vicious' here can be understood twice: as red of polemical claw, and also in the etymological sense of the Latin root *vitiosus*, meaning corrupt and depraved.

> Hear Mr. Lippmann quotes Nietzsche: "the falseness of an opinion is not for us any objection to it ... The question is, how far an opinion is life-furthering, life-preserving, species-preserving, perhaps species-rearing." I see here chiefly a dogma, a dogma about an abstraction called Life. "What Nietzsche has done here is . . ." (says Mr. Lippmann) "to cut under the abstract and final pretensions of creeds". It is not so: what Nietzsche has done is to have built another creed. And I think that perhaps Nietzsche is the most vicious intellectualist of any of us; for having seen that intellectual formulation rests upon something which itself defies formulation, he has endeavoured to formulate the defiance. The man who pulls up a rose bush to peep at the roots need not wonder if the roses wither.[60]

The rose, arresting in its presence here, is a Christian symbol shared with the classical. In its complex beauty it is said to represent God's creation, and is the flower shared by Sappho, Aphrodite and the Virgin Mary.[61]

> Lady of silences   [25]
> Calm and distressed
> Torn and most whole
> Rose of memory
> Rose of forgetfulness
> Exhausted and life-giving
> Worried reposeful
> The single Rose
> Is now the Garden
> Where all loves end
>
>   (T.S. Eliot *Ash Wednesday* II, 1928)

Writing on the dying god Adonis (a name adopted by the ancient Greeks from the Semitic peoples of the southern Mediterranean), Frazer notes in *The Golden Bough* that 'Aphrodite, hastening to her wounded lover, trod on a bush of white roses; the cruel thorns tore her tender flesh, and her sacred blood dyed the white roses forever red'.[62] Nietzsche also wrote poetry, picking roses with a form of intellectual malice.

> *My Roses*
> Yes! My joy — it wants to gladden —,
> every joy wants so to gladden!
> Would you pluck my rose and sadden?
>
> You must crouch on narrow ledges,
> Prop yourself on ropes and wedges,
> prick yourself on thorny hedges!

For my joy — it loves to madden!
For my joy — is malice laden!
Would you pluck my rose and sadden?[63]

A feature of Eliot's critical and poetic work, the rose was also personal. Having written to Ezra Pound in 1959 that Valerie Eliot 'gave me the first happiness I have ever known', he wrote *A Dedication to my Wife* in 1962, speaking of the 'roses in the rose-garden which is ours and ours only'.[64] Following his death, it is said that every week roses were delivered on his behalf to Valerie.

As you step into the Church of Magnus Martyr, a glimpse of the Nietzschean ideas challenged in Eliot's poem can be seen in the theme of structural ruin, the 'bold stare' [232] of the young man carbuncular and the 'sun's last rays' [225]. The bold Nietzschean stare signals the self-belief of his overman as he strides into the future. 'Let us imagine a rising generation with such an undaunted gaze, with such a heroic proclivity for the tremendous. Let us imagine the bold stride of those dragon-slayers, the proud audacity with which they turn their backs on all the weaklings' doctrines that lie within that optimism, in order to 'live resolutely' in all that they do.'[65] The philosopher Richard Rorty comments on such 'weaklings' doctrines', distinguishing between moderate Christianity and extremist aspects of the priesthood.

I am most offended by the passages in which Nietzsche expresses contempt for weakness, and especially by the passages which argue that there is something wrong with Christianity because it originated among slaves. So it did, but those slaves had a good idea: namely, that the ideal human community would be one in which love is the only law. So it would. One can separate this Christian ideal from the ressentiment characteristic of the ascetic priests, but Nietzsche never made that distinction.[66]

The Waste Land is of the same mind. It is ruthlessly critical of the puritan ideological certitude of any belief system, religious or secular. Whereas Nietzsche's rising generation of overmen is charged with effecting a cultural reformation that mandates the destruction of 'weaklings' doctrines' such as a temperate society of the middle way, the classical *via media*.

> How to understand our cheerfulness. — The greatest recent event — that 'God is dead,' that the belief in the Christian God has become unbelievable — is already starting to cast its first shadows over Europe. To those few at least whose eyes — or the *suspicion* in whose eyes is strong and subtle enough for this spectacle, some kind of sun seems to have set; some old, deep trust turned into doubt: to them, our world must appear more autumnal, more mistrustful, stranger, 'older' ... now that this faith has been undermined, how much must collapse because it was built on this faith, leaned on it, had grown into it — for example, our entire European morality. This long, dense succession of demolition, destruction, downfall, upheaval that now stands ahead: who would guess enough of it to play the teacher and herald of this monstrous logic of horror, the prophet of deep darkness and eclipse of the sun the like of which has probably never before existed on earth?
>
> (Nietzsche *The Gay Science*)[67]

PART 1

The CARBUNCLE GEM
and
SATAN

The Visual Language
of the Church of Magnus Martyr

1. *The Reredos in the Church of St. Magnus the Martyr*

The ground stage of the altarpiece represents the biblical Genesis, Exodus, and the Temple of Solomon. The inner Corinthian pillars between the portraits of Moses and Aaron hold the Decalogue, the Ten Commandments, and form a figurative portal into the First Temple and the Holy of Holies.

The round 'Glory' of the second (attic) stage depicts the flooding of the world with the Holy Spirit, representing the Second Temple and the coming of Christ. On top stands a medieval rood, the Calvary scene with Mary and St. John and the dying God.

The carved foliage represents the ancient sacred wood in which spirituality and culture arose prior to temple building. The progression from such primeval sacred groves to the Temple of Magnus Martyr in London represents the doctrine of progressive revelation, a form of religious evolution assisted by the divine.

(Photo courtesy of John Salmon)

The Altarpiece in the Church of St. Magnus the Martyr

2. *The First Priest Aaron, his Breastplate of Judgement, and the Carbuncle Gem*

And thou shalt make the breastplate of judgment with cunning work ... 17 And thou shalt set in it settings of stones, even four rows of stones: the first row shall be a sardius, a topaz, and a carbuncle: this shall be the first row ... 29 And Aaron shall bear the names of the children of Israel in the breastplate of judgment upon his heart, when he goeth in unto the holy place, for a memorial before the Lord continually.

(Exodus 39)

He, the young man carbuncular, arrives,
A small house agent's clerk, with one bold stare,

(*The Waste Land* 231-4)

So spake the Enemie of Mankind, enclos'd
In Serpent inmate bad, and toward Eve
Address'd his way ...
and Carbuncle his Eyes;

(*Paradise Lost* 9:494-500)

Detail: The Portrait of the High Priest Aaron with the Carbuncle Gem

3. *At the Violet Hour*
    Violet Covers over Imagery during Church Mourning
    at Easter

Before Vespers of Saturday preceding Passion Sunday the crosses, statues, and pictures of Our Lord and of the saints ... with the sole exception of the crosses and pictures of the Way of the Cross, are to be covered with a violet veil, not translucent, nor in any way ornamented. The crosses remain covered until after the solemn denudation of the principal crucifix on Good Friday.

(*Catholic Encyclopedia*)

(Photo courtesy of the Church of St. Magnus the Martyr)

At the violet hour, when the eyes and back
Turn upward from the desk, when the human engine waits
Like a taxi throbbing waiting,
I Tiresias, though blind, throbbing between two lives,
Old man with wrinkled female breasts, can see
At the violet hour, the evening hour that strives
Homeward, and brings the sailor home from sea,
The typist home at teatime, clears her breakfast, lights
Her stove, and lays out food in tins.

(*The Waste Land* 215-223)

4. *The Reredos and altar in St. Stephan Walbrook*

The altarpiece in the City church of St. Stephan, with portraits of Moses and Aaron. The altar, by the sculptor Henry Moore, was created following WWII bomb damage.

Stone altars had been prohibited by the English Reformation (and so broken to pieces), meaning this new altar was controversial for some time after installation.

2. The Carbuncle Gem in the Church of Magnus Martyr

The Carbuncle Gem in Literature and Christianity

> ... where the walls
> Of Magnus Martyr hold
> Inexplicable splendour of Ionian white and gold.
>
> (*The Waste Land* 263-5)

Eliot emphatically guides the reader to the interior of the Church of St. Magnus the Martyr in the Notes. 'The interior of St. Magnus Martyr is to my mind one of the finest of Wren's interiors' [264n]. Further, while the finished poem points to the Ionian church style, an earlier draft of the poem directs the reader's eye to the Corinthian architectural order. Had that guidance remained, it would have brought the reader to the visual narrative of the Corinthian altarpiece. 'The lower storey is divided into bays by four attached fluted Corinthian columns with pilasters at either end'.[68]

> / there the walls
> Of Magnus Martyr stood, and stand, and hold
> Inviolable music
> Their Joyful splendour of Corinthian white and gold
> Inexplicable
>
> (Draft of *The Waste Land*, circa 1921)[69]

Altarpieces such as these, which vary in style and narrative according to the church, are called reredos. As a distinct item within such churches, they were exempted from prohibitions against imagery arising from the English Reformation. During the long-running battle of creeds in Magnus Martyr from 1921 over such imagery, a magistrate ruled in 1924 that there 'was a well-recognised distinction between figures forming part of a reredos and figures placed in isolated positions', since reredos 'offered no likelihood of superstitious abuse'.[70] That exemption meant that such an altarpiece could become a statement in support of imagery: it 'is to be concluded ... that the iconography of the altarpieces was anti-Puritan'.[71]

The painting of the first high priest Aaron that precedes this chapter is one of two on that altarpiece, the other being his biblical brother Moses. On Aaron's Breastplate of Judgement are twelve gems, representing the twelve tribes of Israel. Each was inscribed with the name of the Hebrew tribe it represented so that, according to Exodus 39, 'Aaron shall bear the names of the children of Israel in the breastplate of judgment upon his heart, when he goeth in unto the holy place, for a memorial before the Lord continually'. Such gems were akin to intaglios, the carved gemstone prized throughout the ancient and classical world as ornament, talisman, seal, treasure, status symbol and representation of the sacred. Of those gems, over time the carbuncle gem has acquired a particularly rich symbolism.

> He, the young man carbuncular, arrives,
> A small house agent's clerk, with one bold stare,
> One of the low on whom assurance sits
> As a silk hat on a Bradford millionaire.
>
> (*The Waste Land* 231-4)

The carbuncle as a human boil derives its name from the Latin *carbunculus*, meaning both 'little coal' and 'red gem', and also denoting a red inflammation. We will see that Eliot intended the title 'young man carbuncular' to evoke Milton, who makes great use of the carbuncle gem in *Paradise Lost*. In sacred form it adorns Aaron's chest and forms part of the physical fabric of Heaven: in profane form, the gems glow as the coal-red eyes of Satan.

> So spake the Enemie of Mankind, enclos'd
> In Serpent inmate bad, and toward Eve
> Address'd his way ...
> and Carbuncle his Eyes;
>
> (*Paradise Lost* IX 494-500)

Neither Milton's link between the carbuncle gem and Satan nor Eliot's more extensive symbolic load is arbitrary. Nicoletta Asciuto addresses the complexity of the carbuncle gem in Shakespeare, noting that he was aware of its 'common designation for both a precious stone and a boil'. The 'carbuncle, when mentioned in Shakespeare, is often preferred over ruby or other stones precisely for its double connotation'. She writes on the resultant complexity of both the image and the character linked to it in *The Waste Land*. 'This encrusted and scintillating set of carbuncular allusions and connotations makes our 'young man carbuncular' a little more complex a figure than has hitherto been understood. It would be difficult to think that Eliot, an attentive reader of Shakespeare, should not have had this web of allusions in mind, when picking the adjective 'carbuncular' to describe the 'small house-agent's clerk' assaulting the typist'.[72]

Eliot was aware of the carbuncle gem in literature at the time, since it begins a quote from Ben Johnson's *Volpone* in his 1920 book of essays *The Sacred Wood* — 'See, a carbuncle'.[73] The names of characters in *Volpone* suggest the beast fable, Volpone being derived from the Italian for 'sly fox'. The carbuncle gem is offered with other treasures by that decadent predator to Celia to buy her sexual favours. One of the only characters of righteous morality, Celia's chaste refusal drives Volpone to an enraged assault, from which she is fortunately rescued. With Milton's Satan, other aspects of the beast fable in Eliot's poem include Caliban, the malformed human of Shakespeare's *The Tempest* [192n, 257n].

Eliot would have known of the complexity of the gem in the work of Shakespeare, and of the sacred and profane versions of the gem in the work of Milton. Satan travels the heavens on his way to 'Paradise the happie seat of Man, | His journies end and our beginning woe'.

> The place he found beyond expression bright
> with aught on Earth, Medal or Stone;
> Not all parts like, but all alike informd
> With radiant light, as glowing Iron with fire;
> If mettal, part seemd Gold, part Silver cleer;
> If stone, Carbuncle most or Chrysolite,
> Rubie or Topaz, to the Twelve that shon
> In Aarons Brest-plate,
>
> (*Paradise Lost* III 591-633)

Symbolic use of the gem is ancient. In 1867, Charles William King noted that Pliny, the Roman naturalist born in the time of Jesus, 'divides his Carbuncular into male and female, the former of a brilliant, the latter of a duller lustre'. Carbuncle gems were 'engraved in the highest style of art with the heads of Socrates and Plato; a gem which above all other antique remains has served to identify the portrait of the latter philosopher'. The value of the gem 'has greatly fallen since the days of Mary Queen of Scots, the pendent carbuncle to her necklace worn at her marriage with the Dauphin being worth 500 crowns — an enormous sum in that age'.[74]

It is likely that Queen Mary wore the gem because of its significance to the Christian faith, particularly the commitment to sacred imagery of her Catholic creed. Francesca Dell'Acqua notes 'its decorative function in the number of the gemstones that adorned Lucifer when still a cherub'. Her analysis mirrors in Christianity what Asciuto surveys of the gem in literature. She traces accretions of symbolism to the gem such as the blood of martyrs and Christ. St. Augustine thought that 'the carbuncle, the brightness of which is not obscured by the darkness of the night, is like the truth that is not obscured by any falsity', and, 'Jerome compared its colour to a burning charcoal and underlined its capacity to symbolise the luminosity and clarity of Christian doctrine'. The Venerable Bede 'noted that the *carbunculus*, "as its name demonstrates", is a stone with the colour of the fire with which it is possible to clarify the darkness'. In which light, Eliot uses the gem to illuminate the increasing cultural and spiritual darkness brought to the 'violet hour' of dusk [215] by the young man carbuncular.

Dell'Acqua explores the craft of jewelled religious art of the early medieval period, particularly the iconography of crosses, and the extensive use of the carbuncle gem in this. She connects the red garnet, an alternative name for the carbuncle gem, with both Christ and iconoclasm.

As seen in the early Medieval period, in the Mediterranean as well as in northern Europe, on religious jewellery the red garnet signified Christ, his redeeming sacrifice, and the mysterious process of the incarnation especially when associated with pearls. But it might have acquired a deeper significance during the period of Byzantine iconoclasm, when wearing a cross was a clear statement of faith in the incarnation, the central argument in the iconophile justification of sacred images. Therefore, one can assume that Autpertus, inspired by bejewelled crosses, drawing on what appears as a long-attested symbolism that associated Christ with the carbuncle ... created a new "textual icon": an image of the Incarnated God gleaming in the dark like a splendid cabochon-cut red garnet.[75]

Encased in Eliot's inversion of *Paradise Lost* is an interrogation of Genesis II of the Old Testament. There, the seditious Eve and her necessary subordination to men is created, in contrast to Genesis I, in which woman and man are created equal. This vainglorious elevation of Adam at Eve's expense illuminates the type of man Eliot is examining through imagery such as the gem. 'The eye is not shocked in his twilit Hell as it is in the Garden of Eden ... So far as I perceive anything, it is a glimpse of a theology that I find in large part repellent, expressed through a mythology that would have better been left in the Book of Genesis, upon which Milton has not improved'.[76]

Skin for Skin

A contrasting facet of the gem is the carbuncular affliction, a motif of long tradition in literature and theology as an expression of internal sickness. 'For a poet who has been charged with impersonality, Eliot perhaps surprisingly displays in his verse a remarkable fascination with that most personal of organs: the skin. Unlike the heart, the liver, the bones, skin is our advertisement of ourselves to the world, that by which we are known, if only on the surface'.[77]

In this, the high priest Aaron is not the sole biblical link with the pustular clerk in the poem. There is also the near-fatal boil of the biblical iconoclast Hezekiah, the Old Testament destroyer of shrines. He is evoked in the resonance between 'Shall I at least set my lands in order?' [425] and 2 Kings 20 of the Bible. 'In those days was Hezekiah sick unto death. And the prophet Isaiah the son of Amoz came to him, and said unto him, Thus saith the Lord, Set thine house in order; for thou shalt die, and not live'. Hezekiah successfully beseeched God for a reprieve. 'And Isaiah said, Take a lump of figs. And they took and laid it on the boil, and he recovered'.

Alluding to the internal manifestation of such spiritual sores, Part III of *The Waste Land* closes with a reference to St. Augustine's *Confessions*.

To Carthage then I came

Burning   burning   burning   burning
O Lord Thou pluckest me out
O Lord Thou pluckest   [310]

Burning

It is a reference to Augustine's excessive sating of base sexuality, an appetite that left him spiritually starving and his soul covered in sores. 'I came to Carthage and all around me hissed a cauldron of illicit loves. As yet I had never been in love and I longed to love; and from a subconscious poverty of mind I hated the thought of being less inwardly destitute ... My hunger was internal, deprived of inward food ... So my soul was in rotten health. In ulcerous condition it thrust itself to outward things, miserably avid to be scratched by contact with the world of the senses'.[78]

That lack of 'inward food' can be read with the typist's poor nourishment, the 'food in tins' [223], a futurist image used not to criticise her but to represent her impoverished cultural, spiritual and romantic environment. Exercising the base sexual appetite so lamented by Augustine, the pustular clerk brings nothing to her table, his outward boils reflecting the Augustinian lust-sores of his soul. At the same time, Eliot is critical of Augustine's extremist conversion to a puritan attitude toward women, a form of self-emasculation represented by the myth of the self-emasculating Attis of the preamble to the Notes. Echoing the figurative castration of the 'gelded' clerics of *Ulysses*, it is a puritanical charge equally levelled at Nietzsche and his misogny.[79]

Augustine's imagery is acknowledged to be a reference to the boils of Job in the Old Testament. Satan is permitted to infect Job with boils as a test of selflessness. First enduring a series of ever more brutal actions against his wellbeing, such as the killing of his livestock and members of his family, Job maintains his fidelity to God. Satan elevates the test to 'skin for skin'. This is a core argument in egoist thought: that man is ultimately selfish and should act accordingly rather than curtail that instinct for the sake of community. Satan argues that, to save his own skin, Job will sacrifice those around him.

> So Satan answered the Lord and said, "Skin for skin! Yes, all that a man has he will give for his life. 5. But stretch out Your hand now, and touch his bone and his flesh, and he will surely curse You to Your face!" 6. And the Lord said to Satan, "Behold, he is in your hand, but spare his life." 7. So Satan went out from the presence of the Lord, and struck Job with painful boils from the sole of his foot to the crown of his head. 8. And he took for himself a potsherd

with which to scrape himself while he sat in the midst of the ashes. 9. Then his wife said to him, "Do you still hold fast to your integrity? Curse God and die!" 10. But he said to her, "You speak as one of the foolish women speaks. Shall we indeed accept good from God, and shall we not accept adversity?" In all this Job did not sin with his lips.

(Job 2)

Johann Wolfgang von Goethe's early nineteenth century epic poem *Faust* opens with a 'Prologue in Heaven'. Mephistopheles and Lord discuss a similar wager, creating a competition for the romantic, over-reaching soul of Faust.

> THE LORD. Well, go and try what you can do!
> Entice that spirit from its primal source,
> And lead him, if he's not too hard for you,
> To grasp, on your own downward course —
> ...

> MEPHISTOPLES. No doubt; it's a short journey
> Anyway.
> I'll win my wager without much delay.
> And when I do, then, if I may,
> I'll come back here and boast of my success.[80]

That epic struggle closes with the declaration 'Eternal Womanhood | Draws us on high' as Faust is carried heavenward, rescuing him from his dark bargain with Mephistopheles, who becomes carbuncular when witnessing the redemption scene. 'What's wrong with me? I'm out in boils all over, | Like Job. A self-repugnant spectacle'.[81] We will meet Mephistopheles again.

In light of the intense symbolic load of the clerk's affliction, it is significantly unlikely that Eliot would create a character as noxious as the young man carbuncular, pustular with egoism and misogyny, only to then become a writerly version of that character by recounting a series of figurative assaults on women for his own enjoyment. Further, the idea that Eliot is a writer of sustained misogyny unknown to himself is a fundamental misjudgement of his poetic capabilities. He was dismissive of readers who 'peer lasciviously between the lines for biographical confession.'[82] Elsewhere, he writes of those 'who have exerted considerable ventriloqual ingenuity in the replies they have pretended to extract from' poetry.[83]

The misogyny of the characters, scribes and myths in the poem is not his. It forms part of a critique of misogyny engendered by grave scribal error, and scribal manipulation, since the time of the first written records of the Hebrew myths of creation in the Bible, from which a vainglorious Adam with a scribal mandate to control a seditious Eve emerged. This mandate is powerfully reiterated in *Paradise Lost*. We will see the Adam of Milton was later commingled with the far more exciting Satan in the romantic imagination. That hybrid character evolved in ever more errant form until a dark, viciously anti-Christian, culturally destructive and pathologically anti-social Adam arises in the extreme egoisms of modernity such as those of Max Stirner and Friedrich Nietzsche. Misinformed by those scribes, in Eliot's view that dark, decultured new Adam is a boil on the collective body.

Gleaming with its internal fire, the gem and the accompanying imagery in the Church of St. Magnus the Martyr serve to illuminate how the sacred and profane are constructed within creeds and cultures. Through Eliot's pen, the church and the visual narrative of the sacred wood of its altarpiece becomes profoundly eloquent in his poem. What is created is a rich complex of new imagery that ranges far beyond the traditional significances of the carbuncle gem, engendering a wider cultural discourse. Dell'Acqua shows that the carbuncle gem represents iconodule justifications throughout history as Asciuto shows it to gleam in the seeming literary darkness of Eliot's poem. In this way and others, the gem radiates extraordinary symbolic range and intensity in *The Waste Land*. It engenders an argument for art, for the preservation of accumulated culture, for a contemplation of what it is to be human in society, and for the possibility of a spiritual life.

The English Civil War and *Paradise Lost*

In the same essay in which he decries in *Paradise Lost* a theology and mythology he finds 'in large part repellent', Eliot remarks on a 'division, in Milton, between the philosopher or theologian and the poet'. He sees Milton as 'a deliberate propagandist', but that in 'Milton it is much easier to separate the greatness of the poetry from the thought, serious as it is, behind that poetry ... reading Milton we are I think rapt by the splendid verse without being tempted to believe the philosophy or theology'.[84]

In this light, while admitting in 1946 to sharing with Samuel Johnson 'an antipathy towards Milton the man', it is clear that Eliot can and does separate Milton's poetics from Reformation theology.[85] It is also clear that, in Christopher Ricks' phrase, Eliot is an 'anti-Miltonist'.[86] Eliot's opposition to Milton is not only theological, but also cultural and political.[87] It is an opposition to extreme versions of the politics of the Reformation such as zealotry, iconoclasm, and the reliance on the culturally destructive inner voice, with its disdain for tradition and guidance.

A brief look at how the reader is guided to Milton helps establish Eliot's perspective. In the clerk's maladroit title there seems a criticism of what Eliot saw as Milton's prolix and sometimes strained elevated language. He describes an 'individual distortion of the language ... which is pure Milton'.[88] On the connection between his poem and Milton, Eliot commented that the young man carbuncular 'is a conscious derivation from a sonnet of Milton's'.[89] Southam also highlights Eliot's stated intention to link the clerk with Milton: 'not just spotty but 'red like a carbuncle' too, according to Dr. Johnson's *Dictionary* (1755). Odd as the word sounds, it carries a distinguished literary heritage; and Eliot told an enquirer that he intended the phrasing of the 'young man carbuncular' to echo 'that old man eloquent' in Milton's sonnet to lady Margaret Ley'.[90]

That is Milton's Sonnet X, serving as a summary of the politics of the English Reformation. It laments as 'fatal to liberty' the 'sad breaking of that Parliament', the forced dissolution by Charles I in 1629, and lauds the daughter of James Ley for carrying on his 'noble virtues'. An ardent Protestant, Ley was for a period the Lord Chief Justice of the King's Bench for Ireland. He had the *Book of Common Prayer*, from which comes the title of Part I of *The Waste Land*, translated into Gaelic, and forced Irish Catholic nobles to attend Protestant church services. Elsewhere, Charles I imposed the *Book of Common Prayer* and its compromise Anglican practices on the Presbyterian Church of Scotland, which was ardently opposed to such 'innovations'.

There followed the Bishops' Wars, Oliver Cromwell, the victory of Parliament, the trial and execution of Charles I, and resultant English history. The sonnet leads readers of *The Waste Land* to consider not only Milton's theology in *Paradise Lost*, but also the politics surrounding such creed differences as part of the wider schism in society between Puritanism and the *via media*, between zealotry and Eliot's middle way. Since the founding Puritan Revd. Miles Coverdale is interred in Magnus Martyr, that church holds the history of the opposing creeds of the Reformation. This is the cultural civil war that Eliot thought still ongoing in modern society: 'the simple fact is that the Civil War of the seventeenth century, in which Milton is a symbolic figure, has never been concluded'.[91]

The people of Milton's world, divided by a battle of creeds, were relatively new to print and only recently familiar with Coverdale's English version of the previously Latinate Bible. The very power of *Paradise Lost* accentuated the power of Milton's message, making Eve and her mythic machinations so real that it made Milton's reindictment of Eve all the more convincing. Milton claimed his poem to be dream-dictated by a Christianised heavenly muse, so that 'Milton's epic poetry was appreciated and presented to its first generation of readers as an epitome of religious truth that held clear political and social instructional value in late Stuart England'.[92]

Contemporary belief in its veracity can be seen in *Pandaemonium, or the Devil's Cloister*, a 1684 work of demonology that associated Catholicism with witchcraft and strove to show that Milton's demons were real and living in Rome with a harlot Church. 'That the Church of Rome as it is presently, and hath been for the space of nine hundred years odd, is so far wide from the nature of the true Church … it is an idolatrous church, not only an Harlot (as the Scripture calls her) but also a foul, filthy, old wither'd Harlot, and the mother of Whoredom, guilty of the same Idolatry, and worse, then was amongst Ethnicks and Heathen'. Elsewhere he writes 'to prove that what the Papists offer to the Shrine of that which they call the Blessed Virgin, can be nothing less than giving Divine Honour and Adoration to an unclean Spirit'.[93]

In the context of the visual narrative of progressive revelation on the Magnus Martyr altarpiece, it is notable that *Paradise Lost* is also a work of progressive revelation. 'The first four books of *Paradise Lost* derive primarily from pagan authors, who are governed by natural law. The middle books draw heavily on Hebraic revelation beyond nature's law, provided by the "Divine Interpreter," Raphael. The last books attempt to systematically debase the others by submitting both natural law and the Mosaic law to the judgment of Christian experience'.[94] In that, there are structural resonances between these masterpieces, since *The Waste Land* opens with Aphrodite of 'April', and leads to a consideration of the Christian in Part V. They differ in the aspect of the universal. Rather than debasing the heritage of spiritual quest that predates or is outside the Judeo-Christian as Milton does, Eliot's poem preserves and celebrates the diverse mythic heritage of humanity. It forms a composite of different representations over time of the sincere human quest for glimpses of the same godhead, all being essential to the cumulative cultural continuums that ennoble humanity.

In reworking Milton's Eden myth in the typist and clerk scene as Milton reworks the biblical Genesis, Eliot is not the first. The 'desire to create a literary work that is epic in scope but modern in form, and hence different from *Paradise Lost*, haunts romanticism'.[95] Shelley's *Prometheus* 'shares with Blake and Wordsworth an ambition to replace *Paradise Lost*'.[96] Eliot's poem makes that implicit claim: to be the distilled modernist version of the long poems of those such as Homer, Virgil, Dante, Milton and Goethe, now radically compressed through the mythic method.

The Adam and Eve of Miles Coverdale

In schismatic contrast to the rich imagery of its Anglo-Catholic manifestation, inside Magnus Martyr the early Puritan Revd. Miles Coverdale represents antagonism to that church interior as idolatrous.

> When Coverdale died he was buried in Bartholomew-by-Exchange, but this church was demolished in the nineteenth

century, and his remains were transferred to St. Magnus. He would fail to recognise his own church in the present building, erected after the Great Fire by Wren, in what Eliot called the "inexplicable splendour of Ionian white and gold". Undoubtedly Coverdale would disown its present style of churchmanship; but his memorial tablet is to be seen on the east wall, close to the altar.[97]

Coverdale's Reformation Adam and Eve theologically underwrite the Adam and Eve of Milton. The conventional Adam of pre-Reformation Christianity is evoked through the portrait of Moses accompanying that of Aaron in that church. In Eliot's view the dark, godless Adam of Anglo-Nietzschean iconoclastic egoism takes his first steps from the Lutheran pen of the Revd. Coverdale, again from Magnus Martyr.

Coverdale's Adam, like Milton's, is the primary focus of creation. 'And forasmuch as he, being solitary and alone, could not conveniently dwell without a mate, he ... provided for him a wife, even out of the bones of his own body, that she might be the man's help.'[98] This Adam is also against Judaic and Catholic ritual and imagery in the manner of *Paradise Lost*, where in Book IV the first couple's Edenic worship is stripped of ritual:

> and other Rites
> Observing none, but adoration pure
> Which God likes best, into thir inmost bowre.

With Romish forms of worship in mind, it is a theme introduced in Milton's poem in Book I, decrying 'gay Religions full of Pomp and Gold, | And Devils to adore for Deities'. Even the minimised ritual of the compromise *Book of Common Prayer* was rejected by Coverdale.

'His theological development furnishes a paradigm of the progress of the English Reformation ... he parted with the *via media* and adopted a position which might be termed proto-puritan, similar to that of other Marian exiles ... who could not come to terms with the Elizabethan Prayer Book'.[99]

A remarkable aspect of Coverdale's first couple is that they were Protestants in essence in Eden. 'The Old Faith; an evident probation that the Christian Faith hath endured since the beginning of the world'.[100] This allows him to assert that continuing Judaism and ensuing Roman Catholicism constitute a progressive and ever more erroneous idolatry.

> It does not appear certain in what year this work of Bishop Coverdale first appeared. An edition of it appears to have been published in 1541, and another in 1547. Another edition was also published in 1624, under the following title: "Look from Adam, and behold the Protestants' faith and religion, evidently proved out of the holy Scriptures against all Atheists, Papists, loose libertines, and carnal Gospellers: and that the faith, which they profess, hath continued from the beginning of the world, and so is the true and ancient faith."[101]

It is intriguing to think we might still be in Eden had the first couple been Catholic, and so more obedient to authority. Whereas from 'the beginning of the creation there was in Adam a wonderful and excellent efficacy of understanding and remembrance', Eve was never going to benefit from Luther's new idea of rejecting authority in favour of thinking for yourself. Coverdale's Eve carries the same heavy burden she cannot escape in *Paradise Lost*.

Seynge Eve was sore begyled
By the serpentes tentacyon,
Because she Gods worde despysed,
Brought mankynde to destruccyon
(Miles Coverdale *By Adams Fall*)[102]

The White and Gold of the Temple of Solomon

… where the walls
Of Magnus Martyr hold
Inexplicable splendour of Ionian white and gold.
(*The Waste Land* 263-5)

What Eliot achieves in poetry with the Magnus Martyr altarpiece is extraordinary. Yet this is not to claim that it is the overriding centrepiece of *The Waste Land*. Other striking images and complexes of imagery in the poem can claim parity, such as the evening star of Sappho, explored in part two of this book. Rather, as the inner Corinthian pillars of the lower stage of that altarpiece present a figurative entrance into the First Temple, the altarpiece opens a significant portal into the mythic layer of the poem.

The church itself deliberately echoes the First Temple in shape and in colour. The 'white and gold' of Magnus Martyr were also the colours of Solomon's Temple, as Josephus attests in his *Jewish War* of circa 75 CE.

Now the outward face of the temple … was covered all over with plates of gold of great weight, and, at the first rising of the sun, reflected back a very fiery splendor, and made those who forced themselves to look upon it to turn their eyes away, just as they would have done at the sun's own rays. But this temple appeared to strangers, when they were coming to it at a distance, like a mountain covered with snow; for as to those parts of it that were not gilt, they were exceeding white.[103]

An explanation of the First and Second Temple representations on the ground and upper stages of the altarpiece accompanies the Magnus Martyr photographs in this book. That figurative portal in Magnus Martyr also facilitates a visit, in Eliot's poem, to cultures that existed beside and before the Hebrews. It includes ancient characters such as the Northwest Semitic 'Phlebas the Phoenician' and Queen Dido, and a host of other mythic and historical characters whose origins are outside Western and Judeo-Christian culture, while influencing it significantly.

Their inclusion marks an important theme in the poem, a recognition of the fluidity of beliefs within evolving cultural settings. Eliot's taste for the 'distinctive aestheticism of Anglo-Catholicism' can be viewed with 'his response to the artistic heritage of Western Christendom at large, even to its anthropological and sociological origins'.[104] He confirmed that in 1927. 'I am convinced — even from the study of the history of poetry alone — and I think that the history of Christian dogma could be made to support the view — that belief itself has been in constant mutation (not always progress, from any point of view) from the beginning of civilisation'.[105] One significant milestone on the spiritual and cultural path of much of humanity is the storied Temple of Solomon.

It was widely believed that the orders of architecture derived not only from the development of Greek and Roman architecture, but also from the instructions dictated to Moses by God regarding the decoration of the Ark of the Covenant. The character of classical decoration was also related to the decoration of Solomon's Temple, also divinely inspired, and to primitive 'groves', in which it was supposed that the ancients had worshipped. Given the symbolic value of the Corinthian order, it is not surprising that evidence suggests that the majority of altarpieces in late seventeenth-century London utilized it in the chancel decorations.[106]

The mingling of Wren's Ionian architecture and the Corinthian order of the altarpiece in the church is a conversation between the early-modernity of Wren's time and the ancient past, as the Ionian order of classical Greece meets the Corinthian order of the Hebrew First Temple. It is an architectural representation of Arnold's Hebraism and Hellenism and James Joyce's 'Jewgreek is greekjew', and the same conversation resonates in Eliot's poem between modernity, history, and prehistory.[107] As the architectural shape and visual language of this London temple mirrors its ancient template the First Temple, so the carved wood of Magnus Martyr reflects the sacred wood of the interior of its ancient counterpart.

> And he built twenty cubits on the sides of the house, both the floor and the walls with boards of cedar: he even built them for it within, even for the oracle, even for the most holy place.
>
> And the cedar of the house within was carved with knops and open flowers: all was cedar; there was no stone seen ...
>
> And he set the cherubims within the inner house: and they stretched forth the wings of the cherubims, so that

the wing of the one touched the one wall, and the wing of
the other cherub touched the other wall; and their wings
touched one another in the midst of the house.

And he overlaid the cherubims with gold.

And he carved all the walls of the house round about
with carved figures of cherubims and palm trees and open
flowers, within and without.

(1 Kings 6)

In the First Temple, such features were of Phoenician origin.
Through that, both 'Gentile' and 'Jew' [319] are connected to their
figurative ancestor 'Phlebas the Phoenician' [312], who in one
aspect is Eliot's Adam of civilisation.

Here let us look briefly at the biblical texts, mostly the
detailed description of construction in 1 Kings 5-8. The
main points concern the longitudinal shape and tripartite
(three room) plan of the building, with an inner sanctum
at the rear; the construction of finely hewn masonry
combined with carved and gilded wooden panels; and
furnishings consisting of gold-overlaid wooden cherubs
(or winged creatures) and bronze basins and brazier. The
inner walls and the furniture featured several iconographic
motifs: cherubs; palm trees; "open flowers" (lilies?); "chain
work"; pomegranates; gourds; lions; and oxen. The plan of
the building, the chisel-dressed masonry, and the various
decorative motifs are all clearly of Phoenician inspiration,
as we now know.[108]

Such splendour was not only an expression of kingly wealth within
the ancient palace and temple compound, it was a theological

statement. 'Gold was used extensively in cultic contexts in antiquity. It added prestige to sanctuaries and augmented the magnificence of representations of deities. Furthermore, the inalterability and brilliance of gold spontaneously evoked timelessness and luminosity, two of the most essential characteristics of divine beings'.[109]

In Part II of Eliot's play *The Rock*, gratitude is expressed for the 'gilded carven wood' of churches.[110] Notably, the Magnus Martyr altarpiece was also 'gilded carven wood' in an earlier incarnation, described by Thomas Allen in 1828 as being substantially of white and gold.

> The greater portion of the wall is occupied by a magnificent altar screen in two stories ... the two side intercolumniations have full length portraits of Moses and Aaron ... All the spaces on the screen are filled with carvings in relief, by Gibbons, of fruit, flowers, and entwined tendrils, the beauty of which are seen to advantage by the splendid and elaborate gilding and colouring, which have been bestowed upon them. The substantial parts of the screen are coloured in imitation of verd antique and other marbles, the mouldings and dressings white and gold, the foliage white, touched and heightened with gold, forming, on the whole, a resplendent design, in which the utmost profusion of ornament is introduced without gaudiness.[111]

No visual representation of that resplendent altarpiece is in evidence. What can be seen from the photographs in this book is that such altarpieces represented the iconodule stand for imagery, and against Puritanism, of all such churches. Depending on the creed in command of individual churches, such altarpieces experienced periods of deconstruction, destruction of imagery, and reconstruction, mirroring the fortunes of the Jerusalem temples, and the 'broken images' [22] and theme of structural ruin and rebuilding in the poem.

David and Solomon in Culture and Hezekiah the Destroyer of Shrines

Two aspects of the First Temple are notable in the cultural context of *The Waste Land*: its historical time, and its link with reformation. It is significantly more likely that, if the temple existed, the full glory of its construction was realised around the time of Hezekiah, centuries after the period of the putative United Monarchy of Saul, David and Solomon. However, for millennia the legends of David, Solomon and his temple were accepted as historical truth, becoming cultural templates in Western society.

> From the soaring cathedrals and elegant palaces of medieval Europe, to the hushed galleries of world famous art museums, to America's backwoods pulpits and Hollywood epics, the story of ancient Israel's sacred kings, David and Solomon, is one of Western civilisation's most enduring legacies ... They have shaped western images of kingship and served as models of royal piety, messianic expectation, and national destiny ... Yet the legend was not merely a romantic fiction of imaginary personalities and events. It evolved over centuries from a core of authentic memories into a complex and timeless literary creation. In its unforgettable images and dramatic scenes — the battle against Goliath, the rise of David from outlaw to king, the splendor of Solomon's court — the legend of David and Solomon expresses a universal message of national independence

and transcendent religious values that people all over the world have come to regard as their own. Yet, as we shall see, its origins are traceable in the archaeology and history of a single small Iron Age kingdom as it grew from a village society into a complex state.[112]

That understanding has recently arisen as knowledge of the composite and political nature of biblical writings has developed, and archaeology has made new discoveries. Archaeological findings show that 'it is now clear that Iron Age Judah enjoyed no precocious golden age. David and his son Solomon and the subsequent members of the Davidic dynasty ruled over a marginal, isolated, rural region, with no signs of great wealth or centralized administration'.[113] They were retrospectively elevated to the fabled glory of that royal court and temple during the rapid rise of the Kingdom of Judah and its capital Jerusalem around the eight century BCE. It had been ignored by the Assyrian empire that militarily destroyed the more strategically located, populous and prosperously developed Northern Kingdom of Israel. To then, Judah had been a remote rural economy of little significance and sparce population. From then, there was a period of rapid development as Jerusalem filled the resulting power vacuum, evolving from a relatively remote township to an important regional city.

With that new position came the assets of prosperous statehood, including a literate scribal bureaucracy centred in the palace and temple complex, and the funds to hire Phoenician master builders. Like any state, it wanted a founding narrative. This was also the moment of transition from Judahite oral to written culture. That transition is important in the poem, broadly contemporaneous as it is with the same transition up to the time of Sappho on the northern shores of the Mediterranean, also enabled by the newly acquired Phoenician alphabet. The oral folk tales of David as the heroic rebel from around 1000 BCE became a more prestigious written narrative of Judahite stately righteousness. In that script, his son Solomon becomes the kingly inheritor of his position and wisdom through divine right.

For that reason, Solomon was said to have built the temple. It was more likely built — or at least reached the full structural and courtly glory depicted in the Bible — closer in time to the later, newly powerful and prosperous state with its newly literate temple scribes. That period broadly corresponds to the reign of Hezekiah and his descent Josiah: 'the most famous episodes of the Solomon story reflect an accurate historical memory not of Solomon, but of the dramatic era when the kingdom of Judah recovered from Sennacherib's destructive campaign by plunging headlong into the world of imperial commerce. Judah's economic development in the era of Ahaz and Hezekiah was just the beginning'.[114]

Hezekiah is the Old Testament king who destroyed local shrines throughout the kingdom at the urging of temple scribes. In exploring the relationship between the carbuncle gem, Aaron, the young man carbuncular and the carbuncle eyes of Milton's Satan, we saw that Hezekiah is invoked through the correspondence between the line 'Shall I at least set my lands in order?' [425] and his biblical affliction with a near fatal boil. Hezekiah's iconoclast reforms were initiated by 'circles connected with the Temple of Jerusalem intent on exercising religious and economic control over the increasingly developed countryside ... The moment was fortuitous for this; with the expansion of bureaucratic administration came a spread of literacy. For the first time the authority of written texts, rather than recited epics or ballads, had an enormous effect'. Scribal aniconic zealotry radiated throughout the kingdom, enforced by Hezekiah.

Biblical history was, then, 'written by the 'puritanism' of the winners', and so 'fashioned exclusively according to the late

Judahite Deuteronomistic beliefs'.[115] This ideologically shaped history involved a schism, a reformation that saw Hezekiah launch a campaign to destroy the shrines of the preeminent Levantine female deity. She was the powerful Semitic Queen of Heaven of the polytheistic Canaanites, Phoenicians and Hebrews who travelled across the Mediterranean to become Aphrodite and, later again, the Roman Venus. At broadly the time of her destruction, temple scribes also first recorded the myth of a seditious Eve in writing. For perhaps centuries before then the Queen of Heaven had been the divine wife of Yahweh, including in the First Temple, the Temple of Solomon. Speculated to be a storm-warrior god of nomadic Hebrews, Yahweh eventually become the sole deity.

Hezekiah's son Manasseh reinstated the divine couple in the First Temple, a return to 'idolatrous' worship. It was left to Hezekiah's great-grandson Josiah to complete the Yahwehist reformation. Thomas Cranmer, a leader of the English Reformation, called the young Edward VI a 'second Josiah' on his coronation, following the death of his father Henry VIII, to encourage his full commitment to the English Reformation.

3. Sappho I
From Animism to Vespers and 1920s Poetry

Sappho's *Ode to Hesperus* and Escape from the Bell Jar

This is a first visit to the poet-songstress Sappho, as she joins the high priest Aaron as a cultural guide in Eliot's poem. Among the many riches she brings is his preferred Classicism. His view of her place in culture can be seen in the continuum she represents between the vegetation ceremonies of Notes, vespers in Magnus Martyr, and the poetics of the 1920s.

> As poet, as legendary literary figure, Sappho has had an undeniable fascination for readers ever since she composed her poems on the island of Lesbos at the close of the seventh century B.C.E. From Plato's celebration of Sappho as the tenth muse to Robin Morgan's renunciation of Sappho as literary foremother ("get off my back, Sappho"), the life and lyrics of Sappho have haunted the Western imagination. Sappho's intense, burning verses of feminine desire have presided over the Western lyric much the way Homer's epics have occupied their authoritative position in Western literature. Sappho comes down to us as a kind of mother goddess of poetry: imitated, ventriloquized, renounced, worshiped, and feared, as perhaps no other single poet in the Western tradition.[116]

To Ellen Greene's appreciation can be added Eliot's, since he shows us that Sappho figuratively sings in Magnus Martyr, where she meets Aaron, through the traces of her music in Christian song. That striking connection between the Hellenism of Sappho and the Hebraism of Aaron underlies Part III of *The Waste Land*.

> At the violet hour, the evening hour that strives
> Homeward, and brings the sailor home from sea,
>
> (*The Waste Land* 220-1)

Since 'all the women are one woman' [218n] in the poem, the extraordinary Sappho is Eliot's forlorn typist in a different time and place. That she represents guidance in Eliot's poem is embedded in her evening star as shepherd's guide. Eliot extends this theme of stellar guidance to both the 'fishmen' [263] of the Thames and the New England coast of his origins. 'This may not appear as exact as Sappho's lines, but I had in mind the 'longshore' or 'dory' fisherman, who returns at nightfall' [221n]. In that way, Eliot connects these lines to Sappho's *Ode to Hesperus*. Sappho's guiding star Hesperus is the Vesper of classical Rome who, with other allusions in the poem, guides the reader to vespers at the violet hour of dusk in Magnus Martyr.

> Hesperus, you bring home all the bright dawn disperses,
> bring home the sheep,
> bring home the goat,
> bring the child home to its mother.
>
> (Sappho *Ode to Hesperus*)[117]

'Eliot liked to stress that the very nature of poetry is in part music. This is most obvious in his use of musical titles — quartets, song, prelude, rhapsody, 'Words for music', five-finger exercises, invention, suite, caprice, nocturne and humoresque'.[118] In *The Waste Land*, one aspect of the music 'upon the waters' [257] of the Thames is the sound of vespers drifting from Magnus Martyr at 'the violet hour' of dusk. We will see that the journey of humankind in Eliot's poem reaches back to a time before Sappho, to the origins of music and poetry in the primal rhythms of the cultural and spiritual genesis of humanity.

Much could be said on Eliot's agreement with Nietzsche that music offers escape from isolation. In his innovative early work Nietzsche retains traces of the metaphysical and is still a classical scholar, though he approaches it in a startlingly new way. He is also deeply immersed in myth as he seeks the primal sources of music and theatre as expressions of the human condition.

> But the folk song represents for us in the very first instance a musical mirror of the world, an original melody, which now seeks a parallel phenomenon in dream and expresses this in poetry. *So the melody is the first and the universal principle ...* Melody gives birth to poetry, over and over again: this is exactly what the *verse-form of the folk song* tells us ... In this sense we may distinguish two main currents in the history of the Greek people, according to whether language imitates the world of phenomena and images or the world of music ... The world symbolism of music utterly exceeds the grasp of language, because it refers symbolically to the original contradiction and pain at the heart of the original Unity, and therefore symbolises a sphere which exists over and above all phenomena.
>
> (Friedrich Nietzsche *The Birth of Tragedy*)[119]

At that time Nietzsche was captivated by the music of his friend and mentor Richard Wagner, particularly the opera about the tragic love of Tristan and Isolde. Eliot includes quotes from that opera in the poem, and points to it in the Notes: 'V. *Tristan und Isolde*, I, Verses 5-8' [31n].

> *Frish weht der Wind*   [31]
> *Der Heimat zu,*
> *Mein Irish Kind,*
> *Wo weilest du?*

> [Fresh blows the Wind
> Towards the Homeland,
> My Irish Child,
> Where are you lingering?][120]

Wagner's German language opera arises from European culture, since Arthurian romance literature, with its Celtic mythological background, developed from romance origins in France. It depicts the tragic consequences of the marriage of the Irish princess Isolde to King Mark of Cornwall, though she loves the knight Tristan. The reverberating implications of the presence of Wagner and his opera in Eliot's poem, including the recent loss of Ireland to the empire, are beyond the scope of this book except for one aspect.

That is Nietzsche's remarkable passage in which he identifies the human's temporary escape from their ego, and so from the pain of isolation, through the rapture of music. There are a number of remarkable images within this passage. For Nietzsche, Wagner's opera is capable of transporting the listener to their 'primal home amidst the piping of the pastoral metaphysical dance'. This metaphor brings to life the group bonding of the rituals of the primeval community of humanity implicit in the vegetation ceremonies of Eliot's Notes.[121] A second image describes one of the problems of modernity — the pain of isolation caused by the human ego — as the 'wretched bell jar of human individuality'.[122]

> I should like to ask these genuine musicians whether they can imagine a man who could perceive the third act of Tristan and Isolde ... without expiring at the convulsive spreading of their souls' wings? ... How can he bear, in the wretched bell jar of human individuality, to hear the innumerable cries of delight and woe from a 'wide space of the world's night', without inexorably fleeing to his primal home amidst the piping of the pastoral metaphysical dance?
>
> (Friedrich Nietzsche *The Birth of Tragedy*)[123]

In that operatic moment, Nietzsche has been transported from his sense of alienated individuality to the communal. His 'wretched bell jar of individuality' echoes the epigraph of Eliot's poem in which the Sibyl of Cumae is famously trapped in a bell jar and, in philosophy, the opaque spheres of F.H. Bradley that enclose and isolate each individual [411n]. The wretched bell jar of individuality of the Sibyl, Nietzsche and Bradley — the 'prison' [413] of the self — is central to Eliot's poetic exploration of how people such as the typist and clerk cope with their existence within society.

Eliot agrees with Nietzsche that music, as both a universal language and beyond language, has represented an escape from the increasing isolation of the developing human ego since the genesis of the human individual. A dialogue between the classical and modern ego, between the *via media* and extreme egoisms, runs throughout Eliot's poem, including in the romantic rendezvous between the typist and clerk. There is a suggestion that vespers in Magnus

Martyr might be more nourishing and communally uplifting than her romantic supper of 'food in tins' [223].

The Genesis of European Culture
From Sappho to 1920s Modernity

> O violet-haired, holy, honeysmiling Sappho
> (Alcaeus)

The only physical description we have of Sappho is that of her fellow poet Alcaeus from her home island of Lesbos.[124] It is not a reference to dyed hair but to interwoven violets as a floral headdress, a homage to her muse Aphrodite, her divine ally in love.[125] In Homer's hymn to Aphrodite, she is crowned with gold and violets.

> I will sing of stately Aphrodite, gold-crowned and beautiful, whose dominion is the walled cities of all sea-set Cyprus ... there the gold-filleted Hours welcomed her joyously. They clothed her with heavenly garments: on her head they put a fine, well-wrought crown of gold, and in her pierced ears they hung ornaments of orichalcum and precious gold, and adorned her with golden necklaces over her soft neck and snow-white breasts, jewels which the gold-filleted Hours wear themselves whenever they go to their father's house to join the lovely dances of the gods. And when they had fully decked her, they brought her to the gods, who welcomed her when they saw her, giving her their hands. Each one of them prayed that he might lead her home to be his wedded wife, so greatly were they amazed at the beauty of violet-crowned Cytherea.[126]

The contrast between men's enjoyment of and respect for such finely adorned female divinity in the classical world and puritanical ideas of spiritual harlotry aligned with the slanderous Eve myth in Judeo-Christianity is striking. Representations of Sappho through history up to the time of Eliot's poem have been varied. Sappho as prostitute, licentious lesbian and wanton pagan contrasts to the various sanitised and chaste Sapphos, including the Sappho whose lesbian poetry is but the ritual expression of a virgin priestess. 'Most hurtful to Sappho were the majority of her defenders from the seventeenth to the early twentieth century', eager to 'clean up Sappho's act'. There were exceptions such as 'Charles Baudelaire, who paid bitterly for his candor', and William Muir of Caldwell, who admitted Sappho's broad sexuality but termed it 'so foul a blot on the Greek national character'.[127]

Sappho was born around 630 BCE in the Archaic Greek period from which the classical period was emerging. It was a resurgent time of Greek civilisation following the Bronze Age collapse across the Mediterranean that led to the Greek Dark Ages. The Linear B writing script of the Minoans, the first clearly identifiable Greek culture, was no longer used by Sappho's time. That was a writing system of approximately ninety syllabic signs and one hundred ideographs, each of the latter representing an object of some form. According to linguists, the script was used for bureaucratic administration and not for cultural purposes such as art, religion or social communication. Linear B had followed the earlier and as yet undeciphered Linear A. The Minoan language was also expressed in early Bronze Age Cretan hieroglyphs, also yet to be deciphered. Some scholars see Phoenician and other ancient Semitic roots in Linear A.

A new writing system had been adopted from an alphabet originating on the other side of the Mediterranean Sea, that of the North Semitic language of the Phoenicians. 'There is no doubt that the origins of the writing system adopted by Greek speakers centuries after they abandoned Linear B lie in a much earlier script invented to record the languages of the ancient Levant and brought west by merchants from Phoenicia in the eight century BCE ... The Greeks themselves were committed to the foreign origins of their script, and often called their letters "Phoenicians." They added vowels by recycling existing Phoenician letters that had been used for sounds that did not exist in Greek'.[128]

Underwriting most European languages and many others including Hebrew, the Phoenician alphabet emerged from the Proto-Sinaitic script developed at the ancient borders of Egypt. It is thought to be a version of Egyptian hieroglyphs adopted and simplified by Canaanite mine workers, who left a small number of inscriptions both in the mines and in the adjacent temple of Hathor. It would have been known to Eliot, since the script was discovered in 1905 by Flinders and Hilda Petrie. Sometimes called Proto-Canaanite, it is considered close to Paleo-Hebrew. The A of the modern Western alphabet evolved from the *aleph* of that script, in turn said to be derived from the ox or bull-head hieroglyph.

The oral and written Greek of Sappho's time became Koine Greek, the shared language that facilitated the trade and diplomacy of the Mediterranean and beyond. This was also the language of early New Testament writings spread by St. Paul and his acolytes along merchant routes to Corinth and Rome, termed Biblical Greek. As such, the language of Sappho, written in the alphabet of 'Phlebas the Phoenician' [312], facilitated the spread of Christianity throughout Europe. That included Britannia, where it crossed the Londinium bridge of the Romans. We will see that Sappho's music travelled the same path to London, and into the Church of St. Magnus the Martyr in the form of vespers.

Eliot admired Sappho as much as he did James Joyce. He represents to Eliot the summit of modern prose literature; she is the classical poetic genius of literature at the crossover between oral and written culture. As such, Sappho is fundamental to the scheme of his poem, carrying forward the most ancient of incantatory inheritances. Since 'Sappho wrote as she spoke', she wrote from that very ancient wellspring from which arose, at least figuratively, the foundation myths sought by James Frazer and the primal rhythm theorised at the time by Antoine Meillet, the poetic parent meter.[129]

A metaphor from the time of Sappho encapsulates this transition from oral to written culture in an epigram by Posidippus. He writes that 'the Sapphic white pages speak ... here Sappho's fame rests on a page that speaks, a phrase that wonderfully combines the impact of orality and textuality ... the poetry is at once song and script as oral and textual traditions intertwine'.[130]

The earliest Greek verse preserved in writing dates from the 8th cen. BCE, and poetry has continued to be composed in Greek from that time until the present day. But modern research indicates that the Greek poetic tradition is, in fact, far older than the introduction of writing. The nature of the word groupings of which the Homeric epics are largely composed, as well as the content of those epics, imply a preexisting oral tradition of dactylic heroic poetry extending back into the bronze age civilization of the Mycenaeans, which came to an end about 1100 BCE. The aeolic meters that are used in extant Greek poetry, notably by Sappho and Alcaeus, presuppose an even more ancient oral tradition of song, for they show clear affinities with the meters of the Indian Vedas; their ultimate origins may, therefore, date back as far as about 2000 BCE. It is also now generally recognized that Greek poetry emerged from and participated in an ancient Near Eastern and Eastern Mediterranean cultural koine. These links with the music, poetry and culture of the ancient Near East are strongest perhaps in the preliterate and early archaic periods, but various kinds of cultural interaction almost certainly continued to influence Greek verse throughout its history [vice versa].

The introduction of an alphabet specifically adapted to the recording of Greek, which took place no later than the mid-8th century BCE, was no doubt the most important single event in the history of Greek poetry. Greek (and European) literature begins here, at the point where the songs could be fixed in permanent form and transmitted to posterity.[131]

The word that encapsulates the 'cultural koine' noted in this remarkable summation is 'demotic' [212]. Denoting a common language, it encases both cultural and spiritual meanings in *The Waste Land*, as we will see in our visits to the cities of Babel and Pandemonium. Most often the language of international traders and empires, it is a shared language that transcends borders and local cultures. The Koine Greek of the classical Mediterranean was the lingua franca of classical times. The 'demotic French' [212] of the poem alludes to the term lingua franca, the 'language of the Franks', a shared language across much of Europe from medieval times up to the eighteenth century, including in Tsarist Moscow. When Geoffrey Chaucer wrote to Richard II requesting time off from his job — not during his time as clerk of works for the Church of St. Magnus the Martyr but as controller of the London Wool Quay — he wrote in French as 'the primary bureaucratic language of the day'.[132] The idea of a shared language includes music and flows through the unifying continuums of the mythic layer of the poem.

The Princeton schema points to a very ancient and widespread shared oral culture from which the ritual, song and poetry of the various component cultures evolved at different times. Those component cultures in turn contributed to shared culture through shared parent languages, such as Proto-Indo-European. The cultural importance of this concept, and its early-stage inflection by theology, can be seen in Frazer's comment in *Folk-Lore In The Old Testament*. The 'authors of Genesis say nothing as to the nature of the common language which all mankind spoke before the confusion of tongues ... in modern times, when the science of philology was in its infancy, strenuous, but necessarily abortive, efforts were made to deduce all forms of human speech from Hebrew as their original'.[133]

Homer, dated to the end of the eight century BCE, is often proposed as the start point of European literature. Eliot does so when describing the relationship between the individual author and the continuum of European literature: 'the whole of the literature of Europe from Homer and within it the whole of the literature of his own country has a simultaneous existence and composes a simultaneous order'.[134] Studies of Homer's phraseology and meter in the 1920's already suggested that Homer was also the product of oral culture, part of a 'long-standing tradition of ancient Greek singers that led eventually to Homer'.[135] That ancient culture developed within a widespread cultural conversation.

Homer's world is a world touched at every point by the East and South, by Asia Minor, Phoenicia, Crete, Egypt, Libya. Recent excavations on prehistoric sites, Mycenae, Tiryns, Troy, Crete, Egypt, have shown that this contact existed long before Homer. We now know that the whole eastern and probably the western basin of the Mediterranean was, from

Neolithic days, occupied by a people whose civilization was, broadly speaking, homogeneous, and that this civilization continued substantially unbroken from Neolithic down to historic days.

(Jane Harrison *The Religion Of Ancient Greece* 1913)

Eliot wrote of Sappho that what 'matters most, let us say, in reading an ode of Sappho, is not that I should imagine myself to be an island Greek of twenty-five hundred years ago; what matters is the experience which is the same, for all human beings capable of enjoying poetry, of different centuries and languages, the spark which can leap across those 2,500 years'.[136] As the Princeton commentary above shows, Sappho must also be central to any discussion of the genesis of European literature and, for the purposes of Eliot's poem, there are more advantages. She was a woman, and often expresses intensely romantic loves within the poise and spirit of the classical. Both her music and her evening star Hesperus as the Roman Vesper link her to vespers, and so to the Church of St. Magnus the Martyr in 1922. Her evening star brings mythological and classical literary riches to the poem, and her poetics, present in Eliot's poem, are a legacy of the oral cultures of pre-Olympian humanity.

In the figurative schema of his poem, European literature begins when the ancient rituals of animist ceremonies evolve into the genius of the 'holy, honeysmiling' poet-songstress Sappho, to be recorded and preserved through the newly adopted Phoenician alphabet of Phlebas. Regrettably, that preservation is only in fragmentary form, since Barnstone notes that 'Sappho suffered from book-burning religious authorities who left us largely scraps of torn papyrus'.[137] In that, Sappho is another instance when zealot iconoclasts have fragmented and impoverished the cultural continuum to which Eliot is so committed, an impoverishment inbuilt in the structural fragmentation of his poem.

Sappho was also topical at the time of his poem. Erika Rohrbach notes the '1890's boom of interest in her' continued into the early twentieth century when, for 'a number of modernists, much was at stake in the reading of Sappho'; and that 'Woolf and company make Sappho the object of study for the formation of their own insular female "society"'. That said, they shared classical themes with the men of modernism. The fragment poems of Hilda Dolittle, who wrote as H.D., address the self-castrating Attis, and 'H.D. restores Aphrodite'.[138] Among her other influences on modernists, Sappho seems the original Imagist. 'In her own fragment poems H.D. used Sappho to expand her poetic relation to imagism ... H.D. mostly sought refuge in Sappho's lesbianism as a poetic escape from real heterosexual trauma ... H.D. used Sappho as a projection of her own life, not as she wished it to be, but as it was'.[139]

Sappho was particularly important for the women writers of modern literature in the early 1900s in pointing to a female poetic exemplar from less oppressive times. It is clear she served as a rebuke to a male dominated society that stifled women, including their artistic potential. '"Perhaps in Lesbos" Virginia Woolf speculates, "but never since have these conditions been the lot of women"'.[140]

Vespers
From Animism to Sappho and Magnus Martyr

In an echo of Ezra Pound's comment that a 'return to origins invigorates', Eliot wrote in 1919 that 'The maxim, return to the sources, is a good one'.[141] Through Sappho, Eliot returns to the source of

European culture, and to a source of the church music of vespers. While Sappho's evening star Hesperus as the Roman Vesper is the primary allusion to vespers, church evening song is also brought to the poem through a number of other allusions. Critics note the allusion to Dante's *Purgatorio* encased in Eliot's reference to Sappho. Southam writes of the lines opening with 'Homeward, and brings the sailor home from sea' [221] that 'these lines seem to be modelled upon the evening scene at the opening to the *Purgatorio* viii'.[142] Dante's canto opens with the vespers bell at the close of day.

> Now was the hour that wakens fond desire
> In men at sea, and melts their thoughtful heart,
> Who in the morn have bid sweet friends farewell,
> And pilgrim newly on his road with love
> Thrills, if he hear the vesper bell from far,   [8.5]
> That seems to mourn for the expiring day:
>   (*Purgatorio* Canto VIII)

Dante's scene resonates with the theme of maritime guidance in the Notes on 'the 'longshore' or 'dory' fisherman, who returns at nightfall' [221n]. Hearing the sound of bells from shore, Dante's fisherman sings the vesper *Te Luce Ante*: 'To Thee God before the close of day'.

> Both palms it join'd and rais'd,   [8.10]
> ...
> "Te Lucis Ante," so devoutly then
> Came from its lip, and in so soft a strain,
> ...
> Follow'd through all the hymn, with upward gaze

The 'upward gaze' of Dante's sailor leads to a third suggestion of vespers. It is the same heavenward gaze to the 'divine office' suggested at 'the violet hour, when the eyes and back | Turn upwards from the desk' [215]. We will meet the errant angel Mammon in the city of Pandemonium, his eyes covetously downcast to the pavements of gold in Heaven. The desk, an image of the commercial day-time office in which the eyes are downcast, evokes its spiritual evening opposite. That is the divine office of vespers, when the eyes turn upwards from the worldly day to matters of the spirit.

Eliot's play *Murder in the Cathedral* explicitly connects vespers and the divine office when, on the arrival of the murderous knights, a fearful priest advises Thomas Becket, 'My Lord, to vespers! You must not be absent from vespers. You must not be absent from the divine office'.[143] In *Ulysses*, there is 'Father Conmee, reading his office'.[144] In Book II of *Paradise Lost*, Satan and his monstrous daughter are confined to a profane, hateful office. 'Into this gloom of Tartarus profound, | To sit in hateful Office here confin'd'.

Secular or spiritual, the upward gaze signifies the distinction between the animal and the human not so evident in the young man carbuncular, whose 'bold stare' [232] looks down unlit stairs. Ovid makes this explicit in *Metamorphoses*, from which Eliot adopts the dual-gender Tiresias to be 'the most important personage' [218n] of his poem.

> And even though all other animals
> Lean forward and look down toward the ground
> He gave to man a face that is uplifted
> And ordered him to stand erect and look
> directly up into the vaulted heavens
> and turn his countenance to meet the stars;
>
> (*Metamorphoses* I, 118-123)[145]

In *The Rock*, that upward gaze is associated with the lighting of lamps integral to the ritual of vespers as the sun sets. It also gives thanks for the 'gilded carven wood' of churches, recalling Thomas Allen's 1828 description of the 'resplendent design' of a previous manifestation of the Magnus Martyr altarpiece as 'mouldings and dressings white and gold'.[146]

> We thank thee for the lights we have kindled
> The light of altar and of sanctuary;
> Small lights of those who meditate at midnight
> …
> The gilded carven wood, the coloured fresco.
> Our gaze is submarine, our eyes look upward
>
> (*The Rock* Part II)

A fourth allusion to vespers can be seen in the isolation of the typist as she puts a 'record on the gramophone' [256] which, as Rainey points out, rhymes with 'alone' [254].[147] In *Ulysses*, immediately preceding the Hebraic-Hellenic declaration that 'Jewgreek is greekjew', the gramophone is linked with both the coarse propositioning of the chorus of 'Cheap whores' and the sacred classical and Judeo-Christian chorus and choir singing an 'old hymn to Demeter': '*the gramophone begins to blare* The Holy City … THE GRAMOPHONE | Jerusalem! | Open your gates and sing | Hosanna …'.[148] Before he had sight of *Ulysses*, those contrasts, and the motif of sacred song, are also evident in the sacred and secular aspects of music in Eliot's sole prose work of fiction after Harvard, *Eeldrop and Appleplex* of 1917, in which the 'gramophones' are juxtaposed to the communal song of the 'choir of the Baptist chapel'.[149]

This contrast in Eliot's poetry is not isolated, nor is it limited to music. In the opening verse of *Preludes*, again of 1917, there is the significant lacuna before the stanza that opens with 'And then the lighting of the lamps'. It refers to lighting street lamps, and is also an explicit repetition of lighting candles and lamps for vespers, for which the church term is 'the lighting of the lamps'. It arises from the 'hour of lights' of early Christianity known as *Lucenaria hora*, symbolically creating an 'infinite light'.[150] *Preludes* deploys the juxtaposition of urban realism and the sacred he learned from those such as Charles Baudelaire, further compressed and distilled in *The Waste Land*.

> Six o'clock.
> The burnt-out ends of smoky days.
> And now a gusty shower wraps
> The grimy scraps
> Of withered leaves about your feet
> And newspapers from vacant lots;
> The showers beat
> On broken blinds and chimney-pots,
> And at the corner of the street
> A lonely cab-horse steams and stamps.
>
> And then the lighting of the lamps.
>
> (T.S. Eliot, *Preludes*, 1917)

We have seen that the aeolic meter of Sappho's poetry arises from more ancient sources, so that Sappho becomes the musical bridge between Eliot's vegetation ceremonies and the ritual of vespers in Magnus Martyr. In something of an irony, while as a totem of allegedly wanton paganism she has been the object of vituperative scribal misogyny, the music of her poetics rang out in churches. 'In the Middle Ages, the sapphic acquired rhyme and was instrumental in the transition from metrical (quantitative) to rhythmical (accentual) meter ... there are 127 examples in *Analecta hymnica* (Selected Hymns).'[151]

The physical journey of Sappho's music to London and Magnus Martyr can be traced from the earliest Christian music of the Roman Empire in the Levant. Since the Romans had no indigenous system, they used and taught Greek theory and practise in music, of which Sappho is an exemplary practitioner and her near contemporary Pythagoras the theorist. Exported by the Roman Empire, it underlies the mix of Hebrew, Syriac and Graeco-Roman music of the early Christianity of the southern Mediterranean.

From there it followed Pauline Christianity to classical Rome. It became a musical 'demotic' [212], the blend that underwrites all subsequent Christian music. When Rome converted to Christianity, it spread throughout Europe and across Londinium bridge, to underwrite the composition of the music of vespers in the Church of St. Magnus the Martyr.

'Underlying the success of all systems, of course, is sheer naked power. In the case of Western harmony, it began with the muscle of the Roman Empire, which spread diatonic scales, and in due course a system of chants based on the Jewish psalms, throughout the Mediterranean basin.'[152] A key locus of the rise of this new sacred music was east of Jerusalem in Edessa, capital of the 'little kingdom' Osrhoene. Osrhoene has been termed the first Christian state, where a folk legend recounts an exchange of letters between Jesus and its king. The 'Romans conquered Osrhoene and made it part of the empire in the 240s, but before that its Kings had let Christianity flourish.'[153] In his accompanying television series, Diarmaid MacCulloch visits a Syrian Christian church to listen to its music, and speaks of the genesis there of Christian music.

For the last 17 centuries, Christianity has been repeatedly
linked with the state ... and this is where it all started, in the
ancient Christian kingdom of Edessa ... Edessa pioneered
something else that has become inseparable from Christianity.
Church music. Current Syrian church hymns derive from
the poetry of the great 4th century theologian St. Ephrem.
And he was building on an even earlier tradition from these
lands, echoing the music of the Roman Empire. What we
were hearing was the ghost of the music of the streets and
marketplaces seized by the church and turned into psalms
and hymns, taken across the western Mediterranean, turned
into the music of the whole church. Latin and Gregorian
chant, Johann Sebastian Bach, even the tambourines and
guitars of the Pentecostals; all come from here.[154]

Edessa sat at the juncture of empires, so absorbing Hebrew, Greek
and Roman influences from its incorporation into the Roman
Empire. It was also a centre of literary culture for Semitic Aramaic
writings. Later, that merged into a form of Syriac demotic from
which arose some of the early Christian writings. 'Languages like
this became known as Syriac and there was originally a single alpha-
betic script for its literature, Estrangela.'[155] Early Christian writings
were translated into the more international Koine Greek to become
Biblical Greek, and with St. Paul's Greek writings formed the
embryonic New Testament. The 'Alexandria' [374] of the poem later
became the centre of such translation and theology.

Christianity had spread east as well as west ... to Edessa,
a cosmopolitan trading city under the protection of the
Romans ... Christians in Edessa were able to build proper
public church buildings. The earliest public church building

in the world is recorded here ... We tend to think of church music in western terms ... But the real source of western church music probably lies ... in Syria with church leaders like Ephrem of Edessa, who wrote hymns and liturgy in metrical verse and even put new, orthodox lyrics to older popular melodies ... Eastern popes in Rome imported these practices. Western Christians who sing the Agnus Dei, 'Lamb of God, who takes away the sins of the world', are using a Syrian form of words imported by Pope Sergius. And English church music followed suit: there was a Syrian Archbishop of Canterbury, Theodore of Tarsus, of whom Bede says that after he arrived on English shores, 'they began in all the churches of the English to learn Church music'.[156]

The phrase 'At the violet hour' is repeated [215, 220] in the poem, the first suggesting the upward gaze to the divine office of vespers, the second invoking the classical Sappho and her Hesperus, the Roman Vesper. In this way among others, the Hebraic the Hellenic, the Judeo-Christian and the classical, the spiritual and art are entwined in Eliot's modernity. When the Greco-Roman music of Sappho fused with Hebraic and other Levantine folk musical elements to become early Christian hymn, it would have particularly influenced vespers, one of the most ancient Offices of the Christian Church. Before early Christianity became so, it was a reformist sect within Judaism. As a continuation of the Hebrew evening sacrifice of the Old Law, the formal title of vespers is *vespertina synaxis* — 'Synaxis (synaxis from synago) means gathering, assembly, reunion. It is exactly equivalent to the Latin collecta (from colligere), and corresponds to synagogue'.[157]

The theory of Pythagoras, born perhaps in the same year Sappho died, underlies the theory of music.[158] He may have arrived at some of this theory while listening to the compositions of Sappho. It is notable that the *Oxyrhynchus* hymn, the earliest known fragment of Christian music, is notated in Greek. It was found in an ancient rubbish heap near the site of Aphroditopolis in a 1918 archaeological dig in which a significant cache of the fragments of Sappho was also found. Through a version of the classical chorus sung by workmen, Eliot's *The Rock* seems to allude to such zealot iconoclasm.

> CHORUS:
> We wait on corners, with nothing to bring but the song
>   we can sing which nobody wants to hear sung;
> Waiting to be flung in the end, on a heap less useful
>   than dung'.[159]

The *Vigil of Venus* to Welcome Spring

Towards the close of *The Waste Land* Eliot introduces another extraordinary poem, the *Pervigilium Veneris*, the *Vigil of Venus*. Written between 250 and 450 CE, it sits on that significant border in time when the classical world of late antiquity ceded to the early centuries of a christianised Europe. He names the poem in the Notes, and quotes it in the original Latin, meaning 'when will I be like the swallow'.

> *Quando fiam uti chelidon* — O swallow swallow
>   (*The Waste Land* 428)

> *V. Pervigilium Veneris.* Cf. Philomela in Parts II and III.
>   (Notes *on the Waste Land* 428n)

A joyous account of a festival held over several days from the first day of April, it celebrates the bounteous effect of Venus on the spring earth.[160] Recent work on the poem by William Barton helps to illuminate its relationship with *The Waste Land*. Until Barton, it has languished in literary consideration. Like the work of Sappho, it survives in fragments, so that there have been numerous reconfigurations over time.

> *Tomorrow let him love who never has before, and let he who has*
>   *loved also love tomorrow!*
> Spring is new, spring is now full of song, in spring the world
>   was born.
> In spring lovers come together, in spring the birds wed,
> And the wood lets down her hair under nuptial downpours.
> Tomorrow, in the shade of trees, the lover's matchmaker
> Weaves verdant bowers out of myrtle shoots.
> Tomorrow Dione rules enthroned on high.[161]   [5]

We have seen Sappho's poetry and music carry forward the ancient rhythms of Eliot's primeval rituals from oral to written culture through her aeolic meter. It was then carried by the Roman Empire to the early Christianity of the Levant, from where it underwrites subsequent European and Christian music. An aspect of the *Pervigilium* is that it can be seen as a specific instance in this continuum, a crossroads at which we witness the passing of the poetic baton from the Rome of late antiquity to the Rome and Europe of Christianity. Since the *Pervigilium* is written in variations of Roman classical trochaic tetrameter later 'given an injection of energy by writers of early Christian hymns', it joins the poetics of Sappho in the classical continuum into modernity.[162]

A celebration exclusive to women, these are the festival days of the Venus who encourages chastity, Venus Verticordia, whose sacred flower is myrtle. She animates and is suffused within nature as 'the wood lets down her hair in nuptial downpours', so that she is the source of the awakening of the world and all its life in spring.

> *Tomorrow let him love who never has before, and let he who has*
>   *loved also love tomorrow!* [163]
> It is she who paints the purpling year with flowery gems,
> She who encourages the swelling buds with the
>   West Wind's breath
> Into their unfolding nodes; she who sprinkles the
>   moistening waters   [15]
> Of glittering dew that the night breeze leaves behind.
> Look! The trembling teardrops glitter with their
>   unsteady weight;
> And the dripping bead in a small sphere checks
>   its fall.

The intense contrast to the desiccated waste land of Part V of Eliot's poem is more striking because the direction to the *Pervigilium* sits in the notes to Part V.

> Here is no water but only rock
> Rock and no water and the sandy road
> The road winding above among the mountains
> Which are mountains of rock without water
> If there were water we should stop and drink
> Among the rock one cannot stop or think
> Sweat is dry and feet are in the sand

If there were only water amongst the rock
Dead mountain mouth of carious teeth that cannot spit
Here one can neither stand nor lie nor sit
There is not even silence in the mountains
But dry sterile thunder without rain

(The Waste Land Part V 331-342)

The parched reader, arriving at the close of *The Waste Land* thoroughly disconcerted by its clangourous, alienating fragmentation and babel, is guided in the Notes to a spiritual community of women in the classical sacred wood and plenteous, life-giving water. The *Pervigilium* is bounteous in many ways. The refrain 'appeals for universal love' and is repeated throughout the poem, which 'presents itself as a literary hymn to the goddess of love'.[164]

What is witnessed is the classical legacy of the vegetation ceremonies of Eliot's Notes, and not in the crudely sexualised form that more coloured interpretations of polytheism suggest. In this festival of Venus the carnal is rejected, while women and the feminine are celebrated. The most secular of modern women, transported in one of Eliot's timeless moments to this sacred woodland, would have become the participant in an extended celebration exclusive to women of great beauty and joyous grace.

You would now have seen, for three nights of festival,
Chorus bands moving along your paths amongst
    gathered groups
Amongst wreathed flowers and amongst the
    myrtle bowers.   [45]
Neither Ceres, nor Bacchus, nor the god of poets is absent.
The whole should be extended and kept vigil with song.
May Dione reign in the woods! You, Delia, leave!

Tomorrow let him love who never has before,
    and let he who has loved also love tomorrow!
The goddess has ordered her court to be decked with
    Hyblean flowers,   [50]
She presides and exercises jurisdiction, the Graces
    have sat down around.
Hybla, pour out all your flowers, whatever the year
    has brought![165]
Hybla, don your flowery cloak, as far as the plain of
    Aetna extends!
The girls from the countryside will be here, even the
    girls from the mountains,
As well as those who dwell in the woods and the groves
    and the fountains;   [55]
The winged boy's mother commands them all to take
    a seat around
And she instructs the girls to have no faith in
    naked Love.

The 'winged boy' Cupid is viewed with caution, and Venus 'instructs the girls to have no faith in naked love'. The chaste celebratory beauty of this fertility festival is of Venus the Creator as the goddess of purity and chastity. It gives the lie to characterisations of such polytheistic worship as orgiastic, and the characterisation of female participants (and, in other contexts, men who honour a female aspect of the divine) as prostituting themselves in spiritual and actual harlotry.

The Venus of this festival is the Roman form of Sappho's Aphrodite, and is honoured with the same womanly grace and form as Sappho's celebrants at the Kritan altar almost a millennium earlier.

Kritan women once danced supplely
around a beautiful altar with light feet
crushing the soft flowers of grass.

(Sappho *Dancers at a Kritan Altar*)

While the modern visitor would likely be beguiled and immersed,
for the participants of the time it was of another order of intensity.
Venus the Creator not only inspirits the natural world, she flows in
the veins of the celebrants.

She, the creatress, with all-pervading spirit and hidden powers
Hold sway within the minds and the veins.
Through the heavens, the earth and seas, all under her control, [65]
She infused her penetrating influence by the passage of seed
And she ordered the world to know the ways of birth.

The unknown author is well versed in a range of classical poets, many
of whom, with their imagery, are shared with *The Waste Land*, such
as Virgil, Ovid and Horace. Barton shows that it is in the poetry of
Horace in the first century BCE that we first encounter the 'nightingale' [100], the 'swallow' [428], and the 'barbarous king' and
'Philomel' [99] of *The Waste Land*.

The unhappy bird makes her nest
Bewailing tearfully her Itys and the eternal disgrace
Of the Cecropean house, because she wickedly avenged
The barbarous lusts of kings.

(Horace *Odes* IV. XII)[166]

A detailed discussion of the symbolism of the nightingale, the swallow and the Philomela myth is outside the scope of this book. What can be noted is another remarkable resonance between these poems.

> The poem at large demonstrates the conflicted and ambiguous feeling of the poet towards his own song in several ways: he has chosen to write a highly literary poem in a meter often associated in antiquity with popular genres and sub-literary chants. Indeed, some commentators have gone as far as calling it 'the meter *par excellence* of doggerel and jingles'. The conflict between the highly allusive and artificial style of the poem and the meter chosen as its medium has already been noted, and even when the increasing popularity of the meter for more serious literary works in the late antique and early medieval periods is taken into consideration, a certain disconnect remains in the case of the *Pervigilium*. The meter was taken up by Christian writers such as Prudentius and Hilary of Poitiers and became an important meter of early Christian hymnography, yet although the *Pervigilium* is closest to the usage of these authors, it contains no hint of Christian thought or imagery. It is a markedly classical poem. This leaves the *Pervigilium* in a no-man's land: from a Classical point of view the meter is an odd fit with the literary aspects of the poem and in the period when the meter became popular for more serious literary endeavours, the *Pervigilium*'s strong classical themes and allusions do not fit its Christian milieu.[167]

Whether there is a version of the more classical poetic meters of the *Pervigilium* in Eliot's poem remains to be seen. Ezra Pound had worked on and commented on the *Pervigilium*. 'The point is that the *metric* of the *Pervigilium* probably indicated as great a change of sensibility in its day as the change from Viennese waltzes to jazz may indicate in our own'.[168] In noting the popular genres and sub-literary chants and the meter of doggerel and jingles, Barton could be writing of the jazz-age aspects of Eliot's poem.

> O O O O that Shakespeherian Rag—
> It's so elegant
> So intelligent   [130]

Why does Eliot direct the reader to this poem? In its joyous female welcome of spring, the *Pervigilium* undermines theories of *The Waste Land* as unremittingly bleak and despairing. It is a compelling example of how the mythic layer of the poem belies miserabilist, misogynistic ideas of *The Waste Land*.

Hebraism and Hellenism
What has Athens to do with Jerusalem?

> The Catholic Church was derived from three sources. Its sacred history was Jewish, its theology was Greek, its government and canon law were, at least indirectly, Roman. The Reformation rejected the Roman elements, softened the Greek elements, and greatly strengthened the Judaic elements.
> (Bertrand Russell *A History of Western Philosophy*)[169]

The twinning of Aaron and Sappho as guides is Eliot's poetic representation of a core aspect thought to shape Western culture. That is the combined influence of Athens and Jerusalem, a comingling of classical Greek culture and Judeo-Christianity. The idea is older than Eliot and Mathew Arnold's Hebraism and Hellenism. Tertullian, the second century early Christian theologist of Carthage, at the time part of the Roman Empire, asked 'What has Athens to do with Jerusalem?' His question is in part rhetorical, seeking to diminish philosophy in favour of faith because philosophy might undermine faith.

This is not so in *The Waste Land*, where a reconfigured mix of Classicism and Judeo-Christianity form the constituents of Western culture and heritage. Joyce addresses those Judeo-Christian and classical components in *Ulysses*.

STEPHEN

The rite is the poet's rest. It may be an old hymn to Demeter or also illustrate *Coela enarrant gloriam Domini*. It is susceptible of nodes or modes as far apart as hyperphrygian and mixolydian and of texts so divergent as priests hailhooping round David's that is Circe's or what am I saying Cere's altar and David's tip from the stable to his chief bassoonist about the rightness of his almightiness ...

THE CAP

(*with saturnine spleen*) Ba! It is because it is. Woman's reason. Jewgreek is greekjew. Extremes meet. Death is the highest form of life. Ba!

Stephan's 'old hymn to Demeter' is of ancient Greek provenance, and *Coela enarrant gloriam Domini*, 'The heavens expound the glory of the Lord', is the deliberately misquoted opening of Psalm 19 of the Bible. Stephen's comingling of classical Greek and Hebrew ritual celebrants marks no difference between Aaronic priests 'hailhooping' around King David's biblical altar and those around the altar of Ceres, the classical Roman manifestation of the Greek Demeter. Within Joyce's intensely layered meaning, what is represented is his version of the comingled Judeo-Christian and Hellenic mother-lodes of European culture and spirituality.

Christianity has been significantly influenced by Greek thought. Eliot confirmed this perspective in 1933 when he identified Catholicism, the mother church of the Anglo-Catholic creed to which he was by then formally committed, as the creed which best expresses that accumulation of culture. 'I believe that the Catholic Church, with its inheritance from Greece and from Israel, is still, as it always has been, the great repository of wisdom'.[170] They are even more ancient twins. Hellenistic Judaism arose during the Hellenistic period marked from the death of Alexander the Great in 323 BCE to the death of Cleopatra VII in 30 BCE. Classical Greek culture had significantly influenced societies throughout Alexander's widespread empire. Ptolemy I, the founder of the House of Ptolemy that was the pharaonic family of Cleopatra, was a Macedonian Greek general. He was a close ally and friend of Alexander and his successor. Nor was the cultural and sacred exchange one way. The Greek pantheon had been influenced by early Semitic Levantine entities, so that Aphrodite is said to be the Greek manifestation of the Phoenician Queen of Heaven. Looking west, the Romans called their southern regions Magna Graecia, Greater Greece, so significant was the influence of the culture of the Greeks who had settled there from around the eight century BCE, and from where the Greek alphabet learned from the Phoenicians is likely to have spread throughout Italy.

Within that twinning there is also a tension, both in theology and society: that between reason and faith, addressed by those such as Augustine. It is notable that his epiphany on philosophy occurs in the passage that opens with 'To Carthage then I came' [307], his commentary on the Carthaginian 'cauldron of illicit loves' and his internal spiritual ulcers caused by youthful degeneracy, resonating with the carbuncles of Eliot's clerk.

> This was the society in which at a vulnerable age I was to study the textbooks on eloquence ... Following the usual curriculum I had already come across a book by a certain Cicero ... an exhortation to study philosophy ... the book changed my feelings. It altered my prayers, Lord, to be towards you yourself ... for 'with you is wisdom' (Job 12:13,16). 'Love of wisdom' is the meaning of the Greek word *philosophia* ... There are some people who use philosophy to lead people astray. They lend colour to their errors and paint them over by using a great and acceptable and honourable name.[171]

Augustine did not entirely reject philosophy. 'Like a colossus bestriding two worlds, Augustine stands as the last patristic and the first medieval father of Western Christianity. He gathered together and conserved all the main motifs of Latin Christianity from Tertullian to Ambrose ... More than this, he freely received and deliberately reconsecrated the religious philosophy of the Greco-Roman world to a new apologetic use in maintaining the intelligibility of the Christian proclamation'.[172] Following Augustine, in the thirteenth century the influential medieval philosopher-theologist Thomas Aquinas, on rediscovering and reading Plato and Aristotle, concluded in his *Summa Theologica* that great intellect is of universal value. In that way, the debate between Hebraism and Hellenism, between faith and reason, travels from earliest Christianity to modernity, to Mathew Arnold, to Joyce's 'Jewgreek is greekjew', and on to be reworked in Eliot's poem. There, the female Sappho represents Hellenic reason, art and spirituality, and Aaron represents Judeo-Christian imagery and theology.

STEPS of NEW LONDON BRIDGE, S.ͭ MAGNUS, ᴛʜᴇ MONUMENT, AND PART OF THE OLD BRIDGE.

The new London Bridge of 1831, beside the old bridge.

The old bridge was retained and used while the new bridge was built.

(London Metropolitan Archive)

The old London Bridge, terminating at the door of Magnus Martyr.

A photograph from a book as yet unidentified, dated '18—', records that 'The name of this church in antient records has the addition *at the foot of London Bridge*.'[173] The medieval bridge arrived directly at the door of the Church.

4. Pandemonium
The City, the Bridge, and the Stairs

Cities: Babel, Pandemonium and London

> It is not without reason that in 1945 the poem would be likened to the experience of listening to stations on a long-wave radio while tuning the dial between them.
>
> (Matthew Hollis *A Biography of a Poem*)[174]

Cities play an important part in *The Waste Land*. 'Jerusalem Athens Alexandra | Vienna London' [374] are explicitly mentioned, and London is central to the action. Since we are introduced to St. Augustine's *Confessions* in 'To Carthage then I came' [307], Augustine's *City of God* must also be considered. Augustine undertakes to 'write about the origin, the development, and the destined ends of the two Cities. One of these is the City of God, the other the city of this world; and God's City lives in this world's city, as far as its human element is concerned; but it lives there as an alien sojourner'.[175] Central to that book is the 'eternal city' of Rome, in both its classical and early Christian aspects.

Loud in its absence from Eliot's poem, all roads lead to Rome, a central milestone in the poem. It is the fulcrum of the route traced in the geographical continuum from the animist cultures of early humans to the early civilisations of the Mediterranean and on to the mother city of Londinium and the temple of Magnus Martyr in 1922. We will see that Londinium underlies the London of the poem, following a brief visit to Lucifer's infernal city of Pandemonium.

Pandemonium, the name of the capital city of Hell in *Paradise Lost*, was invented by Milton and means 'place of all demons'. Signifying the chaos of Hell, it is modelled in part on the biblical city of Babel. Satan returns triumphant to Pandemonium following his success in Eden. His 'glorious Work' has opened the gates of Hell, and 'made one Realm | Hell and this World, one Realm, one Continent | Of easie thorough-fare'. Having connected Hell to the human world, demonic hordes can now cross Satan's bridge 'to the upper World'. Satan's 'bright star' is the Roman Lucifer, the morning variant of Sappho's evening star.

> Th' other way Satan went down
> The Causey to Hell Gate; on either side   [415]
> Disparted Chaos over built exclaimd,
> And with rebounding surge the barrs assaild,
> That scorn'd his indignation: through the Gate,
> Wide open and unguarded, Satan pass'd,
> And all about found desolate; for those   [420]
> Appointed to sit there, had left thir charge,
> Flown to the upper World; the rest were all
> Farr to the inland retir'd, about the walls
> Of Pandæmonium, Citie and proud seate
> Of Lucifer, so by allusion calld,   [425]
> Of that bright Starr to Satan paragond.
>
> (*Paradise Lost* X)

That Satan has created 'one Realm' comingles the inhabitants of Pandemonium and 1920s London, accentuating the clangourous anarchy of the pandemonic layer of *The Waste Land*. The fragmented babel of voices in Eliot's poem reflects the hubbub surrounding the Throne of Chaos.

At length a universal hubbub wilde
Of stunning sounds and voices all confus'd
Borne through the hollow dark assaults his eare
With loudest vehemence:

(Paradise Lost II 951-4)

Satan negotiates with 'the Anarch old' for uncontested passage on his way to Earth. He promises in return to restore darkness, mirroring the darkness that approaches the world of The Waste Land at its 'violet hour' [215].

To your behoove, if I that Region lost,
All usurpation thence expell'd, reduce
To her original darkness and your sway
(Which is my present journey) and once more   [985]
Erect the Standard there of ancient Night;
Yours be th' advantage all, mine the revenge.
Thus Satan; and him thus the Anarch old
With faultring speech and visage incompos'd
Answer'd. I know thee, stranger, who thou art,   [990]
That mighty leading Angel, who of late
Made head against Heav'ns King, though overthrown.
...
If that way be your walk, you have not farr;   [1007]
So much the neerer danger; go and speed;
Havock and spoil and ruin are my gain.

(Paradise Lost II)

The Bible claims that people spoke one language in Babel. Punished for the vainglorious tower they built to reach the heavens, they fragment into a 'confusion of tongues', the name Babel being derived from the Hebrew for 'confusion'. An aspect of the 'multivocal, multilingual' bedlam of *The Waste Land* is a representation of that collective egoism and the resultant alienated, disparate peoples of mutually incomprehensible languages.[176]

> And the Lord said, Behold, the people is one, and they have all one language; and this they begin to do: and now nothing will be restrained from them, which they have imagined to do ...
>
> let us go down, and there confound their language, that they may not understand one another's speech. So the Lord scattered them abroad from thence upon the face of all the earth: and they left off to build the city. Therefore is the name of it called Babel; because the Lord did there confound the language of all the earth: and from thence did the Lord scatter them abroad upon the face of all the earth.
>
> (Genesis 11:6)

In the first century CE, Josephus explained that it was the vainglorious tyrant Nimrod who convinced the people of Babel to turn from God. Coleridge's concern at the Satanic vanity which fortifies the tyrant and mesmerises his people is explored in the next chapter.

> Now it was Nimrod who excited them to such an affront and contempt of God. He was the grandson of Ham, the son of Noah, a bold man, and of great strength of hand. He persuaded them not to ascribe it to God, as if it was through his means they were happy, but to believe that it was their own courage which procured that happiness. He also gradually changed the government into tyranny, seeing no other way of turning men from the fear of God, but to bring them into a constant dependence on his power. He

also said he would be revenged on God, if he should have
a mind to drown the world again; for that he would build
a tower too high for the waters to be able to reach! and
that he would avenge himself on God for destroying their
forefathers! Now the multitude were very ready to follow
the determination of Nimrod, and to esteem it a piece of
cowardice to submit to God.[177]

In the opening book of *Paradise Lost*, 'Pandemonium, the high Capital
| Of Satan and his Peers' is similarly concerned with architecture.
Unlike Babel, it endures with great architectural prowess and magnificence. The leader of this construction effort is Mammon. Among
fallen angels, he is known for his downward gaze, less concerned with
divine matters than transfixed by the golden pathways of Heaven.
How humans see, and what they look at, is an important theme in
The Waste Land. We have seen that when the 'eyes and back | Turn
upward from the desk' [215], the gaze is directed to the heavens at the
end of the commercial day. The counterpart is Mammon's covetous
downward gaze, also seen in the crowd of sighing City workers 'that
flowed over London bridge'. Each man 'fixed his eyes before his feet' [65]
on his way to the global finance centre this is the City of London.

> Mammon, the least erected Spirit that fell
> From heav'n, for ev'n in heav'n his looks and thoughts
> Were always downward bent, admiring more
> The riches of Heav'ns pavement, trod'n Gold,
> Then aught divine or holy else enjoy'd
> ...
> Anon out of the earth a Fabrick huge
> Rose like an Exhalation, with the sound
> Of Dulcet Symphonies and voices sweet,

Built like a Temple, where Pilasters round
Were set, and Doric pillars overlaid
With Golden Architrave; nor did there want
Cornice or Freeze, with bossy Sculptures grav'n,
The Roof was fretted Gold. Not Babilon,
Nor great Alcairo such magnificence
Equal'd in all thir glories, to inshrine
Belus or Serapis thir Gods, or seat
Thir Kings, when Ægypt with Assyria strove
In wealth and luxurie.

(Paradise Lost I 679-722)

London Bridge, Londinium Bridge and the Bridge from Hell

But hee once past, soon after when man fell,
Strange alteration! Sin and Death amain
Following his track, such was the will of Heav'n,
Pav'd after him a broad and beat'n way
Over the dark Abyss, whose boiling Gulf
Tamely endur'd a Bridge of wondrous length
From Hell continu'd reaching th' utmost Orbe
Of this frail World; by which the Spirits perverse
With easie intercourse pass to and fro

(Paradise Lost II 1023-1031)

The architecture of Milton's city of Pandemonium includes the bridge from Hell to the vulnerable upper world of humanity. In Eliot's poem, that bridge of chaos contrasts to the orderly heritage of Classicism represented by London Bridge and its Roman original in Londinium. That it is constantly in need of reconstruction suggests a relentless contest with destructive forces. 'London Bridge is falling down falling down failing down' [426].

London bridge speaks of its ancient classical heritage, since at broadly the same location it was over the Londinium bridge of the Romans that, at least figuratively and quite probably actually, both Classicism and then Christianity arrived on the northern riverbank of Londinium, where the Roman administration and temples were clustered. Over time, Christianity mingled with and then replaced Roman worship in the immediate area of the bridge. It may be that the sacred site of Magus Martyr was handed on by a Roman deity, since sacred sites often remained so when the religion changed. A jug in the British Museum found at London Bridge is inscribed to 'the temple of Isis at Londinium', and an altar stone of the temple was found repurposed as part of the adjacent Thames wharf.

The Thames wharf was the riverside wharf of Londinium, the 'Lower Thames Street' [260] of the poem. All the London roads in the poem are Roman, such as 'King William Street' [66]. 'Queen Victoria Street' [258] was the site of significant archaeological discoveries and is connected to Watling Street, the Roman road that linked north Britannia through Londinium across London Bridge to Canterbury, the route of Chaucer's pilgrims. The 'Strand' [258] is one of the most significant such roads in Britain. On the *Antonine Itinerary*, the list of roads of the Roman Empire, it is *Iter* VIII to *Calleva Atrebatum*, now Silchester. Near Magnus Martyr, the 'Cannon Street Hotel' [213] was the site of the Roman palace and administrative centre. In that light, it is significant that the word 'Metropole' [214], from the Greek root of metropolis, means 'Mother City', and also demarcates a bishopric.

It is likely that the Roman bridge was the first such permanent crossing of the Thames there, the area being sparsely inhabited to that time. 'The persistent failure to locate any archaeological evidence for a pre-Roman British Celtic settlement in what is now arguably the most extensively excavated provincial capital in the Roman Empire makes it likely that before the Romans, the Thames estuary was a political and economic backwater. One possible etymology for London is from the (plausibly reconstructed, but unattested) British Celtic word landa: 'low-lying, open land'. There is no pre-Roman London to be located.'[178] Ceasar reported that the indigenous population were clothed in animal skins and did not sow corn, instead living on flesh and milk. Returning to Roman Londinium is another return to origins in the poem, the origins of London. There seems to have been no bridge for a long period following the retreat of the Romans as the area returned to nature.

Archaeological evidence suggests that the area of the bridgehead was not occupied from the early 5th century until the early 10th century. Environmental evidence indicates that the area was waste ground during this period, colonised by elder and nettles. Following Alfred's decision to reoccupy the walled area of London in 886, new harbours were established at Queenhithe and Billingsgate. A bridge was in place by the early 11th century, a factor which would have encouraged the occupation of the bridgehead by craftsmen and traders. A lane connecting Botolph's Wharf and Billingsgate to the rebuilt bridge may have developed by the mid-11th century. The waterfront at this time was a hive of activity, with the construction of embankments sloping down from the riverside wall to the river. Thames Street appeared in the second half of the 11th century immediately behind (north of) the old Roman riverside wall and in 1931 a piling from this was discovered during the excavation of the foundations of a nearby building. It now stands at the base of the church tower. St Magnus was built to the south of Thames Street to serve the growing population of the bridgehead area and was certainly in existence by 1128-33.[179]

Like all the imagery of *The Waste Land*, the bridge is fiercely contested. Nietzsche's bridge imagery depicts priests as herders. 'Zealously and with much shouting they drove their herd over their bridge: as if to the future there were but one bridge!'[180] Eliot's crowd on London Bridge is a forlorn herd trudging towards a secular commercial future, a world of false egoist promise in significant part constructed by Nietzsche. 'On a thousand bridges and footpaths they shall throng toward the future, and more and more shall war and inequality be set amongst them'.[181] Among them walks the overman, his new first man of that future. From one such bridge or footpath the young man carbuncular — his 'bold stare' [232] fortified by Nietzsche's advice that women should be but a plaything — steps onto the stairs leading to the typist's bedsitting room.

Eliot's Dantesque march of deadened souls on London Bridge serves as an ironic inversion of Nietzsche's vainglorious image of his overman striding into the future, an antithesis given spice by Nietzsche's comment on Dante as 'the hyena which *poetizes* on graves'.[182] London's bridge, reconstructed numerous times, seems a more fragile construct than Satan's immensely solid bridge from Pandemonium.

> Bound with Gorgonian rigor not to move,
> And with Asphaltic slime; broad as the Gate,
> Deep to the Roots of Hell the gather'd beach
> They fasten'd, and the Mole immense wraught on
> Over the foaming deep high Archt, a Bridge

Of length prodigious joyning to the Wall
Immovable of this now fenceless world
Forfeit to Death; from hence a passage broad,
Smooth, easie, inoffensive down to Hell.

(*Paradise Lost* X 295-305)

A Foul Descent: Heaven's Antagonist and the Stairs of Dante, Milton, Eliot and Joyce

Soul-cleansing imagery, in the form of the stairs, is brought to *The Waste Land* in '*Poi s'ascose nel foco che gli affina*' [427]. 'Then he withdrew into the fire that refines him'. From Dante's fourteenth century *Purgatorio*, it closes the conversation between the poets Guido Guinzelli and Arnaut Daniel in which Guinzelli graciously declares Daniel the greater craftsman.[183] The early critic Cleanth Brooks points to the importance of that imagery.

> The bundle of quotations with which the poem ends has a very definite relation to the general theme of the poem and to several of the major symbols used in the poem. Before Arnaut leaps back into the refining fire of Purgatory with joy he says: "I am Arnaut who weep and go singing; contrite I see my past folly, and joyful I see before me the day I hope for. Now I pray you by that virtue which guides you to the summit of the stair, at times be mindful of my pain."[184]

The conversation takes place on the terrace of lust, the seventh terrace of hell for souls who have sinned through incontinent lust. They are purged of excessive desire, granting the soul salvation and access to the stairs to Heaven. Milton's Satan observes in Book II that 'long is the way | And hard, that out of Hell leads up to light'. Before he can construct the bridge from Hell, he must find the newly created 'Adams abode', and in the opening Argument he is 'describ'd ascending by staires' into Heaven for that purpose. On his way he passes the Paradise of Fools, where those led astray by 'Cowles, Hoods and Habits' and 'Reliques, Beads, | Indulgences, Dispenses, Pardons, Bulls' are held in a limbo of Romish folly. Turning himself into a cherub, he meets the Angel Uriel, who points the way to Eden.

> And long he wanderd, till at last a gleame
> Of dawning light turnd thither-ward in haste
> His travell'd steps; farr distant he descries
> Ascending by degrees magnificent
> Up to the wall of Heaven a Structure high
> ...
> The Stairs were such as whereon Jacob saw
> Angels ascending and descending,
> ...
> The Stairs were then let down, whether to dare
> The Fiend by easie ascent, or aggravate
> His sad exclusion from the dores of Bliss.
> ...
> Satan from hence now on the lower stair
> That scal'd by steps of Gold to Heav'n Gate
> Looks down with wonder at the sudden view
> Of all this World at once.
>
>   (*Paradise Lost* III 499-543)

The stairs as symbol of spiritual assent and descent form an extended theme in Eliot's poetry, including in *La Figlia che Piange*, *The Love Song of St. Sebastian* and *Ash Wednesday*. It is imagery shared with

Joyce's *Ulysses*, which opens as Buck Mulligan looks down a 'dark wind stairs' while mockingly intoning *Introibo ad altare Die* — 'I will go up to God's altar'.[185] Although the intentions of their creators differ, the shadowy descents of Buck Mulligan and Eliot's pustular clerk are both depictions of young men turning from matters of the spirit with disregard. When the clerk departs his assault on the typist, having satisfied his lust and 'vanity' [241], he 'gropes his way, finding the stairs unlit' [248]. In that, he echoes Satan's return to Hell following his assault on Eden. Triumphant, Satan glories in his title the 'Antagonist of Heav'ns Almightie King' as he also descends through darkness. He is lauded by Sin, his daughter and lover who births his son Death, for opening the gate of Hell.

> Whom thus the Prince of Darkness answerd glad.
> Fair Daughter, and thou Son and Grandchild both,
> High proof ye now have giv'n to be the Race
> Of Satan (for I glorie in the name,
> Antagonist of Heav'ns Almightie King) ...
> Mine with this glorious Work, and made one Realm
> Hell and this World, one Realm, one Continent
> Of easie thorough-fare. Therefore while I
> Descend through Darkness, on your Rode with ease
> To my associate Powers, them to acquaint
> With these successes, and with them rejoyce,
> 　　　　　　　　　　　　(*Paradise Lost* III 383-396)

We return to the aspect of *The Waste Land* that is the beast fable. In the drafts of *The Waste Land*, the clerk descends the stairs to the street, pausing by a stable to spit and urinate. This image was removed from the final poem on Ezra Pound's (playfully misspelled) advice as 'probly over the mark'.

And gropes his way, finding the stairs unlit;
And at the corner where the stable is,
Delays only to urinate, and spit.
(Draft of *The Waste Land*, circa 1921)[186]

Encased in this image is the centaur, the mythic man-horse of wild and lustful temperament. Offspring of the deformed Centaurus, they are emblems of humankind's struggle with its animal instincts. The image echoes another cloven-footed beast of myth, the ithyphallic satyr, brought to the poem through the insistent, pitiless satyriasis of 'Albert' [142].

O foul descent! that I who erst contended
With Gods to sit the highest, am now constraind
Into a Beast, and mixt with bestial slime,
This essence to incarnate and imbrute,
That to the hight of Deitie aspir'd;
But what will not Ambition and Revenge
Descend to? who aspires must down as low
As high he soard, obnoxious first or last
To basest things.
(*Paradise Lost* Book IX 163-171)

Charles Darwin's account of human evolution is titled *The Descent of Man, and Selection in Relation to Sex.* The drafts of the poem, read with Milton's 'bestial slime', offer a glimpse of Eliot's intentions with the clerk. In the clerk's descent of the stairs there is another 'foul descent', that of romantic iconoclastic philosophical egoism to brute street-level man. It reflects Satan's vainglorious fall from heaven to his 'imbrute' incarnation as a beast. Now, Milton's Satan of the carbuncle eyes resorts to 'basest things' as, in Eliot's poem, he becomes imbrute in his pustular descendent, the egoist young man carbuncular.

> Keats wanted to write an epic, and he found, as might be expected, that the time had not arrived at which another English epic, comparable in grandeur to *Paradise Lost*, could be written ... Milton made a great epic impossible for succeeding generations; Shakespeare made a great poetic drama impossible; such a situation is inevitable, and it persists until the language has so altered that there is no danger, because no possibility, of imitation. Anyone who tries to write poetic drama, even to-day, should know that half of his energy must be exhausted in the effort to escape from the constricting toils of Shakespeare: the moment his attention is relaxed, or his mind fatigued, he will lapse into bad Shakespearian verse. For a long time after an epic poet like Milton, or a dramatic poet like Shakespeare, nothing can be done. Yet the effort must be repeatedly made; for we can never know in advance when the moment is approaching at which a new epic, or a new drama, will be possible; and when the moment does draw near it may be that the genius of an individual poet will perform the last mutation of idiom and versification which will bring that new poetry into being.
>
> (T.S. Eliot *Milton* II)

5. Satan

The Carbuncle Eyes of Milton's Satan from *Paradise Lost* to *The Waste Land*

Milton's Satan has carbuncle eyes in the figurative glowing sense of the gem, 'little coal', suggestive of the fires of Hell. The mark of that Miltonic beast informs the pustular affliction of Eliot's clerk, who approaches and leaves the typist in the sinister way Milton's Eve is stalked by Satan, who 'toward Eve | Address'd his way ... and Carbuncle his Eyes'.

The questions posed by Eve, Adam and Satan, the trinity that arises from the imagery surrounding the gem in Magnus Martyr, include what might constitute and enculture the ideal human? How are they misinformed by scribes? What danger does the monstrous vanity of Satan, as it makes its way through Romanticism to modern egoisms, pose to the constitution of the human and society of the present and the future?

Eliot's perspective is clear from his critical writing. He sees such egoisms develop through a romantic lineage from a genesis in Luther's theology. In that view, modern egoism emerges from the new primacy of the Lutheran 'inner voice', travelling to England with the Revd. Miles Coverdale of Magnus Martyr and subsequently inadvertently given immense individualist credence by Milton's self-serving Satan. Evolving in ever more errant Byronic, Stirnerian and Nietzschean forms, egoism becomes increasingly vainglorious and disdainful of others and society. Here, we look at the evolution of the romantic Satan through the pens of Coleridge, Goethe and Baudelaire, and particularly Byron.

In an essay on Byron, Eliot refers to Mario Praz's *The Romantic Agony* of 1933. Praz traces Satan's path from medieval imagery to Milton and on to Byron. The book is 'not merely a classic, and not merely a classic of academic literary history — it has a brilliance much greater than needed to achieve that modest eminence — but a classic in a sense which places it among such books as have, in the depths of their insights, power to alter a reader's understanding of the history of his society, and perhaps of his own history'. Kermode describes the subject of the book as 'the pathology of Romanticism', and its importance as such that 'nobody now considers the origins of modern sensibility in ignorance of it'.[187]

In conventional moral terms the Satan of *Paradise Lost* is a degenerate, whose monstrous ego disavows any mortality that does not serve him. Yet he is beloved as a heroic individualist, so that a similar ego informs Byron's Manfred. Satan's subsequent appeal for the Romantics, in ways that Milton did not foresee, is seen in William Blake's *The Marriage of Heaven and Hell*, where the 'devils are almost irresistible — quicker, wittier, bolder and more exciting than the angels, who lose every argument'. Blake enjoys 'walking among the fires of hell, delighted with the enjoyments of Genius'. Writing on 'The Voice of the Devil', he claims that the 'reason Milton wrote in fetters when he wrote of Angels & God, and at liberty when of Devils and Hell, is because he was a true poet and of the Devil's party without knowing it.'[188] Despite his deprecation of Romanticism, Nietzsche has an affinity with the Devil's party. 'The aim should be the sanctification of the most powerful, most terrible, most disreputable forces; to use an old figure of speech, the deification of the Devil'.[189]

Who was Satan before Milton? Satan almost committed the perfect crime, since he was not linked to the Garden of Eden until significantly later in time.

The English word *devil* derives through Old English *deofol* and Latin *diabolus* from Greek *diabolos*, meaning "slanderer" or "false accuser." The Greek term is the translation of Hebrew *śāṭān*, "adversary" or "obstructer" ... the devil has been given a number of names by tradition. Most commonly he is called Satan or Lucifer, but he sometimes takes the name Beelzeboul or Beelzebub, Belial, Azazel, Mastema, Satanail, Sammael, or Semyaza, all of which names derive from the Old Testament or Intertestamental literature. In modern times he also bears the name Mephistopheles. Legend and literature sometimes assign these names to different characters, usually for dramatic purposes; thus frequently in medieval and modern literature, Satan, Lucifer, Belial and others play different parts. In the Old Testament *śāṭān* was originally a common noun (e.g., 2 Sam. 19:22), but gradually it became the title of a particular being. Early biblical references picture a creature of God who prompts evil (1 Chron. 21:1), accuses the righteous (Job 1-2), or even opposes God's will (Zech. 3:1-2). From these passages there developed the more fully defined rebellious angel of later tradition. Two key Old Testament passages which were not originally intended to apply to the Evil One came to be associated with Satan. The serpent of Eden was not identified with the devil until the Intertestamental period.[190]

The Intertestamental period is the roughly four-hundred-year gap from the fifth century BCE to the first decades CE, passing from the Old to New Testament. Protestantism terms it the 'four-hundred silent years' because no new prophets or major Biblical writings appeared. It broadly corresponds to Hellenistic Judaism, when Greek culture and language became influential following Alexander the Great's North African acquisitions. In that light, the intertestamental indictment of Satan as the serpentine agent of sedition in Eden occurs many centuries after the Book of Genesis was first recorded in writing by First Temple scribes from around the eight century BCE.

Those scribes were significantly more conscientious timekeepers in condemning Eve, as is Milton. He reinforces the subordination of woman by showing that if they wander from the oversight of men the cold intelligence of Satan will inevitably win, since woman are vulnerable because of their inferior intelligence and greater vanity. It is for this theological reason that Milton's Eve is narcissistically captivated by her own reflection. That portrait is later repeated by Nietzsche, the intellectually disabling vanity of women being a theme in his work. A facet of the identification of the pustular clerk with Milton's Satan in *The Waste Land* is an inversion of that indictment of Eve. The 'vanity' [241] is his, whereas she is speechless with dismay [249]. The clerk as a dark Adam who assaults the typist as Eve embodies misogynistic Old Testament scribes and their modern fellows through the etymological meaning of Devil shown above: from Old English *deofol* and Greek *diabolos*, the slanderer and the false accuser.

In *The Waste Land*, the Satan of Milton can be seen to escape from *Paradise Lost* to roam the human psyche in the manner that Nietzsche's overman later escapes the works of his genesis. The moral stockades of their creators are too flimsy to restrain their creations. That shared mythopoetic power is not so surprising when, through his romantic lineage, the overman is revealed as a literary descendent of Milton's Satan. One of the dark continuums in Eliot's poem is the Romantic evolution of the Satanic hero from Milton's

Satan to Byron's Manfred and on to Nietzsche's overman, an evolution mapped by Siobhan Lyons.

> John Milton's famous work *Paradise Lost* established a new manner of seeing the figure of the Devil in seventeenth-century literature that would invariably influence the way in which Satan would come to be philosophized. Traditionally, in the Christian faith, Satan is meant to personify evil. Yet Milton set in motion a drastic and fundamental way of interpreting the Devil as a statement of human conflict and paradox that undermined the Christian examination of good and evil as distinct, incompatible entities. It was Milton's representation of the Devil that the Romantic poets utilized in order to establish a bourgeoning philosophy that interrogated the notion of good and evil, and Friedrich Nietzsche's own philosophy is exemplary of this interrogation.[191]

Satan is also the mythic vehicle through which Milton reenforces the Old Testament mandate for the subordination of woman, a mandate Nietzsche also repeats in secular form. As the clerk approaches the typist at the 'violet hour' [220], Satan approaches Eve at dusk, signalled by the 'Starr | Of Hesperus', which we have seen is Sappho's evening star. As the planet Venus in the night sky, the fundamental importance of this star to representations of women in Eliot's poem is discussed in Part II of this book.

> The Sun was sunk, and after him the Starr
> Of Hesperus, whose Office is to bring
> Twilight upon the Earth, short Arbiter
> Twixt Day and Night, and now from end to end
> Nights Hemisphere had veild the Horizon round:

When Satan who late fled before the threats
Of Gabriel out of Eden, now improv'd
In meditated fraud and malice, bent
On mans destruction ...

(*Paradise Lost* Book IX 48-56)

The cultural conversation with Milton's Satan later diverged from the theological, initiated when he escaped Milton's epic into the romantic imagination, to evolve in many forms. Those include the ultimate egoists of modernity, the desiring man of Max Stirner and the overman of Nietzsche.

> Those who restrain desire, do so because theirs is weak enough to be restrained; and the restrainer or reason usurps its place & governs the unwilling.
>
> And being restrained it by degrees becomes passive till it is only the shadow of desire.
>
> The history of this is written in Paradise Lost, & the Governor or Reason is call'd Messiah.
>
> (William Blake 'The voice of the Devil'
> in *The Marriage of Heaven and Hell*)

Blake's revaluation of Satan's egoist drives represents the romantic desire to release the human ego, here expressed through unfettered desire. It is reflected in Eliot's poem in the unfettered desires of the clerk and Albert. To accommodate that, Blake insists on a revaluation of the term 'evil'. Nietzsche's later 'revaluation of all values' also advises man to go beyond good and evil.

> "The more he seeks to rise into the height and light, the more vigorously do his roots struggle earthward, downward, into the dark and deep — into the evil."

"Yes, into the evil!" cried the youth. "How is it possible that you have discovered my soul?"

Zarathustra smiled, and said: "Many a soul one will never discover, unless one first invent it."

"Yes, into the evil!" cried the youth once more.

"You said the truth, Zarathustra."[192]

The Satanic Hero: The Fallen Beauty of the 'Curly-haired Byronic Hero of Milton'

When Eliot compares the Satans of Dante and Milton, he includes the Satanic hero of Byron. Dante's 'vision of Satan may seem grotesque, especially if we have fixed in our minds the curly-haired Byronic hero of Milton'.[193] In part to do battle with the romantic fallen beauty of that figure, Eliot's young man carbuncular enters the same mythopoetic space. Though, according to the drafts of the poem, he is somewhat less groomed.

> A youth of twentyone, spotted about the face,
> One of those simple loiterers whom we say
> We may have seen in any public place
> At almost any hour of night or day.
>
> Pride has not fired him with ambitious rage
> His hair is thick with grease, and thick with scurf,
> (Drafts of The Waste Land, circa 1921)[194]

Eliot's 'curly-haired Byronic hero of Milton' represents the comingling of Adam and Satan in Romanticism. The insipid Adam of Judeo-Christianity and Milton's poem gains rigour when coupled with Satan's muscular egoism. The fascinated romantic aspiration to the contemptuous power of the latter is partly sanitised by the mask of the former. When Eliot points to Byron's 'peculiar diabolism, his delight in posing as a damned creature', the connection is not Eliot's invention.[195] Robert Southey coined the term 'Satanic School' in 1821 to characterise poets such as Byron as of 'depraved imaginations', showing a 'Satanic spirit of pride and audacious impiety'.

In his chapter 'The Metamorphoses of Satan', Praz traces the 'terrifying medieval mask' of Satan, 'like that of a Japanese warrior', from the *Gerusalemme Liberata* of Torquato Tasso to poems such as *The Massacre of the Innocents* by Giovan Battista Marino, recounting Herod's alleged massacre of children.[196] In such poems, Satan is a 'sooty Narcissus' of 'Promethean aspect'. Milton 'had this aspect of Satan in mind', to which he adds a fallen beauty. Praz traces further villainous evolutions. 'Rebels in the grand manner, grandsons of Milton's Satan and brothers of Schiller's robber, begin to inhabit the picturesque, Gothicized backgrounds of the 'tales of terror' towards the end of the eighteenth century'. They are 'on the one hand, descendants of Lucifer and, on the other, precursors of the Romantic hero'. On that evolutionary continuum, Milton's Satan 'transfused with his own sinister charm the traditional type of generous outlaw or sublime criminal'.

> Milton conferred on the figure of Satan all the charm of an untamed rebel which already belonged to the Prometheus of Aeschylus and to the Capaneo of Dante ... With Milton, the Evil One definitely assumes an aspect of fallen beauty, of splendour shadowed by sadness and death; he is 'majestic though in ruin'. The Adversary becomes strangely beautiful, but not in the manner of the witches Alcina and Lamia,

whose loveliness is a work of sorcery, an empty illusion which turns to dust like the apples of Sodom. Accursed beauty is a permanent attribute of Satan; the thunder and stink of Mongibello, the last traces of the gloomy figure of the medieval fiend, have now disappeared.

He adds that 'the sublime criminal of the Romantics, however, is Satanism'. It is this romantic charm and fallen beauty granted to the rebel antihero that informs Eliot's 'curly-haired Byronic hero of Milton'. Praz sees in Byron a thirst for passions and 'the attitude of Satanic defiance, an important quality in Byron … it was Byron who brought to perfection the rebel type, remote descendent of Milton's Satan'. He observes that 'Byron cultivated his character as Fatal Man', and sees the template of that Byronic antihero in the work of the popular gothic novelist Ann Radcliffe in the late eighteenth century. 'The pale face furrowed by an ancient grief, the rare Satanic smile, the traces of obscured nobility ('a noble soul and lineage high') worthy of a better fate — Byron might be said to derive these characteristics, by an almost slavish imitation, from Mrs. Radcliffe.' Byron's 'Giaour, the Corsair, and Lara, therefore, derive … from Mrs. Radcliffe's Schedoni. From Schedoni we can go back to Milton's Satan, and from Milton's Satan to the Satan of Marino, and finally discover the charm of the terrible, demoniac eyes of all these haunted creatures …'[197]

Stephen Greenblatt sees Milton's Satan arise in part from Shakespeare, threatening to upstage Adam and Eve and the poem itself. 'In order to invent a compelling Satan, Milton carefully studied how Shakespeare had done it. The depiction of Macbeth's murderous ambition and despair provided a psychological and rhetorical template for the Prince of Darkness, and Milton added notes he took from Richard III and Iago. He was almost too brilliant a student, for the result was a character so vivid that he threatened to take over the poem, particularly in its earlier books. In the later books Milton choose deliberately to diminish Satan in order to make room for the characters who were at the centre of his lifelong obsession, Adam and Eve'.[198]

Even in the act of poetic creation, Milton's Satan was transgressing boundaries and threatening to overwhelm efforts to contain him. Milton underestimated his own brilliance and the power of his creation, rather than intending to create a proto-Nietzschean revaluation of all values implicit in Praz's query. Heroic energy is also a fundamental characteristic of Nietzsche's overman and, according to Nietzsche, his opposition is the collectively exercised resentment of the weak and degenerate human herd, frustrating the unfettered exercise of the overman's power.

> Is the reversal of values which some critics have tried to discover really to be found in Milton? Is the justification of the ways of God to men only the seeming aim of the poem, the poet himself in reality being 'of the Devil's party without knowing it', as Blake declared? ... And is Satan's cry of revolt the cry of the poet himself, whose genius, inverted, has given a positive value to what objectively stands for the negative — evil — in his poem? At any rate, without accepting so extreme a theory, it cannot be denied that the character of Satan expresses as no other character or act or feature of the poem does, something in which Milton believed very strongly: heroic energy.

Praz goes on to say that 'the Romantics approached to Blake's point of view', and quotes Friedrich Schiller; that automatically 'we take the side of the loser: an artifice by which Milton, the panegyrist of Hell, transforms for a moment even the mildest of readers into a fallen angel'. He also points to the famous advocacy of Milton's Satan by Byron's friend Percy Shelley.

> Nothing can exceed the energy and magnificence of the character of Satan as expressed in *Paradise Lost* ... Milton's devil as a moral being is as far superior to his God as one who perseveres in some purpose, which he has conceived to be excellent, in spite of adversary and torture ... Milton has so far violated the popular creed (if this shall be judged to be a violation) as to have alleged no superiority of moral virtue to his God over his Devil.[199]

Eliot guides readers of his essay on Byron to the opinion of Praz as one he shares. That represents a continuation of his consistent opinion on Romanticism at the time of *The Waste Land* and before. As he conjoins Aaron and Sappho to represent guidance, so Eliot comingles Milton's Satan and Milton's Adam in his comment on the 'curly-haired Byronic hero of Milton', creating a hybrid diabolic entity of rebel charm, fallen beauty and romantic vanity now imbrute in Milton's Adam of Book IV, whose,

> Hyacinthin Locks
> Round from his parted forelock manly hung
> Clustring, but not beneath his shoulders broad.

The resulting Byronic fusion of Satan and Adam is a more interesting and exciting figure than Milton's Adam alone. In Eliot's view, it is this malformed hybrid who escapes Milton into the romantic imagination, terminating in the hybrid egoist who escapes scribes such as Stirner and Nietzsche onto the streets of London and into the typist's room. Uglified as the clerk, he reveals the true progeny of Milton's curly-haired Byronic hero to be the dark, decultured Adam of modernity, pustular with self-regarding romantic vanity.

There is also the theme of hair itself. Female propriety signalled through the control of hair is a theme of pre-biblical, biblical and classical provenance brought to *The Waste Land* [38, 108, 133, 255, 377].[200] Wanton female hair is entwined with the Puritan idea of the harlotry of images and other aspects of spiritual prostitution, an ire expressed through imagery such as the bejewelled romish Whore of Babylon and the Mass ceremony as Mistress Missa.

Puritan concerns with effeminacy meant that the hair of the men of the English Reformation, like that of Milton's Adam, should not fall below the shoulders. The *Homily Against Excess of Apparel*, from the *Books of Homilies* that accompanies the Elizabethan *Book of Common Prayer* which gives Part I of Eliot's poem its title, policed any laxity: 'that yee bee admonished of another soule & chargeable excesse: I meane, of apparell, at these dayes so gorgeous, that neither Almighty GOD by his word can stay our proud curiosity in the same, neither yet godly and necessary lawes, made of our Princes, and oft repeated with the penalties, can bridle this detestable abuse ... Yea many men are become so effeminate, that they care not what they spend in disguising themselues, euer desiring new toyes, and inuenting new fashions'.[201]

The hair of women was not always governed by men. Chiming with the 'violet hour' of the poem, Sappho's favoured headdress was violets, including in her figurative elevation as the tenth muse of Olympus, where the muses were also adorned with violets.

> Rebuff other ways
> As quickly as you can
> And you, Dika, with your soft hands take stems
> of lovely anise and loop them in your locks.
> The blessed Graces love to gaze at one in flowers
> But turn their backs on one whose hair is bare.
>
> (Sappho *On Going Bareheaded*)[202]

The warning implicit in the wanton, serpentine locks of Milton's Eve suggests a more sinister relationship in the Puritan mind between woman and nature than that of Sappho. It reads as a poetic transcription of that part of Reformation theology related to the serpentine Eden myth that Eliot described as repellent.

> Her unadorned golden tresses wore
> Disheveld, but in wanton ringlets wav'd
> As the Vine curles her tendrils, which impli'd
> Subjection
>
> (*Paradise Lost* Book IV)

The *Homily Against Excess of Apparel* is clear on the blonding of such wanton ringlets. 'O vaine excuse, and most shamefull answer, to the reproch of thy husband. What couldst thou more say to set out his foolishnesse, then to charge him to bee pleased and delighted with the Diuels tire? Who can paint her face and curle her hayre, and change it into an vnnaturall colour, but therein doeth worke reproofe to her maker, who made her?'[203]

The Tyrant: Coleridge's Satan

There is another element in Nietzsche, which is closely akin to the objection urged by "rugged individualists" against trade-unions. In a fight of all against all, the victor is likely to possess certain qualities which Nietzsche admires, such as courage, resourcefulness, and strength of will. But if the men who do not possess these aristocratic qualities (who are the vast majority) band themselves together, they may win in spite of their individual inferiority. In this fight of the collective *canaille* against the aristocrats, Christianity is the ideological front, as the French Revolution was the fighting front. We ought therefore to oppose every kind of union among the individually feeble, for fear lest their combined power should outweigh that of the individually strong; on the other hand, we ought to promote union among the tough and virile elements of the population. The first step towards the creation of such a union is the preaching of Nietzsche's philosophy.

(Bertrand Russell *A History of Western Philosophy*)[204]

Another aspect of the structural fragmentation and babel of *The Waste Land* is reflected in Bertrand Russell's comment: the political idea of divide and conquer. In that, there is a striking resonance between Samuel Taylor Coleridge's opinion of Milton's Satan as a template for the tyrant and the closing lines of Eliot's poem. Coleridge identifies the danger of satanic pride in *The Statesman's Manual*, his 'lay sermon' addressed to the 'Higher And Middle Classes Of Society, On The Present Distresses Of The Country'.

But in its utmost abstraction and consequent state of reprobation, the Will becomes satanic pride and rebellious self-idolatry in the relations of the spirit to itself, and remorseless despotism relatively to others ... This is the character which Milton has so philosophically as well as sublimely embodied in the Satan of his Paradise Lost. Alas! too often has it been embodied in real life! Too often has it given a dark and savage grandeur to the historic page![205]

Coleridge is opposed to self-evaluated exemption from common morality. In that he anticipates the egoism of Nietzsche's overman, whose exceptionalism permits the exercise of an amoral will to power over the contemptable herd of humanity, the only good being what is good for his pseudo-aristocratic class. Coleridge exposes the vanity driving the unfettered will, and its moral deficiency. He presents Napoleon as an example, one of Nietzsche's favoured templates for the overman, and notes the tendency of the population to become captivated by such powerful figures.

> And wherever it has appeared, under whatever circumstances of time and country, the same ingredients have gone to its composition; and it has been identified by the same attributes ... Violence with Guile; Temerity with Cunning; and, as the result of all, Interminableness of Object with perfect Indifference of Means; these are the qualities that have constituted the COMMANDING GENIUS! These are the Marks, that have characterized the Masters of Mischief, the Liberticides, and mighty Hunters of Mankind, from NIMROD to NAPOLEON. And from inattention to the possibility of such a character as well as from ignorance of its elements, even men of honest intentions too frequently become fascinated. Nay, whole nations have been so far duped by this want of insight and reflection as to regard with palliative admiration, instead of wonder and abhorrence, the Molocks of human nature, who are indebted, for the far larger portion of their meteoric success, to their total want of principle, and who surpass the generality of their fellow creatures in one act of courage only, that of daring to say with their whole heart, 'Evil, be

thou my good!' All *system* so far is power; and a *systematic* criminal, self-consistent and entire in wickedness, who entrenches villainy within villainy, and barricadoes crime by crime, has removed a world of obstacles by the mere decision, that he will have no obstacles, but those of force and brute matter.

I have only to add a few sentences, in completion of this note, on the CONSCIENCE and on the UNDER-STANDING. The conscience is neither reason, religion, or will, but an *experience* (sui generis) of the coincidence of the human will with reason and religion. It might, per-haps, be called a *spiritual sensation*; but that there lurks a contradiction in the terms, and that it is often deceptive to give a common or generic name to that, which being unique, can have no fair analogy. Strictly speaking, there-fore, the conscience is neither a sensation or a sense; but a testifying state, best described in the words of our lit-urgy, as THE PEACE OF GOD THAT PASSETH ALL UNDERSTANDING.[206]

Eliot explains in the Notes that the close of the poem in 'Shantih Shantih Shantih' is the equivalent of these capitalised words. 'Shan-tih. Repeated as here, a formal ending to an Upanishad. 'The Peace which passeth understanding' is our equivalent to this word' [433n]. These are Paul's words in Philippians 4, central to which is the *via media*, the middle way of moderation.

Let your moderation be known unto all men. The Lord is at hand. Be careful for nothing; but in every thing by prayer and supplication with thanksgiving let your requests be made known unto God. And the peace of God, which passeth all understanding, shall keep your hearts and minds through Christ Jesus.

For Coleridge, such moderation represents the restraint of the conscience cultured by reason and religion, the Hellenic and Hebraic. It acts as an antidote to tyrannical impulses and the amoral lust for unfettered power. For Eliot in his poem, it is all that; it is a reference to Coleridge; and, through that, is an allusion to the romantic Satanic hero as a potential template for the tyrant. Through the link between the Upanishads and Coleridge's argument, the close of *The Waste Land* also closes the universal argument for culture, and for curtailing the brute in humankind through culture, that runs throughout the poem.

It is a reaching across the divide. The firmly classical Eliot and Coleridge, a founder of the Romantic Movement, have common cause in understanding what might constitute a better human, and the society that might engender that human. Both see the ennobling possibilities of culture. Both are concerned with the contrasting brute exercise of the will as power devoid of moral or communal concern. We see the consequences of that brute will in the pustular clerk's treatment of the typist.

Baudelaire's Satan

The contemplation of the horrid or sordid or disgusting, by an artist, is the necessary and negative aspect of the impulse toward the pursuit of beauty.

(Eliot, *Dante* 1920)

Among the figures and themes the poet Charles Baudelaire brings to Eliot's poem are Satan and the *poète maudit*, the accursed poet. 'More enduring is the concept of the Satanic hero, understood as a cursed Cain figure doomed to self-destruction, as in Byron's *Manfred* (1817). This figure draws on John Milton's *Paradise Lost* and J.W. Goethe's *Faust* and prefigures the *poète maudit* as developed later by Charles Baudelaire and his successors'.[207] Ange Mlinko sees Baudelaire as 'the greatest poet-critic of his time ... who will remain a titan as long as there is literature'.

> Defending *Les Fluers du mal* from the charge of immorality brought against it in criminal court, Baudelaire argued that his poetry was not corrupting, but that even if it were, the scope of its influence would be limited by the perfection of his verse, which sailed over the heads of the masses ... He was working on a poetry collection with the title *Les Lesbiennes* and other writing projects — some fiction, a collection of Aphorisms. He was also living a life-style that rock stars a century later imitated ... Richard Sieburth puts it pithily ... "1840 ... first poems. Debts. Prostitutes. Syphilis." ... By 1857 *Les Lesbiennes* had evolved into *Les Fleurs du mal,* exactly one hundred poems in five thematic sections, meticulously assembled and organised, assiduously copyedited, formally perfected. The book was brought out by an anarchist publisher, Poulet Malassis, in an edition of 1,300 copies.[208]

The Waste Land quotes directly from 'To the Reader', the opening poem of that immensely influential book of poetry. 'Hypocrite lecteur! — mon semblable, — mon frère!' [76]: 'Hypocrite reader, — fellowman — my twin!'. As Baudelaire draws you to his shoulder in contemplating both the beauty and the horror of life, so too does

Eliot. Baudelaire's poem links ennui with the Satanic, and the brains of the multitude affected by this devilish condition team with demons, a psychic horde that recalls the demons streaming across Satan's bridge from Pandemonium to the upper world of London in 1922. Ennui is 'frequently translated into English as boredom, but boredom seems not forceful enough for what Baudelaire intends. 'Ennui' in Baudelaire is a soul-deadening, pathological condition, the worst of the many vices of mankind, which leads us into the abyss of non-being.'[209]

> For all of us, greed, folly, error, vice
> exhaust the body and obsess the soul
> and we keep feeding our congenial
> remorse the same way vagrants nurse their lice.
> ...
> Trice potent Satan, cushioned on perdition,
> lulls our enchanted minds incessantly
> ...
> The Devil guides us like a puppet master.
> Disgusting objects please us very well.
> Each day we take another step towards Hell
> ...
> The ranks of demons reveling in our brains,
> Like multitudes of maggots, swarm and seethe
> ...
> there's one most ugly, false and dirty birth!
> ...
> Boredom! Moist-eyed, he dreams, while pulling on
> a hookah pipe, of guillotine-cleft necks.
> You, reader, know this tender freak of freaks—
> Hypocrite reader—mirror-man—my twin!
>
> (*The Flowers of Evil*)[210]

That the romantic legacy of Byron contributes to Baudelaire's idea of the *poète maudit* is also Eliot's view: 'the point is that in Poe, in his life, his isolation and his worldly failure, Baudelaire found the prototype of *le poète maudit*, the poet as the outcast of society — the type which was to realise itself, in different ways, in Verlaine and Rimbaud, the type of which Baudelaire saw himself as a distinguished example. This nineteenth century archetype, *le poète maudit*, the rebel against society and against middle-class morality (a rebel who descends of course from the continental myth of the figure of Byron) corresponds to a particular social situation.'[211]

Interpretation of Baudelaire's poetry has evolved through differing perspectives. Praz notes a tendency to sanitise Baudelaire, ignoring his 'black Venus' in favour of the 'golden-hearted servant-maid'. He writes that 'the Baudelaire of his own age was the satanic Baudelaire, who gathered into a choice bouquet the strangest orchids, the most monstrous aroids from among the wild tropical flora of French Romanticism ... it can be seen from what I have already shown how little there remained for Baudelaire to invent ... Now they have returned to the cemetery of the Past, these ghouls, vampires, and incubi, but the Danse Macabre was prolonged till after the dawn of the present century'.[212]

Both Eliot and Pound had no doubt of its importance. 'Tom hoped his own work, alongside that of Pound and other Francophiles, had changed the literary climate. He asserted it was 'now taken for granted that the current of French poetry which sprang from Baudelaire is one which has, in these twenty-one years, affected all English poetry that matters".[213]

Eliot distinguishes between the diabolism of Baudelaire and what he regards as an element of posturing in the Satanism of Byron. From Eliot's perspective, genuine Satanism such as that of Baudelaire does not always imply a simple bifurcation of good and evil. Satanism can be an expression of an errant, tortured spiritual instinct.

The rebirth of Good and Evil in the nineteenth century is often abortive and never led to a full growth. Its ancestry is mixed, but by an odd accident, Byron (I believe) had something to do with it. With Byron, if you like, everything was pose, but the existence of a pose implies the possibility of a reality to which the pose pretends. One of the constant by-products of this revival of morality is Satanism; but even Satanism — the cultivation of Evil — in any of its curious forms, in part of Baudelaire, in Barbey d'Aurevilly, in Huysmans, in Wilde's *Pen, Pencil and Poison* — is a derivative or an imitation of spiritual life.[214]

Mephistopheles' Boils
The Romantic Faust, and the Eternal Feminine

Johann Wolfgang von Goethe's *Faust* is a poem of twelve thousand, one hundred and eleven lines completed over six decades. Part I was published in 1808, and Part II published after his death in 1832. We saw that Wagner's opera *Tristan and Isolde* emerged from Arthurian legend developed in a conversation within European literature. So too the legend of Faust, which evolved between Germany and England. Goethe's *Faust* owes something to Christopher Marlowe's Elizabethan drama *Dr. Faustus*, perhaps the first to deal with the German folk legend of the late sixteenth century surrounding Johann Faust, a travelling magician and alchemist of dark reputation. Marlowe's Dr. Faustus also becomes impatient with the earthly rewards of success and seeks otherworldly powers, a summons to which Mephistophilis, Lucifer's servant, responds.

Goethe's *Faust* resonates with *The Waste Land* in the experiences of Faust and the modern representative of the devil who holds a claim to his soul, Mephistopheles. Early in the epic, Faust hears the 'dead sound' [68] of church bells and a choir the day before Easter, echoing the sound of vespers in Magnus Martyr and the 'April' of *The Waste Land*. These sounds dissuade him, a cultured, successful but greatly dissatisfied scholar, from drinking a poison suicide elixir, so setting him on his epic journey. Faust then mortgages his soul to Mephistopheles for overreaching powers that transcend humanity.

> FAUST. What lilting tones are these, what notes profound
> Cry to me: do not drink! Have they such power?
> And do these bells with their dull booming sound
> Announce the Easter festival's first hour?
> Is that already the angelic song
> Of solace?[215]

That Eliot was considering the evolution of the Mephistopheles of Goethe and the Satan of Milton at the time is confirmed in an essay of 1920. It also offers a fundamental insight into Eliot's conception of the multifaceted work a character should undertake in a literary work. 'In the nineteenth century another mentality manifested itself. It is evident in a very able and brilliant poem, Goethe's *Faust*. Marlowe's Mephistopheles is a simpler creature than Goethe's. But at least Marlowe has, in a few words, concentrated him into a statement. He is there and (incidentally) he renders Milton's Satan superfluous. Goethe's demon inevitably sends us back to Goethe. He embodies a philosophy. A creation of art should not do that. He should *replace* a philosophy'.[216] These are Eliot's italics, and how characters can *replace* a philosophy is seen in both the typist and the clerk.

The English speaking world is not always aware of the immense impact of Goethe, the German polymath whose range included science, statecraft, theatre, novels and poetry. He occupies a unique position both within and apart from Romanticism, and is fundamental to understanding German culture, from which the overman of Nietzsche later arose. Writing of 'Goethe's modernity and relative proximity to us', Kaufmann summarises his significance.[217]

> In view of his intellectual powers and interests, it is understandable that his ideas should have been related again and again to what came before and after him. From the 143 volumes of his works, diaries, and letters and the 5 volumes of his collected conversations it is not hard to cull a pertinent anthology on almost any subject ... As a member of the state government in Weimar, he took his official duties seriously ... he took an even greater interest in the arts and several of the natural sciences; he made an anatomical discovery, proposed an important botanical hypothesis, and developed an intricate theory of colours; he directed the theatre in Weimar from 1791 to 1817; and he came to be recognised, some thirty or forty years before his death, as Germany's greatest poet. That estimate still stands ... The outstanding fact about Goethe is his development — not from mediocrity to excellence but from consummation to consummation of style upon style. *Goetz* (1773) and *Werther* (1774) represent, and were immediately acclaimed as, the culmination of Storm and Stress. In Goethe's two great plays, *Iphigenia* (1787) and *Tasso* (1790), German classicism reached its perfection. Then, still before the end of the century, *Faust, A Fragment* and *Wilhelm Meister's Apprenticeship* gave a decisive impetus to romanticism, and *Meister* all but created a new genre: the novel that relates the education and character formation of the hero, the *Bildungsroman*. [218]

Goethe had a strong influence on the genesis of the Romanticism Eliot finds suspect. In 1774 he published *The Sorrows of Young Werther*, a key text of 'Sturm und Drang' (Storm and Stress) also considered a founding text of romantic literature. The novel is the story of a young man's unrequited love that ends in suicide. There followed a series of imitator suicides, so that the term 'Werther effect' has been used in police and social analysis to describe a local cluster of suicides. *Werther* is an epistolary novel told in the form of a series of letters of increasing histrionic tone. The tone of the protagonist and the story told through letters are echoed in Mary Shelley's *Frankenstein*, a deep critique of vainglorious Romanticism. In Shelley's book, Doctor Frankenstein usurps God to remake man, and it is children and women who bear the consequences of the resultant agonised creature, who kills as he reads *The Sorrows of Young Werther* and *Paradise Lost*.

'Although J.W. Goethe did not belong to the romantic movement and later condemned its penchant for disorder as "sick," some of his works show a kinship with romantic ideology and aesthetics. In particular *Faust* explored quintessential features of the romantic hero: the sense of being imprisoned in his subjectivity and the yearning for the "real" world, resulting in perpetual restlessness and never-satisfied longings.'[219] Later, Goethe further distanced himself from Romanticism, evident in his rejection of early work such as *Werther* in favour of a renewed Classicism he engendered with Friedrich Schiller, Weimar Classicism.

Marlowe's Mephistophilis successfully claims the soul of Dr. Faustus. Goethe's Mephistopheles is not so successful, since Faust is rescued from his devil's bargain. Mephistopheles breaks out in carbuncles on losing control of that indebted soul as Faust is rescued, in the closing lines of the poem, by 'Eternal Womanhood'.

MEPHISTOPHELES
>What's wrong with me? I'm out in boils all over,
>Like Job! A self-repugnant spectacle ...

CHORUS MYSTICUS
>Eternal Womanhood
>Draws us on high.

(*Faust* II, V, 11809-12111)

We are introduced to Goethe's Eternal Feminine in *The Waste Land* through the reference to Hermann Hesse's essay *In Sight of Chaos* [366n], in which the concept is expressed as the 'Faustian Mothers'. Goethe's Eternal Feminine is of broad scope, populated by Mary Magdalene as Magna Peccatrix, the saint Maria Aegyptiaca (Mary of Egypt), and the Mater Gloriosa, named as 'Virgin, Mother, Queen' and 'Goddess, kind for ever'.

ANGELS [*hovering in the upper atmosphere, carrying* FAUST's *immortal part*]
>This noble spirit saved alive
>Has foiled the Devil's will!
>...

DOCTOR MARIANUS
>What women now draw near?
>...
>I see heaven's Lady pass ...
>Queen and ruler of the world! ...
>Purest Virgin, noblest Mother,
>Queen of our election,
>Goddess yielding to none other
>In thy great perfection ...
>Who can break the chain of lust?

(*Faust* II, V, 11934-12026)

It is in this role as goddess that Goethe's Eternal Feminine steps outside the Christian. Eliot's range is of more universal scope again, opening as he does with Aphrodite of 'April' and closing with such entities as 'Ganga' [395]. That said, it does seem that that for Goethe in *Faust*, as for Eliot in his poem, all the women are one woman. In contrast, for Nietzsche the Eternal Feminine is a useful totem for all that is wrong with women, particularly the independent women he terms *abortive*.

> Isn't it the very worst taste when women prepare to be scientific like this? Fortunately, enlightenment has been a man's business, a man's talent until now — as such, we can remain "among ourselves". And with respect to everything that women write about "woman," we can ultimately reserve a healthy doubt as to whether women really want — and are *able* to want — to provide enlightenment about themselves ... If this is not really all about some woman trying to find a new piece of *finery* for herself (and isn't dressing up part of the Eternal Feminine?), well then, she wants to inspire fear of herself: — perhaps in order to dominate.[220]

This abuse of the Eternal Feminine is viewed through a different lens in *The Second Sex*, Simone de Beauvoir's foundational text of second-wave feminism. She examines the symbolism of the revered and fallen duality of the Eternal Feminine in modernity by highlighting the negative, injurious aspects and consequences of that contradiction. It is a duality also suggested in *The Waste Land* and its drafts. '(The same eternal and consuming itch | Can make a martyr, or plain simple bitch)'.[221]

> There are different kinds of myths. This one, the myth of woman, sublimating an immutable aspect of the human

condition — namely, the "division" of humanity into two classes of individuals — is a static myth ... in place of fact, value, significance, knowledge, empirical law, it substitutes a transcendental idea, timeless, unchangeable, necessary. The idea is indisputable because it is beyond the given: it is endowed with absolute truth. Thus, against the dispersed, contingent, and multiple existences of actual women, mythical thought opposed the Eternal Feminine, unique and changeless. If the definition provided for this concept is contradicted by the behaviour of flesh-and-blood women, it is the latter who are wrong: we are not told that Femininity is a false entity, but that the women that are concerned are not feminine. The contrary facts of experience are impotent against the myth ... In consequence, a number of incompatible myths exist, and men tarry musing before the strange incoherencies manifested by the idea of Femininity ... But if woman is depicted as the Praying Mantis, the Mandrake, the Demon, then it is most confusing to find in women also the Muse, the Goddess, Mother, Beatrice. As group symbols and social types are generally defined by means of antonyms in pairs, ambivalence will seem to be an intrinsic quality of the Eternal Feminine.[222]

In 1920s modernism, the historical tendency of men to opine on women is the target of episode fourteen of *Ulysses*, the symbol being 'mothers', the organ the 'womb', and the location the National Maternity Hospital in Dublin. It satirises a series of prose styles throughout history in which men discuss women's matters, central to which is pregnancy.[223] The idea is also central to the acerbic humour of Victoria Woolf's *A Room of One's Own*. 'Professors, schoolmasters, sociologists, clergymen, novelists, essayists, journalists, men who had no qualification save that they were not women, chased my simple and single question — Why are women poor?'[224]

A twin focus of the evolving modernism of Eliot's time was the gender prejudice of society arising in significant part from Old Testament roots in the Eve myth and the exclusionary nature of an exclusively male god. In light of Eliot's guidance in the Notes that 'all the women are one woman', the Eternal Feminine is present in depleted, exhausted form in the typist, and also represents Eliot's revelation of the former glory of the female divine, ruthlessly suppressed by a lineage of male scribes. She is Eliot's beloved 'Figlia del tuo figlio, | Queen of Heaven' of *The Dry Salvages*, a lifelong veneration he shares with Dante.

As a long-form poem, *Faust* occupies the same literary space as Ovid's *Metamorphoses*, Virgil's *Aeneid*, Chaucer's *The Canterbury Tales* and Milton's *Paradise Lost*, woven with many more into *The Waste Land*. It bears repeating that there is an engagement on the level of form with such long poems throughout history. In 1923 Conrad Aiken described *The Waste Land* as an 'epic in a walnut shell'. Compressed as it is through the intense distillation of the mythic method, Eliot's poem represents a modernist challenge to long form epic poems such as *Faust* — figuratively claiming, in the playful words of Ezra Pound, to be the 'longest poem in the Englisch langwidge'.[225]

The Magnus Martyr Reredos circa 1890

The altarpiece is minimised, with all imagery removed or covered.

(London Metropolitan Archive)

An intermediate stage of the Magnus Martyr reredos

The Magnus Martyr altarpiece with round 'Glory', representing the Second Temple. This may be the form found by the newly appointed Rector, Father Fynes-Clinton, in 1921.

(London Metropolitan Archive)

A Petition against the demolition of Magnus Martyr circa 1921

HE City of London lies before us ; day by day we journey thither, and when the day is ended we leave it behind us, with all its stress of labour, and yet it somehow never leaves us. No city in the world can compare with it for size, for contrasts, for glorious and historic past. To know our London we must look beneath the superficial, we must strike out from its main thoroughfares, we must go back into its past. Here we stand in the midst of its busiest street ; there, down a small courtway, and we are right away back two hundred years or more in the quadrangle of ancient courtyard, or within the walls of hoary temple. The London of the present has its roots deep, deep down in the past. Churches are to be found on every hand, and yet we could not spare one of them—for each and every one has some especial claim to our attention.

Many have already been sacrificed to the City's need for space ; others we are told must go, and yet the City's life is inextricably bound up with these ancient shrines.

Breathes there a man with soul so dead,
Who never to himself has said—
"My God, how wonderful Thou art,
    Thy Majesty how bright ;
How beautiful Thy mercy seat
    In depths of burning light."

So these Churches stand within the fierce light of public scrutiny once again. We are told that the City is ever foremost in the uplifting of humanity, in succouring the needy and downtrodden, the outcast and the oppressed.

Having these words in the ears, we take courage at this time, when **sentence of death** has been passed upon certain City Churches (those Lamps of Faith), which have for centuries guided the feet of past generations into the paths of justice and peace. We feel sure that the men of London, although now only working in London during the day and deriving their income therefrom, will not suffer the golden thread of faith to be drawn out from the fabric of our City's weaving.

"The City prays for the guidance of the Almighty"—may He at this time lead us into the way of Truth. There are, unfortunately, strong materialistic forces at work, undermining and permeating the very foundations of the City's moral, social and religious fabric.

Upon what does British Trade and Commerce rest ? Fidelity to the principles of moral integrity !—and these condemned Churches, even it it were true that some are empty and silent, are yet **witnesses to the foundation principles of our City's life.** They are material evidence of the glorious historic past. They are visible symbols of spiritual power. Remove them, and what is it proposed to put in their place ? The warehouse, the mart ! But what are they without the spiritual influence, purifying and keeping pure the minds which work therein. "Man is the creation of thought." But, oh, what a creation, if the wellspring of thought be fouled, for " that which man thinks that he becomes."

The argument need not be laboured. **S. Magnus the Martyr, standing in Billingsgate, is condemned.** It is to be razed to the ground, and the place wherein it has stood, certainly since 1291, is to know it no more. This spot, consecrated by the prayers of countless millions who stayed one moment ere they entered the ancient city from old London Bridge, which sprang from the Church's very porch, or passed out on pilgrimage bent to a'Becket's shrine, or to trade in Southwark's Fair, this plot of ground which enwraps the bones of so many of London's Civic Lords— John Blount (1307), John Mitchell (1436), the two Gerrards (1555 and 1601), or those of Henry Yevele, the Freemason of Edward III, Richard II and Henry IV, who erected the tomb of Richard II and built Westminster Hall and Eltham Palace, or, yet again, those of Miles Coverdale, who gave to us "our English Bible"—**this spot is to be desecrated** by the erection of shrines in which the worship of mammon will proceed from early dawn till latest even—admittedly for the sake of mere mammon this place must go.

Could this site speak it would tell of the many who knelt in devotion and prayer— it would tell how, on 2nd September, 1666, the dull red glow of a new dawn burst through its windows, brightening as the flames from Pudding Lane spread, and at last engulfed the ancient shrine (but not its undying spirit)—and at last London lay in ashes around—then, out of those ashes the immortal soul of S. Magnus rose up again and, re-enshrined by Wren in 1676, still kept watch and ward over London's Bridge until, in 1831, the Bridge was shifted farther west to its present site.

I must not weary you, but could this Church speak it would call you to spare one moment to examine its beautiful interior—the carving of the Grinling Gibbons School —the antiquities of days when men valued their heritage perchance the more; but no ! midst the City's busy life—midst the coming and going up on yonder bridge, which once sprang from the Church's side, no ear can catch the plaintive cry: " Behold me, and see if there be any sorrow like unto my sorrow."

And this rich treasure, only one 'tis true of nineteen, they no less rich to those who love them—is to be sacrificed for mere monetary gain. It cannot be, it must not be. You, my brother, are called to save this Church; you may not use it, but others do, and if one soul only found rest and peace its preservation is unquestionable. For what shall it profit the powers that be if they gain the whole world by the sale of the site, and yet lose that one soul. This gem of historic antiquarian and artistic worth must be saved.

Will you help ? S.Magnus is a silent witness in Bridge Ward to moral integrity— it is a witness to London City's glorious past. It shall not be destroyed. Let us cry— " Hands off God's heritage ! " We do not ask for money: but we ask your moral support. A Petition lies in the Vestry for signature, or will be sent round to all who are prepared to sign it.

6. Broken Images
The Battle of Creeds Magnus Martyr

The Church

The 'initial appearance of Eliot's interest in identifiably Anglo-Catholic matters is to be found in a letter of 1911'. Spurr notes that 'George Every ... told me that Eliot frequented the High Mass at the City church of St. Magnus the Martyr after the First World War'.[226] For Spurr, the Church offers a haven in *The Waste Land* in a poem that seems otherwise relentlessly bleak.

> Eliot was bound to celebrate it in the midst of the desiccated urban wasteland. 'The interior of St. Magnus Martyr', Eliot wrote five years before his baptism, is the finest among Wren's interiors'. Making this observation and, further, to go into print with it indicates that Eliot had been studying these interiors. Moreover, this was one of the leading shrines of the Anglo-Catholic movement and it is very notable that Eliot should not only refer to it, but, in the midst of a poem of almost unrelieved negativity, present it so positively.[227]

Dig deep in the Church of St. Magnus the Martyr and you will find the history of England. Geoffrey Chaucer was for a period Clerk of the King's Works with responsibility for works to the Church. Thomas à Becket was the patron of the associated chapel on London Bridge from which many pilgrims departed for or arrived from Canterbury. Sir Christopher Wren, who built St. Paul's, rebuilt

Magnus Martyr after the Great Fire of London in the seventeenth century. It was the church of the merchant James Sherley, who ran a business on London Bridge and owned a house near the church. He was an important financier of the Mayflower expedition, and sourced the ship itself and its crew. One of the Puritan Separatists aboard was William 'Bradford' [234], who became governor of the Plymouth colony for thirty years. Also representing the Reformation, the body of the Revd. Miles Coverdale is interred there, looking up in perpetuity at the altarpiece and the vestments of Aaron that he and his fellow ministers refused to wear.

While Eliot was writing *The Waste Land* a battle was raging in the church, a battle both new and ancient. It was newly engaged on the appointment of Father Fynes-Clinton in 1921, the Anglo-Catholic rector who had met with Eliot's mother and brother during their visit to London. He championed imagery such as the portrait of Aaron and representations of the Virgin Mary, imagery which had been prohibited since the Reformation as Roman Catholic idolatry. The clerks of the church were determined the church should remain plain, and so launched a series of court cases between 1921 and 1924 which resulted in a number of forced removals of the imagery installed by Fynes-Clinton. As the altarpiece was exempt from such prohibitions, it became a focus of his resistance.

The battle in that church was also the continuation of an ancient struggle over imagery. It flows back through time to the early Christian councils of Nicaea and their concern with the holiness of sacred wood. In that way, the battle over imagery is inbuilt into both the visual narrative of the altarpiece and the carved wood itself. In the Old Testament, that battle was engaged by temple scribes as they established the primacy of the new God Yahweh, a reformation enforced by the despoiler of shrines King Hezekiah who was afflicted by a near-fatal carbuncle.

The claim of an ancient validation from Hezekiah for the destruction of imagery can be seen in in the 1571 *Homily Against Peril of Idolatry and Superfluous Decking of Churches*. Started in the reign of Edward VI, revoked by Queen Mary and reinstated by Elizabeth I, this series of homilies further developed the compromise Reformation theology of the Elizabethan Settlement. The resultant twenty-one homilies were attached to the *Book of Common Prayer* from which Eliot takes the title of Part 1 of his poem, *The Burial of the Dead*.

Thus you see what authority St. Jerome, and that most ancient history, give unto the holy and learned Bishop Epiphanius, whose judgment of images in churches and temples, then beginning by stealth to creep in, is worthy to be noted.

First, he judged it contrary to Christian religion, and the authority of the Scriptures, to have any images in Christ's church. Secondly, he rejected not only carved, graven, and molten images, but also painted images out of Christ's church. Thirdly, that he regarded not whether it were the image of Christ, or of any other saint; but being an image would not suffer it in the church. Fourthly, that he did not only remove it out of the church, but with a vehement zeal tare it in sunder, and exhorted that a corpse should be wrapped and buried in it, judging it meet for nothing but to rot in the earth, following herein the example of the good king Hezekiah, who brake the brazen serpent to pieces, and burned it to ashes, for that idolatry was committed to it.[228]

Eliot described Calvinism as 'a form of worship from which the office of the imagination and the aesthetic emotions had ... been so ruthlessly evicted'.[229] He saw the antagonism to imagery in the battle of creeds in Magnus Martyr as an eviction of the aesthetic that extends into broader culture, a war on imagery waged in church and mind.[230]

The Murdered Churches of London

In 1921 Eliot wrote of the 'murdered churches' of London that he would 'love to write a book on Wren, or at least on the églises assassinées of London.'[231] He quotes Marcel Proust, who wrote in 'mémoire des églises assassinées' to describe the French cathedrals 'assassinated' by the Germans during the First World War. It is unlikely that Eliot would express so clear a wish on a subject on which he did not already consider himself at least somewhat knowledgeable. In the Notes, Eliot immediately follows the direction to the interior of Magnus Martyr with an instruction to 'See *The Proposed Demolition of Nineteen City Churches*' [264n], referring to a London County Council report on those churches.

> A report in 1920 proposed the demolition of nineteen City churches, including St Magnus. A general outcry from members of the public and parishioners alike prevented the execution of this plan ... T. S. Eliot wrote that the threatened churches gave "to the business quarter of London a beauty which its hideous banks and commercial houses have not quite defaced ... the least precious redeems some vulgar street ... The loss of these towers, to meet the eye down a grimy lane, and of these empty naves, to receive the solitary visitor at noon from the dust and tumult of Lombard Street, will be irreparable and unforgotten." The London County Council published a report concluding that St Magnus was "one of the most beautiful of all Wren's works" and "certainly one

of the churches which should not be demolished without specially good reasons and after very full consideration." Due to the uncertainty about the church's future, the patron decided to defer action to fill the vacancy in the benefice and a curate-in-charge temporarily took responsibility for the parish. However, on 23 April 1921 it was announced that the Revd Henry Joy Fynes-Clinton would be the new Rector. *The Times* concluded that the appointment, with the Bishop's approval, meant that the proposed demolition would not be carried out. Fr Fynes-Clinton was inducted on 31 May 1921.[232]

The report not only found the church to be one of Wren's most beautiful works, it also compliments the reredos. 'The altar-piece extends across the full width of the chancel and is remarkably fine. It is treated with the Corinthian order with entablature and attic stage and a raised pedimented panel over the centre, the whole being richly carved'. This seems to describe an intermediate stage between the minimal, aniconic single-stage altarpiece of around 1890 and a later version holding the round Glory with cherubims. Since this was before the arrival of Fynes-Clinton, it suggests that a previous rector had carried out some restoration. The report also notes that an 'important tablet is erected to the memory of Miles Coverdale, translator of the Bible, who was at one time rector of the church, and whose remains were re-interred therein'.[233]

Eliot wrote in 1921 that there is 'no method but to be very intelligent'.[234] Given his thorough scholarship in myth, ritual, theology and philosophy, it is significantly unlikely that he found the interior of Magnus Martyr 'inexplicable' [265], akin to liking a book cover while feeling no need or ability to read it. This disjunct between his abilities and the alleged impenetrability of the architectural narratives of the church is evident in Spurr's critical analysis. On the one hand, he finds that Eliot presents the church 'so positively (if somewhat uncomprehendingly) in terms of the exquisite beauty of its interior'. On the other, the 'original aesthetic stimulus was combined, in the case of the City churches, for example, with an appreciation of their historical significance ... Once this multi-layered degree of comprehension (aesthetic, historical, moral, theological and spiritual) had been attained, he would have recognised that the churches' beauty was not merely artistically satisfying'.[235]

Those who came to the Church at this time were asked to sign a petition in the vestry appealing against its demolition. This elegantly written petition is undated, but was written either in late 1920 or early 1921. It is more or less concurrent, in time as well as theme, with Eliot's letter of October 1921 to Aldington 'on the églises assassinées of London' — language that mirrors the petition, which decries the 'sentence of death' on the church.[236] This is not to claim that Eliot was involved in writing the petition. The new rector Fynes-Clinton was known to be learned and of great personal fluency, and so was more than capable of writing such an appeal. Eliot would certainly have known of it, and would have read it and most likely signed it, since he also attended protest marches against the demolition.

Breaking Superstitious Imagery to Pieces
Milton's *Eikonoklastes*

> What are the roots that clutch, what branches grow
> Out of this stony rubbish? Son of man,   [20]
> You cannot say, or guess, for you know only
> A heap of broken images

Nietzsche writes that in 'order for a shrine to be set up, *another shrine must be broken to pieces*: that is the law'.[237] The term 'iconoclast' means a 'breaker or destroyer of images'.[238] The Reformation struggle between the aniconic and the iconodule, between those against and those who advocated imagery, can be read with Milton's *Eikonoklastes*, celebrating those who 'broke all superstitious Images to peeces'.

The refurbishment of Magnus Martyr from 1921 was destined to create ire in view of the antipathy to imagery expressed in original form in the *Homily Against Peril of Idolatry* of the Reformation. 'True religion, then, and pleasing of GOD, standeth not in making, setting up, painting, gilding, and decking of dumb and dead images ... these things be vain and abominable, and most damnable before GOD.[239] This struggle over imagery is of ancient provenance and central to Christianity since its inception. The Second Council of Nicaea of 787 CE sought to protect such imagery, including in the form of sacred wood.

> Indeed they had the effrontery to criticise the beauty pleasing to God established in the holy monuments; they were priests in name, but not in reality. They were those of whom God calls out by prophecy, Many pastors have destroyed my vine, they have defiled my portion. For they followed unholy men and trusting to their own frenzies they calumniated the holy church, which Christ our God has espoused to himself, and they failed to distinguish the holy from the profane, asserting that the icons of our Lord and of his saints were no different from the wooden images of satanic idols.[240]

The interest at the Second Council of Nicaea in the 'beauty pleasing to God' is carried forward to Anglo-Catholicism. Mary Bell sums up the core intent behind the struggle for sacred imagery as the 'picture language of the beauty of worship'. Its spiritual function is akin to the *Biblia Pauperum,* the picture Bible for those who cannot read. 'The dawn of Christian hope began to lighten the darkness of the great slums of East London. Leeds, Manchester and Birmingham were touched by it, and later Portsmouth, Brighton, and Swindon and countless others. The beginning of the revival of ritual and ceremonial arose in these churches in the slums, where Religious Truth was taught in the picture language of the beauty of worship'.[241] It aptly expresses the perspective of the new rector, shared with those such as Geoffrey Faber, on what Diarmaid MacCulloch describes as 'the offering of beautiful music in settings of restrained beauty as the most fitting approaches to God in worship'.[242] When Eliot later formally committed to this creed, he brought to that choice his universal cultural and literary appreciation of imagery he had enwrapped with the Church of St. Magnus the Martyr during the creedless moment of his masterpiece.

At the time of *The Waste Land,* such imagery was anathema to Protestantism. In Magnus Martyr, at 'the midday service on 1 March 1922, J.A. Kensit, leader of the Protestant Truth Society, got up and protested against the form of worship'. An article in *The Times* of May 1922 titled *Orthodox Views Changing* shows the church was central to the wider battle of creeds in society. 'A representative deputation waited upon the Archbishop of Canterbury ... bearing nearly 1,400 lay signatures and 500 clerical signatures', including '44 members of both Houses of Parliament. The memorial dealt with the spread of modernism and ritualism in the church during the last 20 years ... Since the Royal Commission of 1903 things have gone from bad to worse ... At St. Magnus Martyr ... there was even the service of the blackening of faces at the communion rail on Ash Wednesday'.[243] Despite such opposition, the rector Fynes-Clinton did manage to restore the altarpiece to near its current glory by

1924. A photograph of that restoration at the London Metropolitan Archives records continued disapproval, pencilled on the back. 'St. Magnus, spoilt by alteration & so called restoration'. MacCulloch sees this tension continue today.

> The Church of England has never decisively settled who owns its history, and therefore of what its colour might be on the world map of Christianity. Within it remain two worlds: One, the sacramental world of theologians like Launcelot Andrewes and William Laud, the world that still values real presence, bishops and beauty; and the other, the world of the Elizabethan Reformation, which rejects shrines and images ... These two worlds contend for mastery within English tradition, and they have created the fascinating dialogue about the sacred which the world calls Anglicanism.[244]

Eliot acknowledged that even in his time such struggles as matters of Church creeds were becoming remote from ordinary people. However, it bears repeating that he saw the struggles of the English Civil War continue into modernity on the wider cultural landscape, representing unseen fault lines within society. 'The fact is simply that the Civil War of the seventeenth century, in which Milton is a symbolic figure, has never been concluded. The Civil War is not ended: I question whether any serious civil war ever does end. Throughout that period English society was so convulsed and divided that the effects are still felt'.[245]

In contrast to the exemption of altarpieces from considerations of idolatry, the new rector was considered to have acted illegally in introducing stand-alone images of the Virgin Mary, regarded by Puritans as cultic and superstitious. From 1922 Mr. W.C.W. Vincent, a church clerk, engaged the rector in recurrent court cases resulting in the forced removal of such imagery. *The Times* reported the judgement of the Chancellor of the Diocese of London.

> The second Holy Table had been taken away, but, in exactly the same place, was a similar table with candlesticks on it, which were lighted when Salve Regina was sung. The original Holy Table had on it a picture of the Madonna and Child. That picture had been removed, and another of the Madonna and Child, with the inscription 'S. Maria de Perpetuo Succursu', substituted ... He came to the conclusion that that was a mere substitution for the original picture, and it must be included in the faculty for removal.[246]

'For many Reformist Protestants, who identified Roman Catholicism with the Antichrist, idolatry meant especially the accoutrements of Roman Catholic worship: the mass, clerical vestments, religious statues and images, paintings of the Virgin Mary and the saints, and sometimes church music'. Lewalski links Milton's iconoclasm to *Paradise Lost*. 'His choice of persona was appropriate, given that idolatry was a central concern for Milton from his first major poem, the "Nativity Ode," through many prose tracts written during the Civil War and Protectorate, to his profound engagement with that issue in his greatest poems, *Paradise Lost, Paradise Regained*, and *Samson Agonistes*'.[247] For his treatise against imagery, Milton chose the title *Eikonoklastes*. In 'choosing this title, Milton was assuming, he explains, the chosen surname of many Greek emperors who *after long tradition of Idolatry in the Church, took courage, and broke all superstitious Images to peeces'*. While there is no record yet evident of what happened to the imagery confiscated from Magnus Martyr in the 1920s, it is likely it was, in like manner, broken '*to peeces*'.

The battle of creeds led to a moment of extraordinary pathos in Magnus Martyr in 1922, in the form of a marmalade pot. Fynes-Clinton obeyed the letter, but doggedly resisted the spirit of the court orders, and made substitutions for the proscribed items removed by clerks.

> The articles of service which were ordered to be removed from the Church of St. Magnus the Martyr, the ancient Billingsgate church, by the Vicar-General at a recent Consistory Court were taken away from the church yesterday by Mr. W. Charles W. Vincent, one of the petitioning church wardens. The articles removed were the tabernacle, the gilded throne, the oil lamp, the water stoup, the votive stand, the small crucifix, and some portions of the catafalque and the sepulchre, which were the subject of much discussion during the Consistory Court proceedings. There was also removed the marmalade pot which, it was alleged, was used for containing holy water at the entrance of the church.

A further article notes that the picture of the Virgin and Child was also ordered removed, taken from the church with the marmalade pot and presumably broken to pieces. It was reported in *The Times* of 4th Dec. 1922 that, when asked about the pot, Fynes-Clinton responded to the court that 'the actual substitute' for the Holy Water basin 'was a marmalade pot, because he could not afford better things'.[248]

Puritanism

The more extreme form of Protestantism is expressed by the term 'Puritan'. It was deployed early in the English Reformation by

Protestants as a pejorative term to denote clergy such as Revd. Miles Coverdale who refused all compromise, including that of the Elizabethan Settlement Eliot so admired. MacCulloch notes that 'those who were prepared to conform to the Queen's wishes named the discontented, in no friendly spirit, as 'Puritans'.[249] It is not the purpose of this book to either define Puritanism or to claim that it is a singular phenomenon. However, a brief look at the term will assist in understanding Eliot's attitude to the battle of creeds in Magnus Martyr and its wider cultural significance.

Eliot regarded the abuses of the thoroughly corrupt Catholic Church to which Luther and others of the Reformation rightly objected to be a temporary historical moment that engendered a perseverating Puritanism. 'As soon as the emotions disappear the morality which ordered it appears hideous. Puritanism itself became repulsive only when it appeared as the survival of a restraint after the feelings which it restrained had gone'.[250] That was in *The Sacred Wood* of 1921, and Eliot was consistent. In a 1946 essay on Milton, he wrote that it is 'now considered grotesque, on political grounds, to be of the party of King Charles; it is now, I believe, considered equally grotesque, on moral grounds, to be of the party of the Puritans; and to most persons to-day the religious views of both parties may seem equally remote'.[251]

Puritanism itself is fragmented. 'Nowhere was puritanism a coherent faith or national church', and even the 'question of whether to award the capital 'P' or not remains a subject of contention among historians'.[252] Stephen Tomkins notes that 'Puritanism was nothing so concrete as a party or sect, but rather a climate of opinion, a mood of discontent ... The Puritans were dissatisfied with the Elizabethan Church and fought its leaders for further Protestant reform, to purify it of 'the relics of papistry'. In these early years, 'puritan' had none of the associations of killjoy morality that have since become its main meaning. Puritans were also, and at first more commonly, known as 'precisians' wanting the church more precisely to model itself on the Bible'.[253]

When Puritans felt an obligation to destroy the imagery of Magnus Martyr in the 1920s as idolatrous, they were following something of a tradition in that church. The *Annals of the Reformation*, a book of 1824 that collected records of 'Queen Elizabeth's Happy Reign', reports the destruction of imagery from the same church in the early days of the English Reformation.

> August the 15th, the roods in St. Paul's were pulled down, and the high altar, and other things pertaining, spoiled ... The 25th day, at St. Rotolph's, Billingsgate, the rood and the images of Mary and John, and of the patron of that church, were burnt, with books of superstition: where at the same time a preacher standing within the church wall made a sermon; and while he was preaching, the books were thrown into the fire. They then also took away a cross of wood that stood in the churchyard. Sept. 16, at St. Magnus, at the corner of Fish-street, the rood, and Mary, and John were burnt, and several other things of superstition belonging to that church.
>
> This visitation did much good, and brought forward the religion very considerably throughout the nation ... In this visitation it was, that all the beneficed clergymen were required to make a subscription with their hands to what the parliament, anno 1558, had enacted, concerning restoring the supremacy to the queen, and the book of divine service, to be according to the word of God: and that was done in this form, as I found it in the MS. library at the palace in Lambhith.

"We do confess and acknowledge, the restoration again the ancient jurisdiction over the state ecclesiastical and the clergy temporal of this realm of England, and abolishing of all foreign power repugnant to the same, according to an act thereof made in the last parliament, begun at Westminster, January the 23d, in the first year of our sovereign lady queen Elizabeth, and there continuing and kept to the 8th day of May then next ensuing; the administration of the sacraments, the use and order of the divine service, in manner and form as it is set forth in a book commonly called *The Book of Common Prayer*."[254]

Such Puritan iconoclasm is made explicit in Eliot's 1934 play *The Rock*. Eliot explained that a 'scene of the Reformation reminds us of the dangers of destruction'.[255]

> *Sound of a Lutheran hymn. The lights change to an angry glow ... On the hill is a* PREACHER *of Reformation Times.*
> PREACHER: Now first of all, brethren, as touching the worship of images, which has long been a gross and Babylonish superstition in the land. God hath said: "Thou shalt not make to thyself any graven image." Therefore look you well to it, that no images abide in your churches, neither let them be carried away by superstitious folk who cling to them; but take them down, take them out yourselves, and destroy them utterly ...
> (*The Rock* II p.72)

In *The Waste Land*, Eliot regards the intemperance that destroyed imagery in the temple of Magnus Martyr during the Reformation, and again in 1922, as of a kind with the destruction of the local shrines of Old Testament Judeah by Hezekiah. It represents the destructive impulses of iconoclastic zealotry and a general taste for destruction universal to humankind to which he objects in principle as a matter of culture and heritage.

The 'heap of broken images' of the poem resonates with Old Testament imagery: 'they have laid Jerusalem on heaps' (Psalm 79). In that, the destruction of church imagery expands to city scale, into the politics of power, and on to the continental scale destruction and industrialised killing of World War I. That war was 'referred to journalistically as the "Anglo-Nietzschean war"' and, as all the women of the poem are one, so all the zealotries are one.[256] For Eliot, zealotry is an inherent risk in the certitudes of any creed, religious or secular, that would reform and reshape the world in its image. He sees the works of those such as Nietzsche as a secular creed, and sees Nietzsche's reformist zeal as of the same puritanism as that of extreme variants of the Reformation.

Max Stirner, who declared the death of God before Nietzsche and is considered with Nietzsche to be an important scribe of modern egoism, understood the power of this destructive process in political polemic. He advocates an attack method that promises reformation through an egoist war on 'false' culture, a destructive scoffing and contempt later deployed with such devastating power by Nietzsche.

In spiritual goods we are (in distinction from the sensuous) injured in a spiritual way, and the sin against them consists in a direct *desecration*, while against the sensuous a purloining or alienation takes place; the goods themselves are robbed of value and of consecration, not merely taken away; the sacred is immediately compromised. With the word 'irreverence' or 'flippancy' is designated everything that can be committed as *crime* against spiritual goods, against everything that is sacred for us; and scoffing, reviling, contempt, doubt, and the like, are only shades of *criminal flippancy*.[257]

In Eliot's view, such secular cultural iconoclasm is an unintended product of the Reformation, in which the subjective Lutheran inner voice gained primacy. The Second Council of Nicaea describes this as men 'trusting to their own frenzies'. From that genesis of individualism arose Romanticism. That version of Romanticism that engenders anarchic, iconoclastic versions of vainglorious individualism was given further expression by the extreme egoisms of modernity, walking forth as the pustular clerk of *The Waste Land*.

> Subjectivity, once let loose, could not be confined within limits until it had run its course. In morals, the Protestant emphasis on the individual conscience was essentially anarchic ... The eighteenth-century cult of "sensibility" began to break it down: an act was admired, not for its good consequences, or for its conformity to a moral code, but for the emotion that inspired it. Out of this attitude developed the cult of the hero, as it is expressed by Carlyle and Nietzsche, and the Byronic cult of violent passion of no matter what kind.
>
> (Bertrand Russell *A History of Western Philosophy*)[258]

The *Via Media*

The perception of Eliot as a reactionary conservative, particularly in his later years, is common. Whereas, at least at the time of *The Waste Land* he was an opponent of extremism in any form. In the absence of formal attachment to any creed at that moment, we can look to

Eliot's intellectual outlook — a universalist perspective central to which is the *via media*, the middle way.

Eliot does not divorce this outlook from every day or secular matters. He looked on all belief systems as forms of creed, even those often felt, or made to feel natural such as capitalism, commenting in 1933 that 'Communism and Capitalism are only forms of the same thing'. In his play *The Rock*, rapacious capitalism is portrayed as a zealot creed as abusive as communism. Lyndall Gordon sees Eliot's social aims as moderate — what he later termed 'temperate conservatism' — in which the individual is respected and protected.[259]

> It has not been customary to take much notice of Eliot's ideological position, yet it seems, from a historical distance, far more reasonable than the sweeping ideologies fashionable in his day. His modest ideal was men's virtue and well-being in community for all, and for a few, the divine beatitude. He wanted a community that would enrich the individual's sense of dignity, and he was indifferent to 20th century social schemes in which the individual was of small worth. Only one or two recognised the reasonableness of Eliot's position. In 1940 Lionel Trilling wrote that, although Eliot might have deceived himself in considering the Church an effective force for social reform, he had provided one moderate answer that favoured morality and human dignity, rare in his time.[260]

Eliot's poem, informed by classical and other myth and literature and art, is a cultural repository of Eliot's learning and spiritual enquiry up to that time. What arises might be termed a literary creed of universal form: as much cultural as spiritual, as much anthropological and classical as Judeo-Christian. Central to all that is a commitment to the *via media*. As the middle way of the Anglo-Catholic creed, the *via media* underwrites the accommodation of all chapels of beliefs through its 'branch theory', holding the unifying hope to return to a form of the pre-schism, universal Church. The *via media* is also the middle way compromise between Roman Catholicism and the Reformation that Eliot so admired in the Elizabethan Settlement, a reason for the presence of 'Elizabeth' [279] in the poem, equidistant as she is from 'both shores' [285].

> The Church of England is the creation not of the reign of Henry VIII or of the reign of Edward VI, but of the reign of Elizabeth. The *via media* which is the spirit of Anglicanism was the spirit of Elizabeth in all things; the last of the humble Welsh family of Tudor was the first and most complete incarnation of English policy. The taste or sensibility of Elizabeth, developed by her intuitive knowledge of the right policy for the hour and her ability to choose the right men to carry out that policy, determined the future of the English Church ... the Church at the end of the reign of Elizabeth, and as developed in certain directions under the next reign, was a masterpiece of ecclesiastical statesmanship.[261]

Geoffrey Faber describes the *via media* as denoting a 'mean between two extremes — the errors of Rome on the one hand, of Protestantism on the other ... a central position between all the many extremes — the Greek as well as the Roman Church, Dissent as well as Protestantism.' In that way, it combines the 'moral earnestness' of religion with 'an intellectual power of analysis and exposition, to a degree long unknown in England.'[262] Eliot wrote that 'the *via media* is of all ways the most difficult to follow. It requires discipline and self-control, it requires both imagination and hold on reality. In a period of debility like our own, few men have the energy to follow the middle way in government; for lazy or tired minds there is only extremity or apathy: dictatorship or communism, with enthusiasm or with indifference'.[263] This is in turn inculcates alienated and exhausted 'indifference' [242] in the citizen.

In cultures, the *via media* is the middle way of Aristotle and of Cicero, and informed the classical Roman way of life. It is also the moderation of the Buddha, whose *Ādittapariyāya Sutta*, the *Fire Sermon*, is an important source for the title of Part III of the poem. It is the middle way of the Upanishads, comingled as *The Waste Land* ends with St. Paul's remark on the peace 'which passeth understanding' — immediately preceded by his advice to let 'your moderation be known unto all men'. The *via media* is also the Golden Mean of Confucius, a philosophy of self-discipline and balance familiar to Ezra Pound through his translation work: 'they then stabilised their hearts, they disciplined themselves; having attained self-discipline, they set their own houses in order; having order in their own homes, they brought good government to their own states; and when their states were well governed, the empire was brought into Equilibrium'. [264] The Confucian idea that self-discipline allows people to 'set their own houses in order' echoes the setting of 'lands in order' [425] of the poem, perhaps encasing a nod to the interests of Pound. Further, Confucius's concern here is with rulers, and we have seen that line also alludes to the biblical King Hezekiah. In that light, the Confucian Golden Mean serves as a counterpoint to the extremism and iconoclasm of rulers such as Hezekiah, as it does to Coleridge's tyrant and Nietzsche's proposed governance by a cabal of contemptuous, pitiless pseudo-aristocrats.

Eliot's European wanderings after his Harvard studies were in significant part motivated by further philosophical enquiry, during which he arrived at a philosophical *via media*. 'Eliot continues to stake out an intermediate position between idealism and realism ... He denounces the "violence of our rushes from pole to pole."'[265] This philosophical quest underpins and compliments his literary and spiritual position, so that, at least at the time of *The Waste Land*, Eliot advocates the *via media* in all things, and is against intemperance in all matters, secular, religious and philosophical. That temperate world is endangered by those such as the pustular clerk of his poem, the selfish, separatist individualists of the extreme egoisms of modernity who would fragment society.

> Eliot discarded popular ideologies of social change — extremist politics and liberal optimism — as solutions to cultural despair ... Eliot was not against liberalism or democracy *per se*; he feared that they would not work: 'It is not that the world of separate individuals of the liberal democrat is undesirable' he wrote, 'it is simply that this world does not exist.' Eliot saw the masses, with their illusion of freedom, manipulated by a society organised for profit which would influence them by any means except their intelligence. Eliot saw in the English Church decency, common sense, and a moderation that, he felt, might provide a corrective to the faddist modern mind. He deplored the kind of facile mind that leapt across existing reality to some simplistic solution — communism; later, fascism — what he called 'the gospels of this world'.
>
> (Lyndall Gordon *The Imperfect Life of T.S. Eliot*)[266]

A Pompous Parade of Erudition, or a *Ulysses* in a Walnut Shell?

Geoffrey Chaucer's job as Clerk of the King's Works included oversight of works at the Church of St. Magnus the Martyr. It may well have provided inspiration for *The Canterbury Tales*, a multivocal poem like *The Waste Land*. Chaucer's pilgrims depart from the Tabard Inn in Southwark, a more anarchic place than the comparatively orderly north side of the Thames. Pilgrims also departed for Canterbury either from the church itself or the Chapel of St Thomas à Becket on the London Bridge of the time, and finished the return journey at the bridge or church. In *The Waste Land*, it is the journey itself and its milestones that is also important, and that theme of human quest is brought to Eliot's poem through 'April' and 'dull roots with spring rain' [1, 4].

> When April with its sweet-smelling showers
> Has pierced the drought of March to the root,
> And bathed every vein in such liquid
> By which power the flower is created;
> ...
> Then folk long to go on pilgrimages,
> And professional pilgrims to seek foreign shores,
> To distant shrines, known in various lands;
> And specially from every shire's end
> Of England to Canterbury they travel,
> To seek the holy blessed martyr,
> Who helped them when they were sick.
>
> (The Canterbury Tales Prologue 1-18)

Eliot's poem extends an invitation in modernity to journey through space and time to 'seek foreign shores' and 'distant shrines'. It is a cultural pilgrimage to the ancient polytheistic civilisations of the Mediterranean, to explore their genesis in the earliest shared symbols, mythologies and poetics of humanity, and see their cultural and spiritual connections to a London temple of the 1920s.

As you depart that temple for those faraway shores, a choice is presented by the paintings of Aaron and Moses, the carbuncle gem and the surrounding imagery, by Sappho, and by the church itself as a deep repository of contesting lodes in English history. It is a choice between two versions of the poet T.S. Eliot. One Eliot deserves his place on the same shelf as James Joyce, the other does not, having allegedly written what a critic in 1923 termed a 'pompous parade of erudition ... the poem as window dressing' in which 'the bright-coloured pieces fail to atone for the absence of an integrated design.'[267]

In fact, Eliot shared that perspective on fragmentation in literature, the fragment poem being a hallmark of romantic poetry. In that light, there exists two possibilities. Either the chaos of the fragmented layer is a structural representation of the world of babel created by the scribes of extreme egoisms, and is undermined by a coherent classical layer that also acts as a criticism of Romanticism and its subsequent philosophies. Or, Eliot disregarded his own perspective on fragmentation to become, in his own words of 1920, a bad poet who throws what he borrows into a poem of no cohesion. This comment alone should make it clear that Eliot would not write a purely fragmented poem lacking coherent unity.

> One of the surest of tests is the way in which a poet borrows. Immature poets imitate; mature poets steal; bad poets deface what they take, and good poets make it into something better, or at least something different. The good

poet welds his theft into a whole of feeling which is unique, utterly different from that from which it was torn; the bad poet throws it into something which has no cohesion.[268]

Consider this poet as he sometimes sat in that church during the creation of the poem. Remember his philosophical training and scholarly investigations into anthropology, literature and other components of culture, his commitment to Classicism and to the mythic method of Yeats and Joyce, and his spiritual yearning and searching. Remember his poetics and his meticulous attention to artistic imagery. Does he recognise the prominent paintings of Moses and Aaron in that church? Does he know that the Breastplate of Judgement which holds the carbuncle gem on Aaron's chest is described in detail in the Book of Exodus in the Bible? Does he intend to create a connection with the 'young man carbuncular'? Does he understand what Aaron represents to that church and all such churches? We know he visited the other City churches. Did he see the similar altarpieces, and the paintings and frescos of Aaron with the carbuncle gem in St. Margaret's Lothbury, St. Stephan's Walbrook and St. Edmund Lombard Street? Is that comprehension isolated, and the surrounding imagery of the Magnus Martyr altarpiece 'Inexplicable' [265], if we are to read that word literally? Or does he understand the architecture, images and carved sacred wood of that church as a whole, narrating as it does a story of culture, spirituality and heritage arising from the ancient sacred groves of the Levant, so connecting that distant past to a temple in the heart of modern London?

In the pew in which he remains oblivious to such imagery, he is said to indulge in a startling level of misogyny in constructing an anarchic, fragmented, miserabilist poem of 'pompous erudition' and self-indulgent personal complaint, all while sitting dumb to the visual language of the church interior. This though we have seen that

Emerson, the essayist connected to the Eliot family and fundamental to American thought, had written admiringly of the work of Christopher Wren, who built the church, and of the carvings of Gibbon, who is said to have carved the altarpiece; and though Eliot's mother Charlotte and his brother Henry had visited and also admired the beauty of the church and its carvings in 1921. Eliot dismissed claims that the poem is a disillusioned complaint as 'nonsense, I may have expressed for them their own illusion of being disillusioned, but that did not form a part of my intention'.[269]

In a different pew, Eliot understands the Magnus Martyr interior. He appreciates the significance of the narrative and history of the altarpiece, and recognises its symbolic importance in the ongoing struggle over imagery throughout the Old Testament, Christianity and the history of humanity. He decries the iconoclastic destruction of such imagery and cultural artefacts, religious or secular, by puritans of any creed, religious or secular. Such destruction leaves us impoverished, so that we must read the extraordinary poetry of Sappho, itself much infused with the sacred, in fragments recovered from ancient rubbish heaps.

Eliot also grasps the resonance with contemporaneous anthropological narratives of the intertwined genesis of spirituality and art in the primeval mind we are about to explore on distant shores. He understands the spiritual and literary significance of the carbuncle gem, including in the work of Milton, and sees the possibilities in that for the mythic method in literature. He has seen that Aaron is also present from the first page of *Ulysses*.[270] While it does refer to an inexplicable aspect to human existence, the word 'inexplicable' in the poem might then also be read as an invitation to explicate.

On this journey, you are invited to join the Eliot who comprehensively understands the church, at that particular moment in history and in his life as a poet. While occasional references are made to Eliot's later criticism and comments, no substantial claim is made about who Eliot became in his later person, creed, life, work and art. The poem was written in an extraordinary moment in the history of literature. Eliot was captivated by the intensity, learnedness, literary bravura and intricately wrought classical discipline that underlies the surface anarchy of James Joyce's *Ulysses*. That Ezra Pound was of similarly firm classical outlook to Joyce is equally clear, since 'Pound didn't want to see Romanticism' in *The Waste Land*.[271]

These aspects give rise to questions of intended and unintended meanings in the poem. Numerous opinions on Eliot's work exist at the intersection between the intense control of meaning of the high modernist and more recent ideas of exponential interpretations. That includes readings of significant unintended meaning that escapes the artist, leaking into and from the text, such as authorial misogyny. This book sees Eliot in control of reverberating meaning of exponential scope and depth with exceptional compression and pointillist accuracy, so that views of the poem which have engendered severely negative perspectives might be reconsidered. *The Waste Land* is an inclusive, small-c catholic poem, reflecting the universal, broad-church aspect of his later chosen creed, Anglo-Catholicism.

> Do you then unchurch all the Presbyterians, all Christians who have no Bishops? ... Nay, we are not judging others ... we do not therefore exclude either from salvation ... Neither do we desire to pass sentence on other persons of other countries ... because similar difficulties may be raised about virtuous Heathens, Jews, or Mahometans.[272]
> (John Henry Newman, for Anglo-Catholicism, *Tract 4*, 1833)

PART II

The CLASSICAL ORDER of the MYTHIC LAYER

7. ORIGIN STORIES

Ritual is Art and Art is Ritual

> That there are no primitive languages is an axiom of con-
> temporary linguistics where it turns its attention to the
> remote languages of the world. There are no half-formed
> languages, no underdeveloped or inferior languages. Every-
> where a development has taken place into structures of great
> complexity. People who have failed to achieve the wheel will
> not have failed to invent & develop a highly wrought gram-
> mar. Hunters & gatherers innocent of all agriculture will
> have vocabularies that distinguish the things of their world
> down to the finest details ... What is true of language in
> general is equally true of poetry and the ritual-systems of
> which so much poetry is a part.[273]

Nine years after publication of Eliot's poem, Jerome Rothenberg
introduced his anthology of poetry under the heading 'Primitive
Means Complex'. A compilation from indigenous African, American, Eastern and Pacific sources, he includes the genesis stories of
the Kato (Cahto) Native American, Aranda (Arunta) Australian,
and New Zealand Māori. Any ideas that such oral accounts of the
world are to be thought primitive in a pejorative sense fade when
viewed with some of the highest literary achievements in Western
culture. The Greek epics the *Iliad* and *Odyssey* are also the products
of oral culture, preceding the written literature made possible for

the Greeks by the Phoenician alphabet. To explore the cultural and spiritual roots of *The Waste Land* is to journey to classical Greece mythology and its origins in preceding cultures such as the Phoenicians, who lent aspects of their mythology to both the Greeks and the Hebrews. In his poem, within the mythic layer that continuum goes further back to prehistory: to the dawn of humankind's first culture and spirituality.

Conditioned by Western thought systems including those of empire and theology, to varying degrees the scholars of the 1920s and before made comparisons between Western culture on the one hand, and both the people of different cultures and early human cultures on the other hand, as that between the complex and the simple, the scientific and the magical, and the reasoned and the superstitious. Some like James Frazer in *The Golden Bough* retained that confidence in the superiority of modern humankind, so that his use of terms such as 'primitive' retain pejorative traces. Others such as Jane Harrison soon recognised that attitude as too simplistic. Eliot shares Harrison's and Rothenberg's view that 'primitive is complex', a perspective that informs the complex mythic layer of his poem and the recognition in his critical work of the value of all human culture since its primeval genesis.

The intense modernist interest in that primeval past during the time of *The Waste Land* and before arose in large part from the theories of Darwin and those of anthropology and archaeology. All shone new light into a newly discovered distant past previously obscured by the assumed age of the earth, calculated from the Bible, of some six thousand years. As Darwin linked all life on earth from its inception, so anthropology, archaeology and comparative religion traced cultural continuations from primeval humanity to the present. Those continuums run through the unifying weave of *The Waste Land*.

Robert Crawford writes that 'Eliot was scientifically interested in religion' and 'continued to relate primitive to civilised man in the period leading up to 1920'.[274] It was a committed interest amounting to a dedicated private study that paralleled his philosophical education. Looking at Eliot's 'programmatic revaluation of the English literary tradition', Jason Harding provides an important insight into Eliot's method. It is an 'adversarial yet reconstructive doctrine of tradition ... saturated in the literature of the past' that stood in contrast to 'extremist modernism ... deficient in tradition'. In contrast, 'several avant-garde movements — notably, Italian and Russian Futurism, and Dadaism — advocated a clean break with the past'.[275] In that adversarial-reconstructive approach Eliot accepts nothing dogmatically and nothing is discarded, nor does he banish or ignore any scribe. He engages in a dialogue, keenly enjoyed with those such as James Joyce, and intensely adversarial with those such as John Milton and Friedrich Nietzsche.

His approach to anthropology and comparative religion is similar, and that adversarial-reconstructive engagement with these relatively new disciplines is in part to counter the relegation of religion to superstition. He wrote in 1916 of the tendency of the new disciplines 'to regard religion as essentially a feature of primitive society, destined to disappear in a world of positive science'. For Eliot, that represented 'a new heresy in religion', resistance to which is an 'important struggle', and that 'the struggle of "liberal" against "orthodox" faith is out of date. The present conflict is far more momentous than that'.[276] He no doubt had Nietzsche's declaration that God is dead in mind. In that, Eliot's position among scholars and literati was somewhat lonesome.

Game, set, and match to "culture." But the corpse of religion had not quite expired. It had one important twentieth-century champion and that was T.S. Eliot. We sometimes overlook the fact that when studying philosophy at Harvard, Eliot was also very much aware of new developments in the new social sciences, that is, sociology, anthropology and psychology ... there was only a very small place for religion ... a good deal of his thinking and writing about society was in large part enacted as acts of resistance to the pervasive secularism of his time and especially the secularist bent in the nature and practices of the social sciences.[277]

A critique of that pervasive secularism forms a core aspect of the mythic layer of the poem, in which cultural and spiritual continuums transcend the current moment in history, pointing to the universal in humanity across time and place. For Eliot, a component of the human mind is a shared inheritance from the cultural evolution of humanity. The universal aspects of myth form an important bridge across time, a perspective central to Frazer's *The Golden Bough*. Eliot commented that '*The Golden Bough* can be read in two ways: as a collection of entertaining myths, or as a revelation of that vanished mind of which our mind is a continuation'.[278] He wrote that Frazer is 'unquestionably the greatest master' of the comparative method in anthropology. 'No one has done more to make manifest the similarities and identities underlying the customs of races very remote in every way from each other ... But I cannot subscribe for instance to the interpretation with which he ends his volume on *The Dying God* ... No method, historical or comparative, will give such results as this'.[279]

Eliot links Shakespeare and Homer to the Upper Palaeolithic cave drawings of the Magdalenian culture of 20,000 BCE. He wrote of that collective heritage in 1921 as the mind of Europe:

'the mind of Europe — the mind of his own country — a mind which he learns in time to be much more important than his own private mind — is a mind which changes, and that this change is a development which abandons nothing *en route*, which does not superannuate either Shakespeare, or Homer, or the rock drawing of the Magdalenian draughtsmen'.[280] An aspect of the rhythms of the primeval vegetation ceremonies which open the poem is a representation of the entwined ritual expression of the cultural and spiritual drives of that Magdalenian culture, and all such early human cultures.[281] Following Darwin, the scholars of Eliot's time searched for the origins of myth and religion not in the Bible but in early humanity. That Eliot regarded such work as central to the poem, and to his time, is evident from his explicit direction to works of anthropology in his preamble to the Notes, and in his sketch of the contemporary intellectual landscape in 1920.

This day began, in a sense, with Tylor and a few German anthropologists; since then we have acquired sociology and social psychology, we have watched the clinics of Ribot and Janet, we have read books from Vienna and heard a discourse of Bergson; a philosophy arose at Cambridge; social emancipation crawled abroad; our historical knowledge has of course increased; and we have a curious Freudian-social-mystical-rationalistic-higher-critical interpretation of the Classics and what used to be called the Scriptures. I do not deny the very great value of all work by scientists in their own departments ... Few books are more fascinating than those of Miss Harrison, Mr. Cornford, or Mr. Cooke, when they burrow in the origins of Greek myths and rites; Mr. Durkheim, with his social consciousness, and M. Levy-Bruel, with his Bororo Indians who convince themselves

that they are parroquets, are delightful writers. A number
of sciences have sprung up in an almost tropical exuberance
which undoubtedly excites our admiration, and we realise
that the garden, not unnaturally, has come to resemble
a jungle. Such men as Tylor, and Robertson Smith, and
Wilhelm Wundt, who early fertilised the soil, would hardly
recognise the resultant vegetation.[282]

Roots and Branches
Edward Tylor's Primeval Continuum to Modernity

What are the roots that clutch, what branches grow
Out of this stony rubbish?   [20]

Mirroring the Darwinian tree of evolution, in *The Waste Land* the
animist vegetation ceremonies of the opening of the poem form the
roots of a figurative cultural tree reaching to modernity. That cultural tree is a central metaphor in the work of one of the founders
of cultural anthropology Edward Tylor, particularly in his *Primitive
Culture: Researches Into The Development Of Mythology, Philosophy,
Religion, Language, Art, And Custom.*

Jane Harrison, who we meet next, noted that Darwin praised
Tylor's book. 'Writing in 1871 to Dr Tylor, on the publication of
his "Primitive Culture", he says ... "It is wonderful how you trace
animism from the lower races up to the religious belief of the highest races. It will make me for the future look at religion — a belief in
the soul, etc. — from a new point of view"'.[283] Entwined with biblical references, an allusion to Tylor's book is encased in the figurative
iconoclastic destruction of the 'stony rubbish' of *The Waste Land.*

Animism characterizes tribes very low in the scale of humanity, and thence ascends, deeply modified in its transmission, but from first to last preserving an unbroken continuity, into the midst of high modern culture ... Animism is, in fact, the groundwork of the Philosophy of Religion, from that of savages up to that of civilized men. And although it may at first sight seem to afford but a bare and meagre definition of a minimum of religion, it will be found practically sufficient; for where the root is, the branches will generally be produced.

(Edward Tylor *Primitive Culture*)[284]

Eliot named Tylor's book and Darwin's *The Origin of Species* as essential reading in his 1923 essay *The Beating of a Drum*. He urges literary critics to expand their reading beyond pure literature to find 'sources which are often remote, difficult'. As with his critical essay on James Joyce of the same year, there seems here again an invitation to reassess his poem through the lens of the mythic method.

If literary critics, instead of perpetually perusing the writings of other critics, would study the content and criticize the methods of such books as *The Origin of Species* itself, and *Ancient Law*, and *Primitive Culture*, they might learn the difference between a history and a chronicle, and the difference between an interpretation and a fact. They might learn also that literature cannot be understood without going to the sources: sources which are often remote, difficult, and unintelligible unless one transcends the prejudices of ordinary literary taste.[285]

Jane Harrison
Darwin, Religion, and the Primal Spiritual Theatre

> What have art and ritual to do together? The ritualist is, to
> the modern mind, a man concerned perhaps unduly with
> fixed forms and ceremonies, with carrying out the rigidly
> prescribed ordinances of a church or sect. The artist, on the
> other hand, we think of as free in thought and untrammelled
> by convention in practice; his tendency is towards licence.
> Art and ritual, it is quite true, have diverged to-day; but the
> title of this book is chosen advisedly. Its object is to show
> that these two divergent developments have a common
> root, and that neither can be understood without the other.
> It is at the outset one and the same impulse that sends a man
> to church and to the theatre.
>
> (Jane Harrison *Ancient Art and Ritual*)[286]

Jane Harrison was a renowned scholar of the time. The first woman
to gain an academic post in England, at Newham College in Cambridge, she is credited as one of the founders of the modern study of
ancient Greece and its myths through archaeological evidence. Eliot
wrote that of the 'Archaeology of the Act Miss Harrison is one of our
most proficient exponents.'[287] Harrison explains her title *Ancient Art
and Ritual* in words that could serve as a thematic mantra for Eliot's
poetic and critical work of that time. 'The point of my title and the
real gist of my argument lie perhaps in the word "and" — that is, in
the intimate connection which I have tried to show exists between
ritual and art. This connection has, I believe, an important bearing
on questions vital to-day, as, for example, the question of the place of
art in our modern civilization, its relation to and its difference from

religion and morality; in a word, on the whole enquiry as to what the nature of art is and how it can help or hinder spiritual life'.[288]

As a field archaeologist and anthropologist, some see her as superior to the 'armchair anthropologist' Frazer. Significantly, those such as Martha C. Carpentier see her as the more serious influence on literary modernists. 'It is clear that Jane Harrison played a much larger role in the modernist understanding of myth and ritual and their relation to classical literature than has hitherto been recognised. One reason Harrison's contribution has been de-emphasized is that scholars have consistently overemphasised Frazer's'.[289] Readers are implicitly introduced to Harrison through Jessie Weston's *From Ritual to Romance*, named in the preamble to the Notes. Weston acknowledges her debt to Frazer's *The Golden Bough* from the outset, and elevates Harrison to a similar position. Further, Weston's comment that the 'perusal of Miss J. E. Harrison's *Themis* opened my eyes to the extended importance of these vegetation rites' most directly reflects Eliot's 'vegetation ceremonies' in the preamble to the Notes.[290] It is notable that Eliot directs to Weston's publisher '(Cambridge)' where he does not do so for Frazer. Harrison was a leading figure of the academic group informally known as the 'Cambridge Ritualists'.

Harrison described the impact of Darwinism in an essay in 1909 called *The Influence of Darwinism on the Study of Religions*. She wrote it to commemorate the fifty-year anniversary of the publication of Darwin's *On the Origin of Species*, the book that irradiates all subsequent thought systems including that of Nietzsche. 'The title of my paper might well have been 'The Creation by Darwinism of the Scientific Study of Religions' but that I feared to mar my tribute to a great name by any shadow of exaggeration'.[291] Following Darwin, scholars such as Harrison sought the origins of myth, ritual and art by tracing the evolution of culture from its genesis to modernity. Within that, Harrison shares with Eliot the idea of the social function of ritual, a bonding of the individual to the communal, yielding insight into another facet of the fragmentation of his poem.

> I have come to see in the religious impulse a new value. It is, I believe, an attempt, instinctive and unconscious ... to apprehend life as one, as indivisible ... the keeping open of the individual soul — that bit of the general life which life itself has fenced in by a separate organism — to other souls, other separate lives, and to the apprehension of other forms of life ... Whether any systematized attempt to remind man, by ritual, of that whole of life of which he is a specialized fragment can be made fruitful or not, I am uncertain.[292]

Not all agree now with Harrison's concept that myth and religion originated from ritual. However, it was understood as revelationary and compelling in the early 1900s, along with the concomitant concept of the genesis of art and culture in the same rituals. It is Harrison who addresses the continuum between ritual and art with the most attention. Like Eliot, she differentiates between modern religious ritualists — a rigid adherence to ceremony — and the primeval ritual in which we witness the genesis of art that leads to those such as Homer and Sappho. Spurr's observation that Eliot 'had become a 'ritualist' long before he officially became an Anglo-Catholic' can be read in light of Harrison's distinction between the modern ritualist and what might be termed the anthropological ritualist, whose compass is all of culture.[293]

> Whether rituals preceded myths or precisely how the two are entwined has never really been the important issue for writers or literary critics: the important discovery was the connection between ritual and *art*, that "they actually arise

out of a common human impulse," and this connection
was made solely by Jane Harrison with the help of Gilbert
Murray. While no one did more to popularise a new
understanding of myths as explanations of fertility rituals
than Frazer, he never came close to making the leap, or to
use Harrison's metaphor, crossing the "bridge" between
ritual and art.[294]

Harrison's work is another origin story, that of the genesis of art
as an abstraction of rituals arising from the re-enactment of valued primeval experiences.[295] She sees the 'germ of history' and
'commemorative ceremonial' as she imagines the transition from
primitive hunt to ritual, to abstraction of that ritual, and from that
abstraction, the emergence of art.

> We have next to watch how out of representation repeated
> there grows up a kind of abstraction which helps the
> transition from ritual to art. When the men of a tribe return
> from a hunt, a journey, a battle, or any event that has caused
> them keen and pleasant emotion, they will often re-act
> their doings round the camp-fire at night to an attentive
> audience of women and young boys. The cause of this
> world-wide custom is no doubt in great part the desire to
> repeat a pleasant experience; the battle or the hunt will not
> be re-enacted unless it has been successful. Together with
> this must be reckoned a motive seldom absent from human
> endeavour, the desire for self-exhibition, self-enhancement.
> But in this re-enactment, we see at once, lies the germ of
> history and of commemorative ceremonial, and also, oddly
> enough, an impulse emotional in itself begets a process we
> think of as characteristically and exclusively intellectual, the

process of abstraction. The savage begins with the particular battle that actually did happen; but, it is easy to see that if he re-enacts it again and again the particular battle or hunt will be forgotten, the representation cuts itself loose from the particular action from which it arose, and becomes generalized, as it were.[296]

Harrison's descriptions of primeval communal ritual might be kept in mind while reading Sappho's *Dancers at a Kritan Altar*, and the *Vigil of Venus* when maidens welcome spring. She expounds another form of origin story, that of hymn, when she links Christian Easter to the most ancient Dionysian ritual cry of the sacred wood. Harrison writes of Iacchos, who is Dionysus.

Some, like Iacchos and probably Bacchos itself, though they ultimately became proper names, were originally only cries. Iacchos was a song even down to the time of Aristophanes and was probably, to begin with, a ritual shout or cry kept up long after its meaning was forgotten. Such cries from their vagueness, their aptness for repetition, are peculiarly exciting to the religious emotions. How many people attach any precise significance to the thrice repeated, stately and moving words that form the prooemium to our own Easter Hymn? 'Alleluia, Alleluia, Alleluia'. They are a homage beyond articulate speech. Then, as now, these excited cries became sacred titles of the worshippers who used them.[297]

Harrison called Nietzsche's *The Birth of Tragedy* 'real genius', and once described herself as a 'disciple of Nietzsche'. At the same time, she is described as having 'researched Dionysian ritual with a scientific rectitude undreamt of by him.'[298] Nietzsche favours Dionysus as the anarchic god of enjoyment who contrasts to what he sees as life-denying Christianity. There are considerable resonances between Harrison's outlook, that of Eliot, and that of the early Nietzsche when he writes of the bonding effect of music.

> Under the spell of the Dionysian it is not only the bond between man and man that is re-established: nature in its estranged, hostile, or subjugated forms also celebrates its reconciliation with its prodigal son, man ... Now, with the gospel of world-harmony, each man feels himself not only reunified, reconciled, reincorporated, and merged with his neighbour, but genuinely one ... In song and dance man expresses himself as a member of a higher communal nature.
>
> (Friedrich Nietzsche *The Birth of Tragedy*)[299]

Eliot's battle with Nietzsche is also fought in those ancient sacred groves. Where Nietzsche ends *Ecce Homo* with the anti-Christian war-cry '*Dionysos against the crucified*', Harrison sees Dionysus as an early expression of the dying god of which Christ is the later Christian manifestation, and we will see Eliot trace the same continuum in the next chapter.

At the time, the boundaries of academic disciplines were significantly more porous, informed by a classical, scholarly outlook of a broad range. Harrison expressed opinions on the interests and direction of arts and literature, so that she was seen as participating in 'the elaboration of Modernism in general'. That worked both ways, since Crawford notes that Eliot, 'pondering myth', 'drew on anthropological reading he had done as a student, and solicited *Criterion* essays from J.G. Frazer, Jane Harrison, F.M. Cornford, G. Elliot Smith, and other anthropologically influenced scholars'.[300] Because of her emphasis on art, classical and modern, Harrison's work may have influenced Eliot more than thought. K. J. Phillips identifies a remarkable resonance between Harrison's opinion on anarchy, order, and a necessary complexity in modern literature that is reflected in the poetic and critical work of Eliot; and a further resonance with Eliot's idea of the tradition made new in modern works.

Harrison recommends two paradoxical combinations which became central to Modernism. First she recommends that writers bring modern life onto the page while remembering tradition; the paradox is novelty with tradition. Second, she advocates that they transcribe chaos into new and difficult language while imposing order; the paradox here is chaos and order. Harrison says, in 1913:

Modern life is not simple — cannot be simple — ought not to be; it is not for nothing that we are heirs to the ages. Therefore the art that utters and expresses our emotion towards modern life cannot be simple; and, moreover, it must before all things embody not only that living tangle which is felt by the Futurists as so real, but it must purge and order it, by complexities of tone and rhythm hitherto unattempted. (*Ancient Art* p.233)

This passage seems to anticipate Eliot's more famous lines in 'The Metaphysical Poets' (1921):

... poets in our civilization, as it exists at present, must be difficult. Our civilization comprehends great variety and complexity, and this variety and complexity, playing upon a refined sensibility, must produce various and complex results. The poet must become more and more comprehensive, more allusive, more indirect, in order to force, to dislocate if necessary, language into his meaning. [301]

Phillips points out a further resonance with Eliot's literary commentary of the time. 'Harrison spells out yet another paradoxical combination of 'tangle' and 'order.' Eliot in '*Ulysses*, Order and Myth' (1923) shares her belief by asking artists to include both 'anarchy' and 'shape' in their art ... Harrison's "living tangle" purged by "order" forecasts Eliot's "anarchy" given "form" by the "mythical method," a union which to some has seemed the essence of Modernism'. Carpentier also comments on the influence of women in modernism.

> The prominence of women in modernist literature is extraordinary. Think merely of Mrs. Wilcox, Margaret and Helen in Forster's *Howards End*, Gudrun and Ursula in Lawerence's *Women in Love*, and Molly in *Ulysses*, to name only the most obvious. I do not think it too rash to assert that female archetypes assume a force in the writing of the Georgian [sic] generation that they have rarely known at any time before or since. By "female archetype" I mean women rendered as symbols of power, both creative and destructive. And since archetypal images are universal and unchanging, female archetypes bear many of the qualities and functions of the three traditional archetypal female forms found in myth: Earth-mother, witch, and virgin (or, more precisely, maiden) ... For writers like Joyce and Eliot, who consciously employed the "mythic method", the comparative methodology of myth criticism is the best way to fully appreciate the meaning of these archetypal figures. [302]

It seems a woman is to blame. Before the high modernist works of Joyce and Eliot, Harrison advocated difficulty in the arts as necessary to reflect the complexity of modernity. After *Ulysses* and before

The Waste Land, her 'spiritual daughter' and long-term travelling companion Hope Mirrlees wrote the extraordinary *Paris: A Poem*. Sometimes called the Ur-text of Eliot's poem, it is also a difficult work of immense scope, complexity and classical discipline within an apparently irredeemably fragmented style. The complexity of high modernist writing, particularly that arising from the mythic method, often perceived as patriarchal literary snobbery, was in part inspired and encouraged by the work and words of an esteemed, scholarly woman; and is in significant part about women.

Origins: Darwin, Christianity, Nietzsche, and the Ape

> The emphasis on change over time was liberating for scientists, including Charles Lyell, author of *Principle of Geology* (1830-3) and Charles Darwin, author of *On the Origin of Species* (1859), who argued that the earth and its inhabitants are immeasurably old and still changing. In subsequent generations, the quest for origins begun in geology and biology led to an explosion of activity in the social sciences, including anthropology, sociology, psychology and religion.[303]
>
> (Jewel Spears Brooker)

At the time of *The Waste Land*, Christianity was under siege from the secular quest for origins. Since Darwin's theory showed the biblical genesis story of the origins of humankind to be myth, it undermined the common idea that morality had been divinely mandated in that moment of genesis. Human morality had been said by scribes to be dictated from the heavens some six thousand years ago, and later in more detail to those such as Moses in the form of the Ten Commandments that sit beside his portrait in Magnus Martyr. Like those such as Joyce, Harrison, Frazer, Weston and Tylor, Nietzsche also investigates origins. *The Birth of Tragedy* is 'concerned with origins', and he writes of another book that the 'subject of this polemic' is his 'thoughts on the *origin* of our moral prejudices ...'[304]

That Nietzsche was significantly influenced by Darwin is reliably confirmed by his hostility. 'Most of what Nietzsche says about Darwin and Darwinism is hostile. Indeed the most striking things he says reach the pitch of denunciation and personal insult. He likes to call Darwin "mediocre," and attacks Darwinism on a host of theoretical and evaluative grounds. But I think this pointed animosity is — here as often elsewhere in Nietzsche's campaigns — misleading. He is so eager to distinguish himself, because he knows how much he has taken over from Darwin — how big a part of his own view, this Darwinism looms.'[305]

Darwin's destruction of the certitudes of the biblical creation story and Nietzsche's subsequent destruction of the certitudes of the divine provenance of morality created what Kaufmann terms a 'crisis in philosophy' in those systems implicitly reliant on some variation of those metaphysical certitudes. Since for Nietzsche that includes much of philosophy and all of theology, in his view all Christianity and much of philosophy are to be considered deluded mistakes. He argues this ruthlessly and at such an intense register that he struck a deep metaphysical blow in tandem with the scientific blow of the theory of evolution.

Nietzsche's writings undermine the idea of morality as anything other than a changeable human construct. His thought developed ever more stridently in opposition to what he saw as the delusional 'slave morality' of Christianity which, among other effects, inhibits the arrival of his overman. Through this attempted genesis of a new Adam of the future who needs no god, Nietzsche compounded what was an extended moment of intense pressure on Christianity, representing an existential threat to the Church. In contrast, the course of Eliot's intellectual enquiries was towards continuity and order. The spiritual aspect of Eliot's philosophical quest is also present from his early years.

> In America, the Harvard Philosophy Department was in the forefront of the challenge posed by Darwin. In the decade before Eliot entered the doctoral program, the department was at the pinnacle of its prestige, primarily due to the eminence of two philosophers, William James and Josiah Royce ... both presented coherent responses to the crisis, which at Harvard included not only the concern with religion but, more generally, with consciousness and morality ... James was more interested in religious experience and Royce in a defence of Christianity ... the issue that was at the core of his thought: the attempt to connect the finite and the infinite, the individual and the Absolute. "The essence of this doctrine of Evolution," he claimed, "lies in the fact that it recognizes the continuity of man's life with that of an extra-human realm whose existence is hinted to us by our experience of Nature."[306]

Father Fynes-Clinton, the rector who met with Eliot's mother and brother on their visit to Magnus Martyr and who undertook the restoration of the altarpiece, described its narrative as 'the whole scheme of redemption'.[307] That imagery includes a visual representation of the doctrine of progressive revelation: the evolution of the soul of humankind, divinely assisted through gradual revelation over time. Eliot weaves this imagery with the cultural continuums in his poem that transcend Judeo-Christian societies, engendering a universal parallel to Darwin's Theory of Evolution. What is suggested is an ennobling cultural evolution of humanity that encases the possibility of an accompanying spiritual evolution that in some way touches an extra-human realm. It seems the most cautious, creedless of suggestions, as universal as the primeval animist intimation of a diffuse spirit in everything.

In contrast, he sees the work of Nietzsche as degenerate. Insistent aspects of Nietzsche's new morality of power are the continued enchainment of women and a need for a cultural cleansing, a reformation. The pustular clerk of Eliot's poem becomes the degenerate embodiment of that zealotry, the egoist new man tasked with the destruction of cultural heritage that for Nietzsche is necessary to clear the path to a world newly ordered to serve his overman. Empowered by the certitude of his inner voice and the egoist creed of the will to power, and rejecting personal and communal restraint, in Eliot's schema that zealot devolves to the brute human, the decultured and unrestrained Darwinian intelligent ape. Eliot asked, 'is man an ape or an angel? ... some reformers are certainly on the side of the Apes'.[308] As he inverts *Paradise Lost* through the typist and young man carbuncular, he also inverts ideas of the Darwinian and Nietzschean evolution of humankind as always progressive.

Variations of this ape roam Eliot's poetry before *The Waste Land*, including the 'Gesture of orang-outang' of *Sweeney Erect* and the 'Apeneck Sweeney' of *Sweeney Among the Nightingales*. Sweeney is the American counterpart of the pustular clerk, a poetic older brother and fellow degenerate. He is explicitly brought to the streets of *The Waste Land* and so, in that aspect of the poem that is the beast fable, links the clerk with the simian theme as he also roams London seeking sex. Mrs. Porter is said in one sense to represent a brothel madam.

But at my back from time to time I hear   [196]
The sounds of horns and motors, which shall bring
Sweeney to Mrs. Porter in the spring.

Like Sweeney, the clerk is a representation of the resurgent brute in that type of man who decultures himself through romantic self-regard, willed ignorance, iconoclasm, extreme egoisms and other zealotries. He is the darkly ironic embodiment of the 'fallen beauty' of the fraternity of individualists engendered by Milton, Byron, Stirner and Nietzsche; the ugly, boil-encrusted, egoist progeny of a continuum of vainglorious romantic imaginings.

Jessie Weston and The Venerable Bede
From Polytheism to Christianity in Britain

> Not only the title, but the plan and a good deal of the incidental symbolism of the poem were suggested by Miss Jessie L. Weston's book on the Grail legend: *From Ritual to Romance* (Cambridge). Indeed, so deeply am I indebted, Miss Weston's book will elucidate the difficulties of the poem much better than my notes can do; and I recommend it (apart from the great interest of the book itself) to any who think such elucidation of the poem worth the trouble.
>
> (T.S. Eliot *Notes on the Waste Land*)

Eliot names Weston's 1920s book of comparative religion with Frazer's *The Golden Bough* in the preamble to the Notes. Her work reiterates the universal links between primeval and modern humanity in the poem by tracing a continuum from ancient rituals to modern Christian ceremonial in Britain. Eliot later wrote of his regret that, because of the Arthurian element of Weston's book, he had inadvertently sent many on a 'wild goose chase' to the grail legend. An early critic wrote in 1926 that there 'is Miss Weston's *From*

Ritual to Romance to read, and its 'astral' trimmings to be discarded — they have nothing to do with Mr. Eliot's poem'.[309]

Weston's book is not a grail story, nor is *The Waste Land* a grail story. Where the poem is concerned, Weston is so often linked with the grail as a cult object that her core interest is overlooked: how Arthurian legend is informed by the fertility rituals of the ancient past, including those of the Ancient Near East. The grail is a minor component of her book, and she explicitly warns against its elevation in isolation. The grail as cup or dish, the lance, the sword and the candelabra should be treated as 'symbols or talismans ... on the same principle as we have treated the incidents of this story, *i.e.*, as a connected whole ... not separated the one *from* the other, and made the subject of independent treatment, but that they be regarded in their relation the one *to* the other, and that no theory of origin be held admissible which does not allow for that relation as a primitive and indispensable factor'.[310] For Weston, the grail in itself is only important in its role within that group of talismans she traces to an accumulation of ritual practices with roots in the ancient Mediterranean and surrounds. It is again a continuum, in which those rituals evolved in transmission between successive cultures across Europe, to then be reshaped to serve Christianity.

Eliot set out that idea of the evolution of religious belief from animist rituals in strikingly direct form in his 1934 play *The Rock*, from which extracts are often published as *Choruses from 'The Rock'*. It is a more universal form of the progressive revelation visually narrated on the Magnus Martyr altarpiece. Where sincere, it is not to be doubted as virtuous spiritual quest along that continuum, and in this we can see the universal human quest that flows through *The Waste Land*.

And when there were men, in their various ways, they
struggled in
torment towards GOD ...
Worshipping snakes or trees, worshiping devils rather than
nothing: Crying for life beyond life, for ecstasy not of the
flesh ...
Invented the Higher Religions; and the Higher Religions
were good
And lead man from light to light, to knowledge of Good
and Evil ...
affirmation of rites with forgotten meanings ...
Bestial as always before, carnal, self-seeking as always before,
selfish and purblind as ever before,
Yet always struggling, always reaffirming, always resuming
their march.[311]

(*Choruses from 'The Rock'* VII:4-25)

Both Weston and Eliot trace the same continuums of myth and
religion examined by Harrison, Tylor and Frazer. In her preface,
Weston advises 'those scholars who may think it a 'far cry' from the
romances of the twelfth century of our era to some 1,000 B.C. to
suspend their judgement till they have fairly examined the evidence
for a tradition common to the Aryan race in general, and persisting
with extraordinary vitality, and a marked correspondence of characteristic detail, through all migrations and modifications of that race,
to the present day'.[312]

What is notable — and specific to Britain and so to the London of *The Waste Land* — is Weston's attention to the transition
from pagan to Christian ritual she excavates from evolving versions
of Arthurian myth. It is a theme she developed from *The Golden*

Bough, in which Frazer attributes Church absorption of pagan symbols to religious pragmatism.

> Taken together, the coincidences of the Christian with
> the heathen festivals are too close and too numerous to be
> accidental. They mark the compromise which the church
> in the hour of its triumph was compelled to make with
> its vanquished yet still dangerous rivals. The inflexible
> Protestantism of the primitive missionaries, with their fiery
> denunciations of heathendom, had been exchanged for
> the supple policy, the easy tolerance, the comprehensive
> charity of shrewd ecclesiastics, who clearly perceived that if
> Christianity was to conquer the world it could do so only by
> relaxing the too rigid principles of its Founder, by widening
> a little the gate that leads to salvation.[313]
>
> (*The Golden Bough*)

Eliot describes this as 'the comfortable compromise between Christianity and paganism arrived at in England'.[314] That compromise,
and Weston's 'evolution from Pagan Mystery to Christian Ceremonial' in Britain, are evident in a remarkable example from English
history. Not only does it resonate with *The Rock*, it also involves the
same historical characters.

The Venerable Bede reports a letter of 610 CE from Pope Gregory to Mellitus, first Bishop of London and Third Archbishop of
Canterbury. In *The Rock*, in another of Eliot's transports in time,
the same Mellitus appears to both seventh century Saxons and to
workmen building a church in modern London. He preaches of
church-building, including St. Paul's, and building London itself.
Eliot explained this scene as 'an "experiment in time" in which the

builders find themselves spectators of the conversion of Sabert, King of London, and his Saxon followers, by the Roman missionary Mellitus'.[315] This transition from Saxon gods to the dying god of Christianity is a form of Weston's evolution from Pagan Mystery to Christian Ceremonial.

> *Enter* SABERT (*King of London*) *with* RETINUE.
> SABERT: Priest of the foreign god, expound again your
>   mysteries, the cross and the god who died like a man but lives
>   again as a god. I will listen and my people will listen with me.
> ...
> I will have your God, and He shall be my God and the God
>   of my people of London, as he is already the God of my
>   brother of Kent and of his people.
> MELLITUS: Blessed be God. Now in the sign of your
>   conversion, my children, and after I have baptised you,
>   you shall build a church to God.
> SABERT: On my hill. Let it be on my hill to the west of London!
> MELLITUS: Be it so. And the church shall be built to the
>   honour of the blessed St. Paul, whom I unworthily follow,
>   and to the glory and worship of God.
>   (*The Rock* Part I, p.16-19)

That same conversion moment is evident in Pope Gregory's letter. It instructs Mellitus to tolerate pagan forms of ritual, including animal sacrifice, and to occupy their places of worship in that transition period.

> The aforesaid envoys having departed, the blessed Father
> Gregory sent after them a letter worthy to be recorded,

wherein he plainly shows how carefully he watched over the salvation of our country. The letter was as follows:

To his most beloved son, the Abbot Mellitus; Gregory, the servant of the servants of God. We have been much concerned, since the departure of our people that are with you, because we have received no account of the success of your journey. Howbeit, when Almighty God has led you to the most reverend Bishop Augustine, our brother, tell him what I have long been considering in my own mind concerning the matter of the English people; to wit, that the temples of the idols in that nation ought not to be destroyed; but let the idols that are in them be destroyed; let water be consecrated and sprinkled in the said temples, let altars be erected, and relics placed there. For if those temples are well built, it is requisite that they be converted from the worship of devils to the service of the true God; that the nation, seeing that their temples are not destroyed, may remove error from their hearts, and knowing and adoring the true God, may the more freely resort to the places to which they have been accustomed. And because they are used to slaughter many oxen in sacrifice to devils, some solemnity must be given them in exchange for this, as that on the day of the dedication, or the nativities of the holy martyrs, whose relics are there deposited, they should build themselves huts of the boughs of trees about those churches which have been turned to that use from being temples, and celebrate the solemnity with religious feasting, and no more offer animals to the Devil, but kill cattle and glorify God in their feast, and return thanks to the Giver of all things for their abundance; to the end that, whilst some outward gratifications are retained, they may the more easily consent to the inward joys. For there is no doubt that it is impossible to cut off every thing at once from their rude natures; because he who endeavours to ascend to the highest place rises by degrees or steps, and not by leaps. Thus the Lord made Himself known to the people of Israel in Egypt; and yet He allowed them the use, in His own worship, of the sacrifices which they were wont to offer to the Devil, commanding them in His sacrifice to kill animals, to the end that, with changed hearts, they might lay aside one part of the sacrifice, whilst they retained another; and although the animals were the same as those which they were wont to offer, they should offer them to the true God, and not to idols; and thus they would no longer be the same sacrifices. This then, dearly beloved, it behoves you to communicate to our aforesaid brother, that he, being placed where he is at present, may consider how he is to order all things. God preserve you in safety, most beloved son. "Given the 17th of June, in the nineteenth year of the reign of our most religious lord, Mauritius Tiberius Augustus, the eighteenth year after the consulship of our said lord, and the fourth indiction."[316]

In that way, early Christianity itself was part of the continuum from the most ancient of rituals. It worked with local polytheistic customs in a conscious manner, often in their temples, gradually replacing disparate pagan rituals and mythologies with those of Christianity throughout Europe. That extended to the ends of the known earth, such as Britain.

A few months later Ethelbert, together with his court and the majority of his subjects, accepted baptism. He thus became the first Christian English king — and a saint to boot. St. Augustine meanwhile established a monastery at Canterbury, which he dedicated to St Peter and St Paul (though it was later to become St. Augustine's) and which was almost certainly the earliest Benedictine foundation outside Italy. Canterbury in turn became the headquarters of Christianity in England, as it remains today. Pope Gregory was delighted. 'By the shining miracles of his preachers', he declared:

God has brought even the ends of the earth to the faith. He has linked in one confession the limits of East and West. Behold, the tongue of Britain, which could formerly utter only barbaric sounds, has lately learned to make the Hebrew Alleluia resound in God's praise.

(John Julius Norwich *The Popes A History*)[317]

8. Sappho II
The Evening Star, the Muses, and April

The Evening Star: Aphrodite, Venus and *Stella Maris*

The work Sappho does for Eliot through a small fragment of her poetry is extraordinary. Alone, Sappho embodies the riches of the Classicism Eliot advocated. Through the link Eliot creates with the Church of St. Magnus the Martyr, her symbolic scope becomes exponential. The old is made new and the classical made modern in some of the most striking and intensely distilled imagery of modernity, and of any time in literature. That imagery opens a second portal into the poem, into the classical world, through Sappho's evening star as the planet Venus in the night sky.

Aphrodite and Venus were in Eliot's poetic considerations of the time. Venus is present in the drafts of the poem as 'Venus Anadyomene', and Eliot's 'Fresca' who 'was baptised in a soapy sea' evokes Aphrodite's birth from the sea foam created by the genitals of Uranus following his castration by Cronus. Hesiod records this myth in his *Theogony*.[318]

> And Heaven came, bringing on night and longing for love, and he lay about Earth spreading himself full upon her. Then the son from his ambush stretched forth his left hand and in his right took the great long sickle with jagged teeth, and swiftly lopped off his own father's members and cast them away ... so soon as he had cut off the members with

flint and cast them from the land into the surging sea, they were swept away over the main a long time: and a white foam spread around them from the immortal flesh, and in it there grew a maiden. First she drew near holy Cythera, and from there, afterwards, she came to sea-girt Cyprus, and came forth an awful and lovely goddess, and grass grew up about her beneath her shapely feet. Her gods and men call Aphrodite, and the foam-born goddess and rich-crowned Cytherea, because she grew amid the foam.[319]

The evening star represents many other manifestations of the female divine in history. Frazer connects the Christian Mary and Isis: 'to Isis in her later character of patroness of mariners the Virgin Mary owes perhaps her beautiful epithet of *Stella Maris*, 'Star of the Sea', under which she is adored by Tempest-tossed sailors'.[320] A Marian hymn sung at vespers from the eighth century is titled *Ave Maris Stella* — 'Hail, star of the sea'. Its modern version is the hymn *Hail Queen of Heaven, the Ocean Star*. From Eliot's homeland, a photograph of Our Lady of Good Voyage in Gloucester, Massachusetts is identified as the *Mater Dolorosa*. 'Eliot particularly embraces the idea of Mary as *Mater Dolorosa*, the Mother of Sorrows, in reference to the women who suffer while their menfolk undertake hazardous, life-threatening work at sea. But she is also there, crowned, as the 'Queen of Heaven'.[321]

Isis is 'the many named', 'the thousand named' and in Greek inscriptions 'the myriad-named'.[322] She is brought to the poem as Part II opens in the form of her self-declared earthly doppelganger Cleopatra, the 'Eastern Star' of Shakespeare's *Anthony and Cleopatra*.[323] Worship of Isis existed for centuries alongside early Christianity throughout the Roman Empire. At Philae in lower Egypt, the last temple to Isis was closed by the Byzantine emperor

Justinian I in 537CE, prior to which its celebrants practised along-side Christianity. In the north of the empire, we have seen that a jug found by London Bridge held the inscription to 'the temple of Isis at Londinium'. That an altar stone of that temple was found to have been reused as part of the Thames riverside wall suggests that the temple of Isis was near the site of the later Church of St. Magnus the Martyr; and possibly even on the same site, since sacred sites often remain so when the creed or religion changes.

In the first century CE, Pliny confirmed the pervasive influ-ence of that star, including through its evening and morning names, Vesper and Lucifer. That it 'sprinkles everything with its genial dew' and 'stimulates all living things' recalls *the Vigil of Venus* from our first chapter on Sappho, when 'the wood lets down her hair in nuptial downpours'.

> Below the Sun revolves the great star called Venus, wander-ing with an alternate motion, and, even in its surnames, rivalling the Sun and the Moon. For when it precedes the day and rises in the morning, it receives the name of *Lucifer*, as if it were another sun, hastening on the day. On the contrary, when it shines in the west, it is named *Vesper*, as prolonging the light, and performing the office of the moon. Pythagoras, the Samian, was the first who discovered its nature, about the 62nd Olympiad, in the 222nd year of the City. It excels all the other stars in size, and its brilliancy is so considerable, that it is the only star which produces a shadow by its rays. There has, consequently, been great interest made for its name; some have called it the star of Juno, others of Isis, and others of the Mother of the Gods. By its influence everything in the earth is generated. For, as it rises in either direction, it sprinkles everything with

its genial dew, and not only matures the productions of the earth, but stimulates all living things.[324]

The mythic range of the evening star is not limited to Mary, Isis, Aphrodite, Venus and Juno. Its ancient lineage was noted as early as 1200 BCE by Sanchoniatho, the Phoenician author whose work survives in fragments paraphrased by later authors.

> The origin of this story of the star of Venus may be traced to a Phoenician or Trojan source; for we find, in the fragments of Sanchoniatho, the following account: "But travelling about the world, she found a star falling from the sky; which she, taking up, consecrated in the Holy Island Tyre. And the Phoenicians say, that *Astarte* is she who is amongst the Greeks called *Aphrodite*" ... This Tyrian or Trojan deity was the Marine Venus, and is to be distinguished from Venus Urania, the heavenly, the greatest; who, according to Cicero, and other authority, was the Syrian Astarte, and the Ashteroth of sacred Scripture.[325]

In *The Histories* of circa 450 BCE, Herodotus gives an account of an invasion from the north by the Central Asian Scythians. He also confirms the Phoenician origin of Aphrodite.

> From there they marched against Egypt: and when they were in the part of Syria called Palestine, Psammetichus king of Egypt met them and persuaded them with gifts and prayers to come no further. So they turned back, and when they came on their way to the city of Ascalon in Syria, most of the Scythians passed by and did no harm, but a few remained behind and plundered the temple of Heavenly

Aphrodite. This temple, I discover from making inquiry, is the oldest of all the temples of the goddess, for the temple in Cyprus was founded from it, as the Cyprians themselves say; and the temple on Cythera was founded by Phoenicians from this same land of Syria. But the Scythians who pillaged the temple, and all their descendants after them, were afflicted by the goddess with the "female" sickness: and so the Scythians say that they are afflicted as a consequence of this and also that those who visit Scythian territory see among them the condition of those whom the Scythians call "Hermaphrodites".[326]

Of note is the link between the Phoenician Astarte and the biblical Ashtaroth. 'Her name derives from the deliberate conflation of the Phoenician Ashtart with the Hebrew word *boshet* ("shame")'.[327] As the Hebrew Queen of Heaven she was called Asherah, and was the divine partner of Yahweh, including in the First Temple, before her shrines were destroyed by Hezekiah. 'Likewise Canaanite 'Anat became Greek Athena, the warlike patron of deity of Athens. And Canaanite-Israelite Asherah appears later as Greek Aphrodite and Roman Venus, the latter also goddesses of beauty, love, and sexual pleasure. The similarities are unequivocal: Asherah and Aphrodite are both connected to the sea, and doves are symbols of both'.[328] In that light, the Aphrodite who opens Eliot's poem in 'April' originates in part in the Queen of Heaven of the polytheistic First Temple of the Hebrews.

The Waste Land is universal and not limited to the Judeo-Christian or classical, since the poem also incorporates 'Ganga' [395], the Hindu goddess of purification and forgiveness. Other manifestations of this divinity in the poem include Cybele through her consort Attis, and the Roman Artemis through her Greek counterpart Diana in her sacred grove that opens *The Golden Bough,* and her pavilion at the centre of the 'Hofgarten' [10]. The blinding of 'Tiresias' [218] brings Juno to the poem through Eliot's corresponding note on the 'great anthropological interest' [218n] of Ovid's corresponding passage. Demeter and the 'Queen of Hades' Persephone are suggested, among other allusions, through the 'hyacinths' [35] Persephone was gathering before her abduction by Hades.

As for the masculine, the castration aspect of Aphrodite's birth introduces from the first word of the poem the motifs of emasculation and potency. Like everything in the poem, these work on many levels. A facet of this theme is a critique of those who seek to distance themselves from women through religious or secular zealotry. The mandated celibacy of the Catholic priest (and the reformed, puritanical St. Augustine) becomes a self-emasculation in the manner of the self-castrating Attis myth, repeating Joyce's running theme of the 'gelded' priest in *Ulysses.* In secular philosophy, the themes of emasculation and potency are deployed throughout Nietzsche's work to devalue common morality, the communal citizen, women, and Christianity. Eliot portrays his consistent and cherished misogyny that accompanies his cries for reformation as a form of self-emasculation. That includes his use of the Old Testament trope that the rebellious woman is abortive or barren, which might be read with Reformation feminisations of Catholicism in such tropes as the Whore of Babylon and the Mass as the harlot Mistress Missa.

That such imagery is deeply hidden in *The Waste Land* (as it is in *Ulysses*) may reflect the idea, shared with *Ulysses,* of an equal female aspect of the divine hidden from society through the dogmatic and censorious Judeo-Christian emphasis on a male God. As it was for Old Testament Deuteronomist scribes who insisted that Hezekiah enact a reformation, so according to Puritans any attention to female divinity represents idolatry, explained in the Reformation *Homily Against Peril of Idolatry and Superfluous Decking of Churches.*

> Alas, we seem in thus thinking and doing to have learned our religion, not out of God's word, but out of the Pagan poets, who say, Excessere omnes adytis, arisque relictis, Di, qidbis imperium hoc steterat, etc. That is to say, All the gods by whose defence this empire stood, are gone out of the temples, and have forsaken their altars. And where one saint liath images in divers places, the same saint hath divers names thereof, most like to the Gentiles. When you hear of our lady of Walsingham, our lady of Ipswich, our lady of Wilsdon, and such other; what is it but an imitation of the Gentiles idolaters? Diana Agrotera, Diana Coryphea, Diana Ephesia, &c. Venus Cypria, Venus Paphia, Venus Gnidia. Whereby is evidently meant, that the saint for the image sake should in those places, yea, in the images themselves, have a dwelling, which is the ground of their idolatry. For where no images be, they have no such means. Terentius Varro showeth, that there were three hundred Jupiters in his time: there were no fewer Veneres and Dianae: we had no fewer Christophers, Ladies, and Mary Magdalens, and other saints. Cenomaus and Hesiodus show, that in their time there were thirty thousand gods. I think we had no fewer saints to whom we gave the honour due to God. And they have not only spoiled the true living God of his due honour in temples, cities, countries, and lands, by such devices and inventions, as the Gentiles idolaters have done before them: but the sea and waters have as well special saints with them, as they had gods with the Gentiles, Neptune, Triton, Nereus, Castor and Pollux, Venus, and such other:

in whose places become St. Christopher, St. Clement, and
divers other, and specially our Lady, to whom shipmen sing
Ave, maris stella.[329]

April and the Muses

"I sing the seasons, and their causes, and the starry signs that
set beneath the earth and rise again, drawing my lore from
annals old. We have come to the fourth month in which
thou art honoured above all others, and thou knowest,
Venus, that both the poet and the month are thine." The
goddess was moved, and touching my brows lightly with
myrtle of Cythera, "Complete," said she, "the work thou
hast begun." I felt her inspiration, and suddenly my eyes
were opened to the causes of the days.

(Ovid's *Fasti*, '*On the Roman Calendar*')[330]

Like Ovid, Eliot also invokes the muse Venus. Ovid's Venus is of the
same all-pervading, life-giving power she represents to the female celebrants of the *Vigil of Venus*. When Sappho spoke to the evening star as
Aphrodite, it was to a being of the same numinous and very real presence, substance and personality, with the kind of extraordinary power
that had real world effects including in love. As Barnstone observes,
she 'chatted with Afroditi', sometimes 'conversing almost fiercely with
her ally the love goddess', an intensity that also inspirits the women
of the *Vigil of Venus*.[331] The same spiritual intensity pervades Ovid's
Fasti, in which he explains the origins of each month of the calendar.
This is the April that opens the classical mythic layer of Eliot's poem.

James Frazer observes in his translation of *Fasti* that Ovid
'expressly says that he had written the *Fasti* in twelve books, each

book dealing with a separate month ... The matter of the poem falls, roughly speaking, into three sections, the historical, the astronomical, and the religious ... The religious section of the poem embraces the notices and explanations of those fixed festivals and sacred rites which were recorded in the calendar. This is for us moderns by far the most interesting and valuable part of the work, for our knowledge of Roman religion is comparatively meagre and fragmentary, and in the absence of more detailed and authoritative expositions, such as were doubtless to be found in some of the lost books of Varro, the *Fasti* of Ovid must always rank as a document of the first importance'.[332]

The link between the month of April and Venus is central to that work. Further, Ovid sees the origin of that link in that between April and Aphrodite, born from a foaming sea. 'But I surmise that the month of Venus took its name from the Greek language: the goddess was called after the foam of the sea. Nor need you wonder that a thing was called by a Greek name, for the Italian land was Greater Greece'.[333]

> She indeed sways, and well deserves to sway, the world entire; she owns a kingdom second to that of no god; she gives laws to heaven and earth and to her native sea, and by her inspiration she keeps every species in being. She created all the gods — 'twere long to number them; she bestowed on seeds and trees their origins. She drew rudeminded men together and taught them to pair each with his mate ... The same force preserves all living things under the broad bosom of the deep, and fills the waters with unnumbered fish. That force first stripped man of his savage garb; from it he learned decent attire and personal cleanliness ... everywhere the goddess is powerful and her temples are thronged with worshippers.[334]

The intensity of the experience of Venus can only have been heightened by the elixir Ovid tells us was part of that encounter with the divine. 'Nor grudge to take poppy pounded with snowy milk and liquid honey squeezed from the comb; when Venus was first escorted to her eager spouse, she drank that draught'.[335] Cliches of pagan wantonness can be avoided in favour of shared rituals by noting the presence of cannabis residues on early Hebrew altars, with archaeological similarities indicating this may at some stage have also been a ritual practice in the First Temple.

Ezra Pound sent his edit of a draft of *The Waste Land* to Eliot with the comment, 'Complimenti, you bitch. I am wracked by the seven jealousies'.[336] He included a light-hearted private poem, which opened:

These are the Poems of Eliot
By the Uranian Muse begot;
A Man their Mother was,
A Muse their sire.

The Uranian Muse is a classical name for Aphrodite and her Roman counterpart Venus in their roles of granting inspiration to poets. Recitals in ancient Greece often began with an appeal to the muses of Mount Olympia, where they dwelt with Aphrodite. The assistance of such a goddess is invoked in both the *Iliad*: 'Sing, O goddess, the destructive wrath of Achilles', and the *Odyssey*: 'Tell me, O muse, of that ingenious hero who travelled far and wide after he had sacked the famous town of Troy'.

Like many of the classical poets, Eliot also invokes the muses. In that facet of the poem that is a universal chronicle, the story of humankind told through its gods, the incantatory opening of his poem holds a predominantly female pantheon, such as the ultimate earth mother Gaea, of 'Earth' [6]. Muses who compliment Sappho's muse Aphrodite are suggested through 'Memory' [3]. The titaness Mnemosyne ('memory') and her three daughters Aoidē ('voice' or 'song'), Meletē ('contemplation' or 'practice'), and Mnēmē (also 'memory') are the muses considered by classical scribes to be fundamental to the composition of poetry and song. Pre-dating the pantheon of Mount Olympia, Aoidē, Meletē, and Mnēmē are the Boeotian muses of Mount Helicon, the earliest known muses. The mnemonic, originating from the same Greek root *mnēmē*, meaning 'memory' or 'remembrance', underlies the ritual and song of the oral culture of ancient humanity represented in the opening of *The Waste Land*. Originally epics of oral culture, the *Iliad* and the *Odyssey* would have been recited from memory.

When the home of the muses moved to Mount Olympia, they became nine in number: 'convention has the Muses "crowned with violets" and presenting gifts of knowledge.' They are later figuratively joined by Sappho as the 'tenth muse'.

> Some say there are nine Muses, but this is too few;
> For behold, Sappho from Lesbos is the tenth.
>
> (Attributed to Plato)[337]

As such, Sappho becomes an adopted daughter of Mnemosyne, and 'lingers between the human and divine worlds'. [338]

> Memory was astounded when she heard
> the honey-voiced Sappho, and she wondered
> whether mankind had a tenth muse.
>
> (Antipatros of Sidon)[339]

Eliot's appeal to the muses is neither a poet's affectation of classical style nor a posture. However creedless, however catholic rather than Catholic, however troubled by doubt, he seems to experience — or seeks to experience — the continuum of culture, art and spirituality with the same intensity as Sappho in her relationship with Aphrodite, and Ovid's experience of Venus and the muses. Further, however relatively chaste his personal experience was, his immersion in the span of culture is as earthy as that of Sappho, Ovid, John Donne, Baudelaire, and the scandalous *Satyricon* from which the epigraph of *The Waste Land* is taken.[340] That continuum between the earthy and the divine is part of the vast map of humanity, sacred and profane, noble and degenerate, that underlies and unifies the poem.

The Boeotian muses honoured in the opening of Eliot's poem represent a continuum from a time older again than Homer, Sappho and their Aphrodite. The Boeotian legacy informed the later spirituality, poetics and music of Homer and Sappho. As such, Aoidē, Meletē, Mnēmē, and Mnemosyne represent a cultural bridge between the rhythms of early human cultures and those of later classical Greek culture preserved for us in writing through the alphabet of 'Phlebas the Phoenician' [312], transported to us by the poet-songstress Sappho.

The Morning Star
Lucifer, Jesus, Attis, and the Death of God

Jewel Spears Brooker writes that 'the single most important pattern in early Eliot is that of the dying God'.[341] When Eliot states in the Notes that male character 'melts into' male character [218n], he is suggesting a universal examination of man in the same manner that 'all the women are one woman' in the same note casts light on universal ideas of women.

We have seen Jane Harrison link the most ancient Dionysian exultation in the sacred wood to the Christian alleluia. She observes that we 'realise, for example, that Dionysos is not only the beautiful young wine-god, but also an ancient tree-god, worshipped as a draped post'.[342] That locates the origins of Dionysus in the primeval vegetation ceremonies of Eliot's Notes, from which the anthropomorphic dying gods arose — as did the concept of sacred wood itself, flowing from the inspirited tree of animism through various mythologies to later be expressed in both the Christian cross and the sacred wood of the Magnus Martyr altarpiece. As such, Dionysus is an early manifestation of the dying gods Adonis, Attis and Osiris of the preamble to the Notes. In certain classical times he was regarded as so close to Osiris that a Greco-Egyptian syncretic deity emerged called Dionysus-Osiris, as there was an Isis-Aphrodite.

In this aspect the poem is timeless, and as all the goddesses are one and all the temples are one, so all the dying gods are one. Complementing the extensive range of female divinities linked to Sappho's evening star, there is a male mythological line linked to the star in its morning variant, the planet Venus in the morning sky. As the Virgin Mary is brought to the poem, so is Jesus. *The Golden Bough* explains the origins of the god who dies yearly and is resurrected.

Under the names of Osiris, Tammuz, Adonis, and Attis, the peoples of Egypt and Western Asia represented the yearly decay and revival of life, especially of vegetable life, which they personified as a god who annually died and rose again from the dead. In name and detail the rites varied from place to place: in substance they were the same.

The worship of Adonis was practised by the Semitic peoples of Babylonia and Syria, and the Greeks borrowed it from them as early at least as the seventh century before Christ. The true name of the deity was Tammuz: the appellation of Adonis is merely the Semitic *Adon*, 'lord', a title of honour by which his worshippers addressed him. In the Hebrew text of the Old Testament the same name Adonai, originally perhaps Adoni, 'my lord', is often applied to Jehovah. But the Greeks through a misunderstanding converted the title of honour into a proper name ... The tragical story and the melancholy rites of Adonis are better known to us from the descriptions of the Greek writers than from the fragments of Babylonian literature or the brief reference of the prophet Ezekiel, who saw the women of Jerusalem weeping for Tammuz at the north gate of the temple. Mirrored in the glass of Greek mythology, the oriental deity appears as a comely youth beloved by Aphrodite.[343]

The ancient Mesopotamian dying god Tammuz evolved to manifest in the trio of dying gods Adonis, Attis and Osiris of Eliot's Notes. The scribes of the Old Testament raged against him. 'Then he brought me to the door of the gate of the LORD'S house which was toward the north; and, behold, there sat women weeping for Tammuz. Then said he unto me, Hast thou seen this, O son of man? turn thee yet again, and thou shalt see greater abominations than these'.[344] Yet Hebrew traces of Tammuz or Tamuz continue, as both a month of the civil year and a month of the ecclesiastical year on the Hebrew calendar. Jane Harrison writes of the universal nature of that dying god, noting both the annual wound of Tammuz in Ezekiel's imagined temple in the Bible, and his presence in Milton's *Paradise Lost*.

The god who died and rose again is not of course confined to Egypt; he is world-wide. When Ezekiel (viii. 14) "came to the gate of the Lord's house which was toward the north" he beheld there the "women weeping for Tammuz." This "abomination" the house of Judah had brought with them from Babylon. Tammuz is Dumuzi, "the true son," or more fully, Dumuzi-absu, "true son of the waters." He too, like Osiris, is a god of the life that springs from inundation and that dies down in the heat of the summer. In Milton's procession of false gods,

"Thammuz came next behind,
Whose annual wound in Lebanon allured
The Syrian damsels to lament his fate
In amorous ditties all a summer's day."[345]

Harrison sees Tammuz as a variant of Dumuzi, a West-Semitic variant of the older Sumerian dying god known as Dumuzid, one of the most ancient dying gods of springtime rejuvenation of the earth. Later, Adonis, whose name we have seen is adopted from the Hebrew honorific title for Jehovah meaning 'Lord', is the dying god of Sappho.

Afroditi, delicate Adonis is dying,
What should we do?
Virgins, beat your breasts
And tear your garments.[346]

(Sappho *Death of Adonis*)

Later again the dying god is Christ, who is linked to the morning star as is Lucifer. Sappho's evening star as Hesperus is the son of the Greek dawn goddess Eos and half-brother of her other son Phosphorus, the 'Morning Star'. The Latin name for the morning star is Lucifer, meaning 'light bringer'. Eliot, reviewing a performance of

The Rites of Spring in 1921, termed Stravinsky the 'Lucifer of the season, brightest in the firmament ... The effect was like *Ulysses* with illustrations by the best contemporary illustrator'.[347] In the Bible, he becomes a dark figure whose anarch egoist pride is his ruin. 'How art thou fallen from heaven, O Lucifer, son of the morning! How art thou cut down to the ground, which didst weaken the nations!' (Isaiah 14.12). That Levantine symbolism of light is shared with a classical entity, linked with the Roman Vesper in Pliny's *Natural History*. 'Each Planet hath a several colour; Saturn is white, Jupiter clear and bright, Mars a fiery red, Venus glowing, when Lucifer; when Occidental, or Vesper, resplendent'.[348]

The planet Venus as the morning star in the Graeco-Roman sense of light bringer is also associated with Christ. 'I Jesus have sent mine angel to testify unto you these things in the churches. I am the root and the offspring of David, and the bright and morning star' (Revelations 22:16). That idea of the light-bringer can be read with the connection shown in chapter two between Christ and the carbuncle gem, which throws light into the darkness; the darkness Satan promises the 'Anarch old' he will bring to the 'upper world' in *Paradise Lost*; and the invasive 'young man carbuncular' at the 'violet hour' of dusk. Spurr observes that, like Milton, 'having thought of the idea of a poetic work on the death of Christ, Eliot did not pursue it'.[349] That may not be so, since the Christian Christ seems woven into the 'violet hour' [215] of *The Waste Land* through his links to the carbuncle gem, the morning variant of Sappho's evening star, and the dying gods Adonis, Attis and Osiris.

The annual death of Jesus at Easter is also evoked through violet, the mourning colour of covers placed over imagery in Magnus Martyr and all such churches between Passion Sunday and Good Friday, seen in the photographs in this book. 'Before Vespers of Saturday preceding Passion Sunday the crosses, statues, and pictures of Our

Lord and of the saints ... with the sole exception of the crosses and pictures of the Way of the Cross, are to be covered with a violet veil, not translucent, nor in any way ornamented. The crosses remain covered until after the solemn denudation of the principal crucifix on Good Friday'.[350] This is the same veiling of imagery in Hope Mirrlees's *Paris: A Poem* of 1920, in which she writes 'In the Churches during Lent Christ and the Saints | are shrouded in Mauve veils'.[351]

In addition to suggesting the mournful church coverings of Easter and twilight as the hour of vespers, the colour violet also evokes the yearly death and resurrection of Attis, as Frazer writes that 'violets were said to have sprung from the blood of Attis'. Eliot's Notes link the 'Hanged Man' [55] of the poem with the 'Hanged God of Frazer' [46n], who in *The Golden Bough* is Attis. Frazer remarks on the close parallels between Attis and Christ. 'Christians and pagans alike were struck by the remarkable coincidence between the death and resurrection of their respective deities ... the pagans contending that the resurrection of Christ was a spurious imitation of the resurrection of Attis, and the Christians asserting with equal warmth that the resurrection of Attis was a diabolical counterfeit of the resurrection of Christ'.[352]

Nietzsche announces a different death of God. Inverting the resurrection schema of those spring gods who revive the waste land, he instead claims a triumph over the winter of Christianity through the anarchic high spirits, unrest, and contradictions of the Dionysian overman. 'This book ... seems to be written in the language of the wind that brings a thaw: it contains high spirits, unrest, contradiction, and April weather, so that one is constantly reminded of winter's nearness as well as of the triumph over winter that is coming, must come, perhaps already has come'.[353]

Nietzsche's death of god takes its place among the dying gods of history. In Eliot's schema, theomachy is present from the outset of his poem in 'April', since the birth of Aphrodite arose from the castration of Uranus that led to the violent overthrow of the Titans. It is further suggested in the death of the pantheon of the Semitic gods of Dido and Phlebas, figuratively commenced at the battle of 'Mylae' [70]. The gods of the Roman victors triumphed, to then be supplanted in Rome by Christianity. In Britain, Christianity first arrived along Roman roads and across Londinium bridge, killing off the Roman gods of Londinium. Those Roman gods had previously in significant part killed off the Celtic pantheon that underlies Arthurian legend. Later again, Roman Christianity supplanted the Saxon gods in its second arrival. That saw the founding of Canterbury, to where pilgrimages departed from the Church of St. Magnus the Martyr across London Bridge.

As such, the mythic narrative of *The Waste Land* carries the suggestion that, whereas the universal godhead is eternal, the death of a representational god or gods has been common throughout history, and that may even be a form of evolution aided by the divine. Eliot later committed to Anglo-Catholicism as the 'less false' creed, carrying the idea that it is not necessarily to be considered the full or final truth. Continuing the battles of the heavens, that cycle of theomachy is represented in his dying gods Adonis, Attis and Osiris, who eventuate in the Christian Christ and are of primeval origin in the vegetation ceremonies from which Nietzsche's beloved dying god Dionysus also arose.

The *Stella Maris* of James Joyce and Hope Mirrlees

Ezra Pound writes of the city of Dublin and its characters in James Joyce's novel that the 'details of the street map are local' but that Leopold Bloom 'is ubiquitous' and his 'spouse Gea-Tellus' is the 'earth symbol.'[354] Gea-Tellus is the Greco-Roman 'mighty mother', a recurring presence in *Ulysses* that includes the Christian Mary as *Stella Maris*. The significant presence of this entity in both works suggests a more significant conversation between these two masterpieces of high modernism than thought, on this and other subjects.[355]

The marine form of the ancient goddesses is introduced from the outset in *Ulysses* as the 'mighty mother' when Stephan Dedalus and Buck Mulligan look out over Dublin Bay.

> — God! He said quietly. Isn't the sea what Algy calls it: a great sweet mother? The snotgreen sea. The scrotumtightening sea. *Epi oinopa ponton.* Ah Dedalus, the Greeks! I must teach you. You must read them in the original. *Thalatta! Thalatta!* She is our great sweet mother. Come and look.
>
> Stephan stood up and went over to the parapet. Leaning on it he looked down on the water and on the mailboat clearing the harbourmouth of Kingstown.
>
> — Our mighty mother! Buck Mulligan said.[356]

The Nausicaa episode, the symbol of which is the 'virgin', sets Bloom by the sea at the violet hour of dusk. 'A star I see. Venus? Can't tell yet ... Land of the setting sun this'. Bloom's star is 'symbolic of divine guidance or favour; the Virgin Mary as Queen of Heaven is crowned with twelve stars ... the star is symbolic of her title Stella Maris (Star of the Sea)'.[357] Other resonances between the imagery of Joyce and Eliot include sounds drifting 'upon the waters' [257], vespers, and the radiance of Dante's Mary.

> Far away in the west the sun was setting and the last glow of all too fleeting day lingered lovingly on sea and strand, on the proud promontory of dear old Howth guarding as

ever the waters of the bay, on the weedgrown rocks along Sandymount shore and, last but not least, on the quiet church whence there streamed forth at times upon the stillness the voice of prayer to her who is in her pure radiance a beacon ever to the stormtossed heart of man, Mary, star of the sea.[358]

Pound wrote that 'the atmosphere of the Gerty-Nausika episode with its echoes of the vesper service is certainly "conveyed," and conveyed with a certitude and efficiency that neither James nor Proust have excelled.'[359] The resonance with Eliot's 'Figlia del tuo figlio | Queen of Heaven' 'whose shrine stands on the promontory' of *The Dry Salvages* is also compelling, since both allude to Dante's *Paradiso*, merged by Joyce with the figure of Eve who 'sold us all' for a penny apple. Joyce's mythic and theological tension between the venerated Mary and the fallen Eve is echoed in Eliot's poem, including in the contrast between the typist and Sappho.

She hath an *omnipotentiam deiparae supplicem*, that is to wit, an almightiness of petition because she is the second Eve and she won us, saith Augustine too, whereas that other, our grandam, which we are linked up with by successive anastomosis of navelcords sold us all, seed, breed and generation, for a penny pippin ... vergine madre, *figlia di tuo figlio*.[360]

The meld of female divinities is also explicit in the work of Hope Mirrlees, the long-term companion of Jane Harrison. By the time Mirrlees' poem was written after her visit to Florence in 1959 she had long been a Catholic convert, whereas Eliot at the time of *The Waste Land* is creedless. That said, in their consideration of

Aphrodite and other divine females manifest in Sappho's evening star as prior, partial realisations of the Christian Queen of Heaven Mary, the literary and anthropological thinking of these two poets is similar. Mirrlees's *Maris Stella* is also the planet Venus as Sappho's evening star Hesperus.

> But the Archangel as he kneels perceives
> That it was not the treacherous sea
> But *Maris Stella*, the sea's star,
> Whom Sappho without knowing it implored,
> For stars are 'steadfast'.
> And that, by myths of man for long concealed,
> The pagan mother-goddess stands revealed
> As mirror both of mercy and of truth
> In whom can be no shadow of deception,
> The dark, chaotic, treacherous *Anima*
> Made pure and luminous at last —
> Mary, the Immaculate Conception,
> No goddess, but the Virgin Mother of God's Love.
>   (*A Meditation on Donatello's Annunciation*
>   *in the Church of Santa Croce, Florence*)[361]

The lost divine female was not only a literary consideration but also political, seen in an article in Dora Marsden's 'little journal' *The New Freewoman*, precursor of *The Egoist* at which both Pound and Eliot worked. Under the general title 'The Eclipse of Women' and titled 'The Earth Goddess', it points to St. Augustine's account of the fall of the earth goddesses, sees a need for more involvement of women in Church governance, acknowledges the role Elizabeth I played in the English Church and, strikingly in such a journal, expects the revival of veneration of the Virgin Mary.

The question is of practical importance at the present moment because this worship of the Earth Goddess is intimately connected with the political rights of women. Saint Augustine informs us (in the City of God, xviii, 9) that the introduction of the Olympian Gods at Athens, and the consequent eclipse of the old Earth Goddesses, was accompanied by the change from matriarchal to patriarchal government. The women were deprived of votes, and children who had formerly borne the name of their mother's family, were now given their father's instead ... If the general tendency in the past has been for these religious and political changes to go together, it follows that the recovery by women of their political rights is likely to be accompanied by a revival of their influence in the religious sphere. To put it in the plainest light, women will be empowered to legislate for the Church of England. As that Church was governed by a woman during the forty years that really settled and stamped its character, there should be no reason for alarm as to the probable future. But we may reasonably expect the worship of the Virgin to be revived.[362]

Joyce deploys the 'mighty mother' as 'a favorite phrase of the Irish poet-Theosophist-economist George William Russell'.[363] He does so to echo Russell's lament at the destruction of the divine female by a male only religion of so little understanding and care of women that they are driven to insanity, a theme that runs throughout *The Waste Land*. Russell's comment that a woman is considered to be 'distinctly an evil influence' where 'there be enchantment in her eyes and her laugh, and if she bewilder too many men' is echoed in the Eve myth, in Catholicism, in the Old Testament harlot imagery of Puritanism, and in the works of Nietzsche — Nietzsche as a new priest of modernity also being central to the opening chapter of *Ulysses*. Joyce, Russell, Marsden and Eliot see that lineage of misogyny as void of spiritual and philosophical validity because at its core, however disguised by the scribe, is a brute will to power over women.

> I have often wondered whether there is not something wrong in our religious systems in that the same ritual, the same doctrines, the same aspirations are held to be sufficient both for men and women ... The ancients were wiser than we in this, for they had Aphrodite and Hera and many another form of the Mighty Mother who bestowed on women their peculiar graces and powers. Surely no girl in ancient Greece ever sent up to all-pervading Zeus a prayer that her natural longings might be fulfilled; but we may be sure that to Aphrodite came many such prayers. The deities we worship today are too austere for women to approach with their peculiar desires, and indeed in Ireland the largest number of our people do not see any necessity for love-making at all, or what connection spiritual powers have with the affections. A girl, without repining, will follow her four-legged dowry to the house of a man she may never have spoken twenty words to before her marriage ...
>
> What the loss to the race may be it is impossible to say, but it is true that beautiful civilizations are built up by the desire of man to give his beloved all her desires. Where there is no beloved, but only a housekeeper, there are no beautiful fancies to create the beautiful arts, no spiritual protest against the mean dwelling, no hunger to build the world anew for her sake. Aphrodite is outcast and with her many of the other immortals have also departed. The home life

in Ireland is probably more squalid than with any other people equally prosperous in Europe. The children begotten without love fill more and more the teeming asylums. We are without art; literature is despised; we have few of those industries which spring up in other countries in response to the desire of woman to make gracious influences pervade the home of her partner, a desire to which man readily yields, and toils to satisfy if he loves truly. The desire for beauty has come almost to be regarded as dangerous, if not sinful; and the woman who is still the natural child of the Great Mother and priestess of the mysteries, if she betray the desire to exercise her divinely-given powers, if there be enchantment in her eyes and her laugh, and if she bewilder too many men, is in our latest code of morals distinctly an evil influence.[364]

9. All the Women are One
'Plain Simple Bitch' or Eternal Feminine?

The Cult of Masculinity from the Eve Myth to Christianity and Modernity

> Modern life is a tale told by an idiot;
> flat-chested, crop-headed, chemicalised women, of
>   indeterminate sex,
> and wimbly-wambly young men, of sex still more
>   indeterminate,
>
> (D.H. Lawrence A Tale Told by an Idiot 1929)

Matters of sexuality, gender and gender distinction at the time of *The Waste Land* were cultural considerations in part carried forward from nineteenth century *fin de siècle* Aestheticists, the British form of the French Decadent and Symbolist movements. The gender blurring erotic drawings of Aubrey Beardsley were shocking at the time and for some time following, so that the owners of an art gallery were prosecuted for displaying his drawings in 1966. Among creeds, John Bull Protestantism characterised emerging Anglo-Catholicism as effeminate.

Eliot sees Lawrence's overly masculinised gender essentialism as a form of satyriasis infused with sadism, its everyday representatives in the poem being the pustular clerk and Albert. 'Lady Chatterley's Lover which otherwise seems and essentially is, the gibbering of an illiterate erotomaniac, becomes more intelligible, though hardly more acceptable, when we understand Lawrence's ideas and his perversities ... He is a Sadist, like Hardy ... Love or Sex always associated with Pain, with Sadism or Masochism ... Sadism and Snobbery combine in his perpetual coitions between well born ladies and savages'.[365] Lawrence's modern anti-hero emerges from his 'Real Man' self-image, and both the author and reader 'can go on with this indefinitely and get nowhere. Immature. Joyce interested in relations of man with God. Lawrence's notions of relations man and woman sensible though tainted with his Real Man conception of himself — 8-cylinder man with plenty of spare parts'.

It seems unlikely that Eliot would highlight such ideas in Lawrence while, if it is so, remaining insensible of such instincts pervasive in *The Waste Land*. It seems equally unlikely that he was aware of sadistic drives in his poem and merely deeply hypocritical. In response to a critic who termed Joyce's work a libel against humanity, Eliot commented that if *Ulysses* were such a libel against humanity 'it would simply be a forged document, a powerless fraud'.[366] In the same way, if his poem is an expression of personal misogyny and so a libel against women as half of humanity, it is a forged document, a powerless fraud. This leads to a core question to be asked of the poem: is it an unconscious, symptomatic eructation of Eliot's alleged misogyny or a more complex, classical poem that includes an attack on vainglorious scribal error throughout history? Eliot figuratively portrays the work of Nietzsche as just such a libellous fraud against women, showing that he claims to revalue all values yet so relishes the dark values he inherited from the original libel, the Eve myth, that he refuses any reconsideration.

In that light, it is somewhat ironic that Dora Marsden modelled her 'freewoman' on Nietzschean ideas of the overman. She was the intellectually fierce feminist, also fearlessly courageous in action, who was founder and co-owner of *The Egoist* at which Eliot worked for a period. However, my enemy's enemy is my friend, and the idea of a gender-surpassing new woman was her response to oppressive ideas of gender essentialism and male supremacy. Before her little journal became *The Egoist* it was titled *The New Freewoman: An Individualist Review*. She wrote there that the 'story of Adam and Eve is the exact reverse of the truth'; that 'the religious, political and industrial eclipse of woman is the result of a great revolution, in which Christianity is the latest episode'; and that 'woman will never obtain the religious franchise from a masculine God'.[367]

We have seen that representations of woman and man across the cultural spectrum of western literature at the time were sometimes mediated through the figures of Eve and Adam. Widespread recognition of these mythic archetypes meant they served as cultural shorthand for an examination of aspects of modern culture in its creation. Before Marsden, Mary Wollstonecraft also inverted the Eden myth. She writes of male infantilization of women as 'fragile' and so needing protection from the intellectual: 'if men eat of the tree of knowledge, women will come in for a taste; but, from the imperfect cultivation which their understandings now receive, they only attain a knowledge of evil'.[368] For her stance, Wollstonecraft was characterised as a 'philosophical wanton' and her book as a 'scripture archly fram'd for propagating whores'.[369] She views the biblical genesis myth as an assertion of a scribal will to power over women, one effect being to reduce women to a plaything. 'Probably the prevailing opinion, that woman was created for man, may have taken its rise from Moses's poetical story ... it proves that man, from the remotest antiquity, found it convenient to exert his strength to subjugate his companion, and his invention to show that she ought to have her neck bent under the yoke, because the whole creation was only created for his convenience or pleasure.'[370]

This theme of fragility is often repeated by Nietzsche, either as evidence of a deficiency of intellect in women or an accusation of guile that is also central to the Eve myth. His strongman ideas are based in the Darwinian intelligent ape that Eliot embodies in the pustular clerk and Sweeney.

> *The strength of the weak.* — All women are subtle at exaggerating their weaknesses; indeed they are inventive at weaknesses in order to appear as utterly fragile ornaments that are harmed by even a speck of dust: their way of living is supposed to remind men of their clumsiness and burden their conscience with this. Thus they defend themselves against the strong and 'the law of the jungle'.[371]

Much effort is expended to excuse such opinions as a product of his time, but Nietzsche had met many courageous women notably free of such cliches, not least Lou Salome, who twice refused his proposals of marriage. It bears repeating that his reaction to independent women and feminists was to consider them afflicted with the Old Testament curse of barrenness. "I am the first psychologist of the eternal-womanly. They all love me — an old story: excepting the *abortive* women, the 'emancipated' who lack the stuff for children."[372]

East of Eden: The Wanderings of Eve

The examination of the myth of the first couple as a lens to view the constitution of modern humankind includes the theme of the fall from Eden. Banished for their disobedience, the first couple now wander 'east of Eden' in a world of struggle and pain in which, for many, the salve of belief in eternal life is no longer available.

Eliot originally proposed an epigraph for his poem from Joseph Conrad's *Heart of Darkness* but was discouraged by Ezra Pound, a decision he regretted according to Valerie Eliot. Central to Conrad's novel is such a primal journey. 'We penetrated deeper and deeper into the heart of darkness ... We were wanderers on a prehistoric earth, on an earth that wore the aspect of an unknown planet. We could have fancied ourselves the first of men taking possession of an accursed inheritance, to be subdued at the cost of profound anguish and of excessive toil.'[373] This Adamic imagery of the banished first man is repeated in *Ulysses*. In what might be termed a sequel to the biblical expulsion from Eden, Joyce's squalid Dublin couple are also the first couple, now in a place where woman is particularly afflicted and betrayed by man: oppressed and prostituted, with a 'shefiend's whiteness under her rancid rags'. That 'shefiend' is the biblical Lilith, the similarly used up and burned out 'Lil' [139] of *The Waste Land*.

> Shouldering their bags they trudged, the red Egyptians ... With woman steps she followed: the ruffian and his strolling mort. Spoils slung at her back. Loose sand and shellgrit crusted her bare feet. About her windraw face hair trailed. Behind her lord, his helpmate, bing awast to Romeville. When night hides her body's flaws calling under her brown shawl from an archway where dogs have mired. Her fancyman is treating two Royal Dublins in O'Loughlin's of Blackpitts.[374]

Joyce's vignette resonates with the relationships between the typist and clerk and Lil and Albert. All represent the immiseration of woman in the service of the decultured man, whether Joyce's fancyman pimp or, in Eliot's poem, the pustular clerk whose street vanity is informed by his lineage of advisors from the Old Testament to Christian creeds and philosophy. Joyce's street couple is not so far removed in circumstances from Eliot's couples, nor from the fraught woman who, through her maddening circumstances, is near to becoming a streetwalker: 'I shall rush out as I am, and walk the street | 'With my hair down, so.' [132-3].

In her 1923 poem *Marriage*, not quite an endorsement of that binding ritual, Marianne Moore wonders 'what Adam and Eve | think of it by this time'. Her male character 'stumbles over marriage', thinking it 'a very trivial object indeed'. Much of the implicit subordination of the female in Moore's poem again has its roots in the Eden myth. She shares a theme with *Ulysses*: that Adam is not born of woman. In that way Adam is completely separated from the female and so, implicitly, is the vainglorious invention of male scribes who exclude the 'Unhelpful Hymen'.

> that shed snakeskin in the history of politeness
> not to be returned to again —
> that invaluable accident
> exonerating Adam
>
> ...
> the ease of the philosopher
> unfathered by a woman.
> Unhelpful Hymen!
>
> (Marianne Moore *Marriage*)[375]

The Typist of *The Waste Land* is the Eve of Dora Marsden, Mary Wollstonecraft, Marianne Moore and James Joyce, subordinated to the male of Genesis II and Milton's *Paradise Lost*. In contrast, Eve was an equal partner within the primal couple in the first version of the Genesis myth. Why did Eve suffer such a disastrous fall at the hands of scribes from the first version of Genesis to the next? In another of his works, James Frazer notes that collapse in Eve's status.

ATTENTIVE readers of the Bible can hardly fail to remark a striking discrepancy between the two accounts the creation of man recorded in the first and second chapters of Genesis ... In the first narrative the deity begins with fishes and works steadily up through birds and beasts to man and woman. In the second narrative he begins with man and works downwards through the lower animals to woman, who apparently marks the nadir of the divine workmanship.

(James Frazer *Folk-Lore In The Old Testament*)[376]

It was from these discordant Genesis accounts that the early medieval myth of Jewish folklore developed in which Lilith was the first wife of Adam. Divorced because she refused to be subordinate, she fled. No doubt Eve regrets not having followed that example. It is this theology of subordination that Eliot decries as the 'theology that I find in large part repellent, expressed through a mythology that would have better been left in the Book of Genesis, upon which Milton has not improved'. That scribal will to power over the female in the Bible, and in the subsequent reiterations by the Revd. Coverdale and Milton, later becomes the secular theology of Nietzsche, throughout whose work can be found variations of Milton's Reformation perspective.

> For well I understand in the prime end   [540]
> Of Nature her th' inferiour, in the mind
> And inward Faculties, which most excell,
> In outward also her resembling less
> His Image who made both, and less expressing
> The character of that Dominion giv'n
> O're other Creatures;
>
> (*Paradise Lost* Book VIII)

Desire: Geoffrey Faber and Homosexuality

We have met Mnemosyne and her three daughters Aoidē, Meletē and Mnēmē, the Boeotian muses of Mount Helicon, the earliest known muses. The spring of Mnemosyne flows at the Oracle of Trophonius in Boeotia in Greece, marking a classical entrance to the underworld. Since Harrison sees 'Mnemosyne as revelation rather than mere memory' and, as 'renewed consciousness, is a new Life', there is in her presence an oracular aspect.[377] Her memory is all encompassing and timeless, holding past and future and knowing the world's true order and origins. Mnemosyne is also linked with 'desire' [3] in Hesiod's *Theogony*, and together they sing songs pleasing to the heavens.

> Then in Pieria did Mnemosyne (Memory), who reigns over the hills of Eleuther, bear of union with the father, the son of Cronos, a forgetting of ills and a rest from sorrow ... she bare nine daughters, all of one mind, whose hearts are set upon song and their spirit free from care, a little way from the topmost peak of snowy Olympus. There are their bright dancing-places and beautiful homes, and beside them the Graces and Himerus (Desire) live in delight. And they, uttering through their lips a lovely voice, sing the laws of all and the goodly ways of the immortals, uttering their lovely voice. Then went they to Olympus, delighting in their sweet voice, with heavenly song, and the dark earth resounded about them as they chanted, and a lovely sound rose up beneath their feet as they went to their father.
>
> (Hesiod's *Theogony* 'Hymn to the Muses')

Himerus is the god of pressing sexual desire, one of the winged gods the Erotes who, with his twin brother Eros, is born of Aphrodite.

Desire can also allude to his brother Pothos, representing a yearning or longing that can include a spiritual dimension. The Erotes express the range of desire from the carnal to the spiritual, echoing the same scope in *The Waste Land*. Eliot writes that Baudelaire reaches out towards something beyond the human in desire, and points to a contrasting deficiency in Romanticism: 'in much romantic poetry the sadness is due to the exploitation of the fact that no human relations are adequate to human desires, but also to the disbelief in any further object for human desires than that which fails to satisfy them.'[378] An important aspect of desire in his poem is entwined with the sacred and the cultural, ennobling humanity. We see the spiritual aspect of desire in Sappho's poetry.

Afroditi and Desire
It is not easy for us to equal
the goddesses
in beauty and form Adonis

desire
and
Afroditi

poured nectar from
a gold pitcher
with hands Persuasion

the Geraistion shrine
lovers
of no one

I shall enter desire[379]

It might be said that Sappho is the first known non-binary literary author. The homoeroticism of some of her poetry suggests her same-sex loves within her circle of women. The mythic layer of *The Waste Land*, so enamoured as it is with Sappho, shows no concern with who Sappho chose to love. It is concerned only with her poetry, her spirituality, and her all governing relationship with the divine through Aphrodite. This seems to reflect Eliot's perspective at the time. Rachel Potter comments that Eliot implies 'structural as well as visionary cohesion' through the dual-sex Tiresias, and that 'Eliot insists that femaleness produces a significant unity of being in the poem'.[380] The contrasting hypermasculinity of the aggressive male characters in the poem fragments that unity, creating an impoverished, remorseless, alienating environment. That binary opposition suggests that the presence of Tiresias might be read as an argument for the wisdom of the communal unity of man and woman, rather than some form of closeted homosexuality on Eliot's part. Mark Ford sounds a note of significant caution on homosexual readings of the poem. He crystallises what seems to be Eliot's disregard, in the sense of a lack of concern, for sexual preferences.

> Eliot, as Miller himself insists time and again, spent much time, both in Boston and London, in circles where straight, gay and bi mingled freely. And it's a bizarre sort of literary criticism that makes the act of alluding to the work of another writer mean you share their sexual preferences, particularly when the poem in question is a dramatic monologue. While Miller tirelessly insinuates that overwhelming guilt at his unmentionable homosexuality is the key to the mystery of Eliot's life and poetry, he never once considers the possibility that Eliot might have known what he was about when he included in his early poems incidents such as Mr Eugenides's invitation to the male

narrator of 'The Fire Sermon': 'To luncheon at the Cannon Street Hotel / Followed by a weekend at the Metropole'.[381]

An aspect of the presence of Tiresias represents the metaphysical dissolution of gender differences outside the temporal fragmentation of human experience. That is related to the Absolute, the philosophical idea of a timeless, genderless universal whole in which all difference disappears. The reader is guided to the Absolute through the philosopher F.H. Bradley [411n], and the effect of this theory on the fragmentation of the poem is addressed in a subsequent book in this series. One consequence is that Teresias renders sexual preferences inconsequential. Gail McDonald also advises caution when considering Eliot's youthful friendship with Jean Verdenal, who died in the Great War and to whom *Prufrock and Other Observations* is dedicated.

> This brief but intense attachment has been the focus of arguments positing Eliot's homosexual attraction to Verdenal, a possibility sometimes milked to strengthen an argument that Eliot was "really" a homosexual. At various points in his life after Eliot left Vivien, he shared housing with three homosexual men, one priest, and, at greatest length (some eleven years), with John Hayward, who declared himself "the most un-homosexual man in London." These flat shares occurred in a period in which Eliot claimed to be celibate, having taken a vow of chastity in 1928. No reliable evidence has arisen to suggest he broke this vow.[382]

This indicates a notable level of acceptance on Eliot's part, and this is implicitly supported by those close to him. Eliot's friend Conrad Aiken, who considered himself something of a younger brother to Eliot, remembers his visits to Harvard. 'When he paid his infrequent visits here, we invariably met to get drunk together. There was a splendid occasion when he and I and our wives dined at "The Greeks'" after he'd received a silver bowl from the Signet Society; he was wearing a cowboy hat, and we all got plastered. We went on to the Red Lion Grill, after many drinks at the Silver Dollar Bar, the two toughest and queerest joints in Boston. He couldn't walk, for his ankles were crossed, so Valerie lifted him into the taxi'.[383]

Mark Thomas Krone writes of '1950s Gay Boston' in *Boston Queer History*. 'Boston was a more active port of call for sailors then and they were regular visitors to Scollay Square bars, especially the Lighthouse, Half Dollar, and Silver Dollar. Gay men and sailors could meet at one of these bars and take a room at one of the cheap, nearby hotels. And if you were down on your luck or too drunk to go home, you could spend the night at the Rialto, a 24-hour movie theatre where men met for sex'.[384] Excepting double-bluff arguments, visiting one of the toughest and queerest joints in Boston with his wife and friends does not seem like the socialising of a man squeamish about or hiding his own sexuality, or with censorious perspectives on the sexuality of others.

Closer to the time of the poem, there is also the attitude of Geoffrey Faber, Eliot's publisher in the years following *The Waste Land* and his 'employer and friend'.[385] In 1933, in a book on the Oxford Movement, Faber wrote an enlightened and enlightening commentary on homosexuality. The book, dedicated to 'T.S. Eliot with affection and respect', examines the personalities of the movement that fought for the right of Anglo-Catholics to their form of worship. As an indication of their sympathy of mind, Faber points to the origins of the *Book of Common Prayer* in 'primitive and medieval liturgies and a close English cousin of the Roman service books', notes the 'depressing conditions' of churches before the proto-Anglo-Catholic Tractarians and Oxford Movement, and twice remarks on the poetry of Byron as a form of poison.[386]

In general, Faber's book is concerned with spirituality and personalities rather than literature, providing significant insight into the thinking of people closest to Eliot in society. In the context of 1933, it is notable that Faber's discussion of homosexuality is not censorious and is significantly more inclusive than the practised psychology of the time. It includes the argument that a same sex relationship can be equally ennobling of the person if spiritually informed: what he terms 'the ideal of the sanctification of earthly loves by the love of God'.

There have been two attempts, in the west, to study the nature of homosexuality — In Athens of the fifth and fourth centuries before Christ by Socrates and his followers, and in the twentieth-century Europe by psychologists of various schools. The methods of approach in the two cases differ *toto coelo*. In Athens, and in a number of other Greek cities, homosexuality was not regarded with public horror. On the contrary the tendency was to regard physical connection between men and women as no more than an animal act, pleasing in itself and involving a momentary emotion, or as a social duty, for the continuance of the race. Love between people of the same sex was thought by most Greeks to be of a higher, more ideal character. The typical Greek romance was not a story like that of Tristan and Iseult, but a story of passionate friends like Achilles and Patroclus, Orestes and Pylades, Harmodius and Aristogeiton ... and it was thought no shame if the friendship was accompanied by physical intimacy. It was as much 'the thing' for a man to be in love with a youth as it is for a young Englishman or American to be in love with a girl ... But it was the spiritual, ideal love which interested Socrates. The physical act, if it did not in itself disgust him, was at best a concession to animalism, impeding love's gift to the soul.[387]

Faber refers to Plato's *Phaedrus* — either a set of dialogues or a single dialogue depending on the scholar — in which Socrates debates various matters with Phaedrus, including same sex love. The dialogues are also about rhetoric, about debate itself. Faber goes on to contrast that Greek perspective with the 'invert' pathologized by the psychology of his own time.

> Very different is the modern psychological approach. Regarding love as no more than an emotional accompaniment or refinement of the sexual instinct, and the sexual instinct as obviously existing for the sole purpose of procreation; acting, also, under the powerful pressure of social opinion; psychology has tended to treat homosexuality as a disease, out of which nothing good can come, or at best only an inferior kind of good. It is true that this is not quite the whole story. Most psychologists will agree that no man is perfectly 'normal'. Most, if not all, psychologists will agree that every human being, in his progress towards 'normality', passes through a definitely homosexual stage. Many will go so far as to admit, with McDougall, 'that, in some small proportion of human beings, the sex instinct is innately inverted, is innately homosexual'. And some may even be bold enough to suggest that emotional attachments between persons of the same sex have as much intrinsic right to existence and recognition as emotional attachments between persons of opposite sexes.[388]

This is the opinion of a man close to Eliot as a friend, in the business of literature, and in creed, yielding insight into the enlightened, private perspectives of those close to Eliot. Faber decries the harshness of psychological characterisations of homosexuality as a disease in favour of equality, regardless of gender or preference, based on 'love's gift to the soul'. It is an argument remarkable in its time and would be notable for its spiritual, religious and cultural inclusiveness if made today. Gail McDonald writes of the role of perspective in contemporary analysis of gender and sexuality in Eliot's work.

> Analyses focused on gender and sexuality will inevitably be shaped by the kinds of questions being asked; those questions will stem not only from the texts under consideration but also from current critical practices. Two examples will suggest the interpretive differences that arise from different premises. Tony Pinkley's *Women in the Poetry of T.S. Eliot: A Psychoanalytic Approach* (1984) frames his study of Eliot according to the psychoanalytic theories of D.W. Winnicott and Melanie Klein, and finds that violence towards women is constitutive of Eliot's poetics: "any Eliot text has to, needs to, wants to in one way or another, do a girl in; and if it fails to achieve that goal, it is itself murderously threatened by the girl." Pinkley's argument may or may not convince a given reader, but its effectiveness depends on accepting certain premises of psychoanalysis.[389]

McDonald's essay resonates with the caution of Mark Ford, examining how different critical approaches at different times deliver different perspectives. Implicit is the question to what extent critics are empowered by their theoretical approach, and to what extent that approach might encode their analysis.

Sappho, Aphrodite, Mary, and Love

The enlightened outlook of Geoffrey Faber is another instance of the *via media*, the idea of moderation in all things, and elucidates Eliot's view on humanity. If anything, in his own life Eliot mirrored Sappho's sacred governance of love, since in his poem, in which 'all the women are one woman', Sappho's divine helper and advisor Aphrodite is also the Christian Mary. Sappho is central to ideas of women in positive and beautiful ways in *The Waste Land*. Her thoughts on who to love, guided as they are by her all-governing sacred relationship with her Queen of Heaven Aphrodite, seem of no concern in the poem or to its author, who had a lifelong relationship with his own Queen of Heaven. On his relationship with Valerie Eliot, Eliot wrote to Geoffrey Faber, 'I have found my own love for a woman enhanced, intensified and purified by meditation on the Virgin'.[390]

Eliot opened a 1926 lecture on metaphysical poetry with a quote from Dante's *La Vita Nuova*: 'Ladies, the end and aim of my Love was but the salutation of that lady of whom I conceive that ye are speaking; wherein alone I found that beatitude which is the goal of desire'.[391] We return to the spiritual dimension of the word 'desire' [3] in considering gender and sexuality in the work of Eliot. To Eliot, as to Geoffrey Faber, human desire should be entwined with desire for spiritual elevation, so that the human is ennobled in the act of love. This is a continuum from classical thought, since in *Fasti* Ovid makes clear, as he describes the relationship between the month of April and Venus, that it is the love of women and the female divinity that civilises men. 'She drew rudeminded men together and taught them to pair each with his mate … The same force preserves all living things under the broad bosom of the deep, and fills the waters with unnumbered fish. That force first stripped man of his savage garb; from it he learned decent attire and personal cleanliness'.[392] In Eliot's case, such love is mediated by the Mediatrix, the Virgin Mary as the modern embodiment of the divine female.

It is clear that it is the spiritual aspect of love and its physical expression that matters to Eliot, not the choice of gender partner. In the creedless moment of his poem there seems no fundamental distinction between Sappho's Queen of Heaven Aphrodite, the Venus of the Romans, and Eliot's Queen of Heaven Mary as *Stella Maris*. Nor is there any distinction in the continuum between the poets Sappho and Eliot as they consult the sacred feminine on human love; regardless, as Geoffrey Faber notes, of preference.

Epilogue
As Good in its Way as *Ulysses* in its Way

His poem is as good in its way as Ulysses in its way — and there is so DAMN little genius, so DAMN little work that one can take hold of and say 'this at any rate stands, and makes a definite part of literature'.

(Ezra Pound to publisher Scofield Thayer, 9th March 1922)

To look back at the Church of St. Magnus the Martyr and the bridge that once terminated outside its door is to see the bridge and the temple portal that have transported you to the ancient past and the genesis of human culture and spirituality. In that, this book may seem different to other readings of *The Waste Land*. As a classical reading, it is in fact significantly the more cautious, since it follows Eliot's preferred Classicism.

He consistently advocated and worked towards classical order and unity. It is testimony to the genius of the poem that even its discordant, fragmented layer represents in itself an extraordinary poem. As such, it is often read as an expression of resigned acceptance of personal alienation and despair in a hopelessly fragmented world, an existential literary manual for life in a relativist spiritual void.

An alternative reading of that discordant layer is as a warning that the cult of the individual will create an ever more atomised, fragmented society of isolated individuals stripped of bonding narratives — a multivocal babel ever closer to anarchy. Not the romantic political anarcho-utopia of Max Stirner and the Nietzschean H.L. Mencken, but the real anarchy of the industrialised killing of the recent Great War. In that, the poem has been prophetic as history repeated itself, published less than two decades before the Second World War.

His poem shows the monstrous and noble to co-exist in humans. The danger is the destruction of the iconoclast, the chaos of the anarch, the vain appetite of the tyrant. In his theme of structural ruin and reconstruction, Eliot shows culture to be meticulously constructed over time, only tenuously keeping chaos at bay. Eliot advises that all culture should be preserved as heritage, from the rock drawings of the Magdalenian culture of over twenty millennia ago to the City of London of 1922, built as it is on the site of Roman Londinium. Shared imagery and narratives bond a culture that can be destroyed by iconoclasm. The accumulation of culture is the mirror through which we come to know ourselves, and the stuff we use to construct our societies. As it is through their mirrors, shaped by their worlds, that the women of the poem come to know themselves.

The intertwined strands of the cultures of all humanity since its primeval genesis form the mythic layer that unifies the poem. *The Waste Land* represents the ennobling repository of humankind's cultural and spiritual efforts, and shows us Eliot's idea of a universal, shared world. It reveals itself over time in the poem in the manner of the doctrine of progressive revelation expressed in visual form on the Magnus Martyr altarpiece. It is also the way of anthropology and archaeology: the gradual revelation of a mythic continuum from fragments, the 'broken images' of cultures unearthed with 'the broken fingernails of dirty hands'.

If you consider the mythic layer flowing through the poem to be literature of extraordinary craft and beauty, like the mellifluous flow of music, it is as Eliot intended. If emotions of alienation and confusion arise from the discordant fragmented layer, that is also as Eliot intended. To borrow from his *Eeldrop and Appleflex*, it is the clangour and babel of a 'mob of individualists' and their scribes. The opposition of those layers in the poem suggests that it is only through a careful relationship with our heritage that we can order, make sense of, and bring beauty to the fragmented experience of life. It is the difference, in his words, between the complete and the fragmentary, the adult and the immature, the orderly and the chaotic.

Through Sappho, and the splendour of Magnus Martyr, and the imagery throughout the poem, *The Waste Land* becomes a meditation on art, in all its expressions, as essential to humans and their cultures since the primal dawn of consciousness. Eliot heeds Jane Harrison's words that it is at the outset one and the same impulse that sends a man to church and to the theatre, as he heeds her stipulation that art should be complex to reflect the complexity of the times. The rituals, images, texts and structures which collectively constitute a bonding cultural tradition should, with care and vigilance, self-perpetuate and evolve. Anarchic impulses such as iconoclasm and zealous reformation — a new world order in which a new Adam can start afresh by, in the words of Milton, breaking images to peeces — strike at that heritage, fragmenting it. So that we are left with only fragments of some of the greatest poetry ever written, that of Sappho.

How is the new Adam shaped without the guidance and restraint of the collective repository of tradition? How is the new Eve shaped? How is she treated in the world of the male egoist empowered by the Eve myth? How is she treated in a world of romantic self-exceptionalism described by Bertrand Russell as the Byronic cult of violent passion of no matter what kind? How does she respond to that vainglorious misogynist, the new Adam of Nietzsche?

Eliot insisted at that moment in time on the mythic method of W. B. Yeats, given extraordinary further expression in James Joyce's

Ulysses. That he considered it to be 'the most important expression which the present age has found' seems an invitation to look again at his poem through the mythic lens, rendering it complete, adult and orderly. Either that or, despite that it would be a complete betrayal of his critical writings, he ignored his own advice and wrote an irredeemably fragmented, despairing poem. If the poem is that, it runs many gauntlets to accusations of failure. Through his own pen, as the critic who wrote that the bad poet throws his borrowings into something which has no cohesion. Through the eyes of the 1923 critic who wrote of the poem as a pompous parade of erudition, the poem as window dressing in which the bright-coloured pieces fail to atone for the absence of an integrated design. Through the pen of Nietzsche, who dismissed modern poets as incapable of representing anything other than a little lust and a little boredom. And through the eyes of Ezra Pound — *il miglior fabbro*, the better craftsman — his friend, mentor and editor of the time who viewed poetic incompleteness as impotency.

The question is whether, read as a fragmented complaint, the poem can sit on the same shelf as *Ulysses*. When he wrote that *The Waste Land* is as good in its way as *Ulysses*, was Pound comparing a seemingly irredeemably fragmented poem with no mythic schema — in the words of Yeats, a 'mere chronicle of circumstance' — to the scale, intellectual bravura, mythic depth and modernist classical cohesion of Joyce's masterpiece? Or did Pound make that observation because he understood Eliot's poem as a work of similar scope, genius and discipline, underwritten by a similarly cohesive mythic layer? To equate Eliot's poem to *Ulysses* is high advocacy from Pound, a fellow poet of exceptionally acute and firmly classical poetic sensibilities, indicating that the poem can claim to be, to paraphrase Conrad Aiken, a *Ulysses* in a walnut shell.

Pervasive and brutal as it is, if the misogyny of the poem is Eliot's it is vulgar, no matter the poetics: as base in its way as his young man carbuncular. It would sit many bookshelves below Joyce's effort to understand women. The sources of the misogyny in the poem are not in Eliot but elsewhere. It is not Eliot who assaults the typist, it is the pustular clerk. It is not Eliot who has so physically and mentally degraded Lil, nor is it Eliot who, as a false friend, castigates her lack of ability to perform in a relentless male world. It is not Eliot who cuts out Philomel's tongue. It is not Eliot who names the typist, the suicidal woman leaving the pub, and the Cleopatra figure as sluts and fallen women. He wrote that 'the maxim return to the sources is a good one', and a fundamental source of Western misogyny lies in the Old Testament Eve myth.

Regrettably, those who control the Christian creeds cherish the Eve myth and its slanderous import. In Eliot's poem, all the women are one woman. Through Sappho's evening star, Aphrodite is Venus, is Isis, is the Old Testament Queen of Heaven and, as James Frazer and Hope Mirrlees tell us, is also the Christian Mary as *Stella Maris*, star of the sea. Those divine and secular females are also linked in modernity with the typist, shocked into muteness, and the exhausted Lil. How the mighty and venerated have fallen: from the bounteous world of Sappho and the *Vigil of Venus* to a London bedsitting room and a romantic rendezvous with a clerk pustular with selfish egoism.

Eliot identifies perspectives such as misogyny to question, like Nietzsche, the very nature of human perspectives: how they are created, manipulated and governed by scribes, and often marred by grave scribal error. Eliot reworks such perspectives as a means of revelationary critique, asking questions of scribes such as those of the Old Testament, Milton, Nietzsche and other scribes brought to the poem. Central to that is the question posed to Nietzsche:

why the self-proclaimed revaluer of all values resolutely refuses to revalue his virulent, Old Testament and Reformation misogyny, and how that reflects on his other claims. In that, Eliot encourages us to revalue Nietzsche, guiding the reader to Nietzsche's enchained Eve. Where we find her, we find his vainglorious Adam, the overman. We see that the heresiarch Nietzsche, one of modernity's most extraordinary of writers and genius though he is in many ways, gifts his overman with an egoist philosophical manual. It is of puritan pseudo-aristocratic temper, and disdainful of any society save that of a cabal of overmen freed to ruthlessly deploy power to advance that self-evaluated exceptionalism.

The overman quickly escaped Nietzsche's flimsy moral compound as Satan escaped that of Milton to evolve into what Eliot described as the curly-haired Byronic hero of Milton. In modernity, now further fortified by the bold stare of the overman and his philosophy, this romantic character exempts himself from the constraints of society. The pustular clerk is Eliot's similarly mythopoetic figure, created in part to battle the curly-haired Byronic hero of Milton, his predecessors, and his progeny such as the overman. He represents for Eliot the most likely brute, street-level manifestation of the anarchic individualism released by the Reformation that terminates in the extreme egoisms of modernity.

Nietzsche acknowledged that his elevated overman has never arrived in the real world, 'never as willed', the Godot of romantic philosophical fiction. The overman's degenerate imitator has arrived, in the form of the typist's romancer. Fortified by the certitudes of egoism, he is freed to indulge in Russell's Byronic cult of violent passion of no matter what kind. As a portrait of a type of man, the young man carbuncular contrasts to those who might be engendered through the guidance of the Hellenic Sappho and the Hebraic Aaron, who wears the sacred carbuncle gem. He is not the Adam imagined by either Milton or Moses, the said scribe of the Book of Genesis who is Aaron's brother in portraiture in Magnus Martyr.

Notes

1 Michael North *Reading 1922* (Oxford University Press 2002) p. 3, 6.

2 *The Letters of T.S. Eliot* Vol. 1 revised edition, Eds. Valerie Eliot and Hugh Haughton, John Haffenden (Faber & Faber 2009) p. 625, fn.1. Hereafter, Letters 1.

3 James Joyce *Ulysses* Eds. Hans Walter Gabler, Wolfhard Steppe, Claus Melchior (The Bodley Head London 1993) 15.1471/1544/1631.

4 Friedrich Nietzsche 'Conclusion' *The Antichrist* Trans. R. J. Hollingdale (Penguin Books 2003) p. 199.

5 Nietzsche's idea of a revaluation of all values was also in Pound's mind at the time, less as iconoclasm than as a means of dismantling cultural clichés such as those that contributed to the First World War. Pound 'took to heart Carlyle's vision of the poet as the 'Hero-soul' living each day *direct from the inner facts of things*. In 1911 he gave such a figure a name of his own, and called him 'over-man' – brother most certainly to the *Übermensch*, to the poet-hero, to Aristotle's magnanimous man'. Matthew Hollis *A Biography of a Poem* p. 190.

6 Matthew Hollis *A Biography of a Poem* (Faber & Faber 2022) p.25.

7 Frances Dickey 'The Stale Dregs of Revolt' *T. S. Eliot Studies Annual* (Liverpool University Press 2017) p. 85.

8 Ronald Schuchard and Jewel Spears Brooker 'Introduction' *The Complete Prose of T. S. Eliot: The Critical Edition: Apprentice Years, 1905–1918* (Baltimore: Johns Hopkins University Press and Faber & Faber Ltd 2014) p. 478. Hereafter CP1.

9 Robert Crawford *Eliot After The Waste Land* (Jonathan Cape 2022) p. 1.

10 CP1.xxviii, Introduction.

11 *Writers at Work* Ed. George Plimpton, intro. Van Wyck Brooks, Second Series (Penguin Books 1982) p. 110. Original interview in the *Paris Review*.

12 Christopher Ricks and Jim McCue *The Poems of T.S. Eliot: Volume I* (Faber & Faber 2015) p. 671.

13 John Betjeman *Coming Home* (Vintage 1998) p. 345.

14 Geoffrey Faber *Oxford Apostles: A Character Study of the Oxford Movement* (Faber & Faber 1974) p. 85.

15 Ralph Waldo Emerson 'Wealth' *The Selected Writings of Ralph Waldo Emerson* (The Modern Library New York 1992) p. 546.

16 Lawrence Rainey *The Annotated Waste Land* 2nd Edition (Yale University Press 2006) p. 108, 222.

17 Michael North *Reading 1922* (Oxford University Press 2002) p. 183.

18 *The New York Times Book Review* Sunday 4th Jan. 1914, p. 775. *The House of Mirth* by Edith Wharton, 1905.

19 *The New York Times* Tuesday, March 8, 1921, 32 pages, P. 1. timesmachine.nytimes.com.

20 *The Collected poems of W.B. Yeats* Intro. Cedric Watts (Wordsworth Editions 1994) p. 158.

21 Jewel Spears Brooker *Mastery and Escape: T. S. Eliot and the Dialectic of Modernism* (University of Massachusetts Press 1994) p. 6, 20.

22   T.S. Eliot 'A Commentary' 1927, *The Complete Prose of T.S. Eliot* Vol. 3, Eds. Francis Dickey, Jenifer Formichelli, Ronald Schuchard (John Hopkins University Press, Faber & Faber 2021) p. 104 fn.18. Hereafter CP3.

23   Matthew Arnold *Culture and Anarchy* Ch. 4, 'Hebraism and Hellenism' *Selected Prose* (Penguin Books 1970) p. 274.

24   Charles Baudelaire *Intimate Journals 1821-1867* Trans. Christopher Isherwood (Hyperion Press 1978) p. 95. First printed London: Blackamore Press, 1930.

25   Peter Nicholls *Modernisms* (Palgrave Macmillan 2009) p. 1.

26   Charles Baudelaire *The Flowers of Evil (Les Fleurs du mal)* Trans. Aaron Poochigian, Introduction Dana Gioia, Afterword Daniel Handler (Liveright Publishing 2022) p. xv.

27   Lawrence Rainey 'With Automatic Hand: *The Waste Land*', *The New Cambridge Companion to T.S. Eliot* Ed. Jason Harding (Cambridge University Press 2017) p. 80, 78.

28   John Gunstone *Lift High the Cross: Anglo-Catholics and the Congress Movement* (Canterbury Press 2010) p. 16.

29   Christopher Ricks and Jim McCue *The Poems of T.S. Eliot: Volume I* (Faber & Faber 2015) p. 664 [III] 222-23.

30   Gilbert Seldes 'T.S. Eliot, 'Nation', (New York)' *The Dial*, 6 Dec. 1922.

31   Friedrich Nietzsche *Thus Spoke Zarathustra* Trans. Graham Parkes (Oxford University Press 2008) Book I, §18, p. 57.

32   Brian Leiter *Nietzsche on Morality* (Routledge 2003) p. xiv.

33   Walter Kaufmann *Nietzsche: Philosopher, Psychologist, Antichrist* (Princeton University Press 2013) p. 42, 308.

34   Max Stirner *The Ego and Its Own* Ed. David Leopold (Cambridge University Press 2006) p. 276.

35   T.S. Eliot 'Three Reformers' CP3.506.

36   'Education'; 'Milton' *The Complete Works of Ralph Waldo Emerson: Natural History of Intellect, and Other Papers* [Vol. 12] VII. (Houghton Mifflin Boston: New York 1903-1904) p. 275.

37   Ralph Waldo Emerson *The Conduct of Life* [Vol. 6] IV. 'Culture' p. 145; VII. 'Considerations by the Way' p. 266.

38   Friedrich Nietzsche *The Gay Science* Ed. Bernard Williams (Cambridge University Press 2001) Book III. §125 p. 120.

39   Helen Gardner 'The Waste Land: Paris 1922' in *The Waste Land* (Norton Critical Edition 2001) Ed. Michael North p. 78.

40   T. S. Eliot *The Function of Criticism* CP2.460.

41   Northrop Frye *T.S. Eliot An Introduction* (University of Chicago Press 1981) p. 2. First published 1963.

42   T. S. Eliot 'Introduction' *The Sacred Wood* 1920 (Faber & Faber 1997) p. xiv.

43   Kaufmann *Nietzsche: Philosopher, Psychologist, Antichrist* p. 136.

44   Bertrand Russell *A History of Western Philosophy and Its Connection with Political and Social Circumstances from the Earliest Times to the Present Day* (Simon and Schuster New York 1945) p. 764.

45   Leiter *Nietzsche on Morality* p. 293 fn. 7.

46   Kaufmann *Nietzsche: Philosopher, Psychologist, Antichrist* p .84.

47 Walter Kaufmann *From Shakespeare to Existentialism* (Princeton University Press 1980). First printed 1959.

48 Friedrich Nietzsche *Beyond Good and Evil* Eds. Rolf Peter Horstmann and Judith Norman, Trans. Judith Norman (Cambridge University Press 2002) §62 p. 57. (Allowing the possibility that the poem is proto-Anglo-Catholic).

49 Russell *A History of Western Philosophy* Preface.

50 *The Complete Prose of T. S. Eliot: The Critical Edition: The Perfect Critic*, 1919–1926 Vol 2 Eds. Anthony Cuda and Ron Shuchard (Baltimore: Johns Hopkins University Press and Faber & Faber Ltd 2014) p. 516. Hereafter CP2.

51 Letters 1.155. Reviewing *the Philosophy of Nietzsche* by A. Wolf (Constable & Co. 1915), in which Eliot comments on Nietzsche's writerly qualities as a hybrid philosopher, and identifies what he sees as philosophical absences in Nietzsche's thought.

52 Leiter *Nietzsche on Morality* p. 290. 'More recently, there has been a growing backlash to both the Kaufmannesque whitewash and the "French" trivialization of Nietzsche'. P. 291.

53 Letters 1.132.

54 Friedrich Nietzsche *Beyond Good and Evil* Eds. Rolf Peter Horstmann and Judith Norman, Trans. Judith Norman (Cambridge University Press 2002) §234 p. 125.

55 Frank Kermode 'T.S. Eliot' in *Modern Essays* (Fontana Press 1990) p. 312. First published 1971; Rachel Potter 'Gender and Obscenity in *The Waste Land*', *The Cambridge Companion to The Waste Land* p. 133; Mark Ford, review of *The Poems of T.S. Eliot: Volume I*, by Christopher Ricks and Jim McCue, London Review of Books Vol. 38 No. 16 · 11 August 2016, pages 9-12.

56 T.S. Eliot 'The Relationship between Politics and Metaphysics' CP1.90-91.

57 Leiter *Nietzsche on Morality* p. 290.

58 Russell *A History of Western Philosophy* p. 767.

59 T.S. Eliot 'A review of *The Philosophy of Nietzsche*, by A. Wolf' 1916, *The International Journal of Ethics,* 26 (Apr 1916) 426-27, CP1.401.

60 T.S. Eliot 'The Relationship between Politics and Metaphysics' CP1.90.

61 Although violets are the symbol of the classical Muses, 'roses are the Muses gift to Sappho, and the flower has a symbolic association with desire, loveliness, the *locus amoenus* [idealised waterside grove], and sensuality; the rose is something of a signature image for Sappho ... she applies the metaphor "roses of Pieria" to poetic competence, linking the Muses and Aphrodite as sponsors of divinely sanctioned song'. Angela Gosetti-Murrayjohn 'Sappho as the Tenth Muse in Hellenistic Epigram' *Arethusa* Vol. 39 No. 1 (Winter 2006) pp. 21-45, p. 22.

62 James Frazer *The Golden Bough* Ed. and Introduction Robert Fraser (Oxford University Press 2009) p. 332.

63 Nietzsche *The Gay Science* p. 13.

64 *The Poems of T.S. Eliot* p. 219, 1061.

65 Nietzsche 'Attempt at a Self-Criticism' *The Birth of Tragedy* Trans. Shaun Whiteside, Ed. Michael Tanner (Penguin 2003) p. 11, 88.

66 'What does Nietzsche mean today?' Peter Bergmann, Teodor Münz, Frantisek Novosád, Paul Patton, Leslie Paul Thiele, Richard Rorty, Alan D. Schrift, Jan Sokol *Kritika & Kontext* 15 February 2008.

67   Friedrich Nietzsche *The Gay Science* Book V, §343, p. 199.

68   stmagnusmartyr.org.uk

69   Valerie Eliot *The Waste Land: A Facsimile and Transcript of the Original Drafts* (London: Faber & Faber 1971) p. 37.

70   Appendix .

71   David Chaundy-Smart 'The Moral Shecinah: The Social Theology of Chancel Decoration in Seventeenth Century London' *Anglican and Episcopal History*, June 2000 Vol. 69, no. 2. pp. 193-210. P. 193.

72   Nicoletta Asciuto 'T.S. Eliot's 'Young Man Carbuncular': Precious Gemstone or Infected sore?' *Notes and Queries* Sept. 2017 (Oxford University Press) p. 2-3, 4.

73   T. S. Eliot 'Ben Jonson' *The Sacred Wood* 1920 (Faber & Faber 1997) p. 96.

74   Charles William King*The Natural History of Gems Or Decorative Stones* (Bell & Daldy Covent Garden 1867) p. 39.

75   Francesca Dell'Acqua 'The Carbunculus (Red Garnet) and the Double Nature of Christ in the Early Medieval West' *Konsthistorisk tidskrift/Journal of Art History* 2017, 86:3, p. 158-172, 166.

76   T. S. Eliot 'Milton 1' *The Complete Prose of T. S. Eliot: The Critical Edition: Tradition and Orthodoxy 1934-1939* Eds. Iman Javadi, Ronald Schuchard and Jayme Stayer (Baltimore: John Hopkins University Press 2017) p. 376. Hereafter CP5.

77   Kevin Rulo 'Eliot and Skin' (Liverpool University Press) p. 93.

78   St. Augustine *Confessions* Trans. Henry Chadwick (Oxford World Classics 2008) p. 35.

79   *Ulysses* 3.117, 5.217.

80   Johann Wolfgang Goethe *Faust* Part I, Trans. David Luke (Oxford University Press 2008) 'Prologue in Heaven' 323 – 335, p.12.

81   Johann Wolfgang Goethe *Faust* Part II Trans. David Luke (Oxford University Press 2008) 11827 – 12110, p. 230-239, n.237, p. 283.

82   T.S. Eliot 'Valéry' CP2.561.

83   T.S. Eliot 'Modern Tendencies in Poetry' 1920 CP2.212

84   T. S. Eliot 'Poetry and Propaganda' *The Bookman* (New York) Feb 1930.*The Complete Prose of T. S. Eliot: The Critical Edition,* Vol. 4. Eds. Jason Harding and Ronald Schuchard (Johns Hopkins University Press 2015) p. 27. Hereafter CP4.

85   T.S. Eliot 'Milton II' *The Complete Prose of T. S. Eliot: The Critical Edition: A European Society, 1947–1953* (Baltimore: Johns Hopkins University Press, 2018) Eds. Iman Javadi and Ronald Schuchard. P. 23.

86   Christopher Ricks *Milton's Grand Style* (Oxford University Press 2001, first print 1963) p. 16 & etc.

87   Eliot was later said to have retracted that antipathy in a lecture in America, so that *Time* magazine claimed Eliot now thought 'Milton is O.K'. However, he explained to Emily Hale that 'my supposed 'recantation' refers to my lecture on Milton (which only recants on a few minor details, otherwise the title is merely sensationalism)'. Christopher Snow Hopkins 'Picturing Paradise: T. S. Eliot, John Milton, and Jean-Honoré Fragonard' frick.org.

88   T.S. Eliot 'Mystic and Politician as Poet: Vaughan, Traherne, Marvell, Milton' CP4.103/102.

89   *The Poems of T.S. Eliot* p. 665.

90 B. C. Southam *A Guide to The Selected Poems of T.S. Eliot* 6th Ed. (Harvest 1994) p. 173.

91 'Milton II' CP7.23

92 Steven Cowser 'Richard Bovet's PandæMonuim (1684) as Early Political Engagement With '*Paradise Lost*', *Notes & Queries* Volume 70, Issue 1, March 2023, p. 35.

93 *Pandemonium or the Devil's Cloister* 1684.

94 *The Princeton Encyclopaedia of Poetry & Poetics* 4th edition. Editor in Chief Roland Greene, Gen ed. Stephan Cushman, Associate ed. Clare Cavanagh, Jahan Ramazani, Paul Rouzer; Assist. ed. Harris Feinsod, David Marno, Alexandra Slessarev (Princeton University Press 2012) p. 599-600. Hereafter *Princeton*.

95 *Princeton* p. 122.

96 Harold Bloom 'Urbanity and Apocalypse' in *Shelley's Poetry and Prose* Second Norton Critical Edition, Ed. Donald H. Reiman and Neil Fraistat (W. W. Norton & Company 2002) p. 569.

97 Celia Hughes 'Coverdale's Alter Ego' *Bulletin of the John Rylan's University Library of Manchester* 65 Autumn 1982 p. 123.

98 *Writings and Translation of Miles Coverdale* The Parker Society (Cambridge, The University Press 1864) p. 16.

99 Celia Hughes 'Coverdale's Alter Ego' p. 100.

100 *Writings and Translation of Miles Coverdale* p. ix.

101 *Writings and Translation of Miles Coverdale*, preamble to first chapter.

102 *Remains of Bishop Coverdale* The Parker Society (Cambridge, The University Press 1866) p. 556.

103 Titus Flavius Josephus *Jewish War* 5.222.

104 Barry Spurr *Anglo-Catholic in Religion': T.S. Eliot and Christianity* (Lutterworth Press 2010) p. 41.

105 T.S. Eliot 'A Note on Poetry and Belief' CP3.19.

106 David H. Chaundy-Smart, 'The Moral Shecinah: The Social Theology of Chancel Decoration in Seventeenth Century London'. *Anglican and Episcopal History*, June 2000 Vol. 69, no. 2. pp. 193-210. P. 207.

107 *Ulysses* 15.2097.

108 William G. Dever *Did God Have a Wife?* (Wm. B. Eerdmans 2005) p. 97.

109 Nissim Amzallag 'Beyond Prestige and Magnificence: The Theological Significance of Gold in the Israelite Tabernacle' *Harvard Theological Review* 2019, 112:3 p. 297. Nietzsche has Zarathustra declare that only 'as an allegory of the highest virtue did gold assume the highest value'.

110 T.S. Eliot *The Rock* (Faber and Faber 1934) Part II p. 85.

111 Thomas Allen *The History and Antiquities of London, Westminster, Southwark, and Other Parts Adjacent* Volume 3 (George Virtue, Ivy Lane 1828) p. 179.

112 Israel Finkelstein and Neil Asher Silberman *David and Solomon* (Free Press, Simon & Schuster 2006) p. 5-6.

113 Israel Finkelstein and Neil Asher Silberman *The Bible Unearthed* (Touchstone/Simon and Schuster 2002) p. 238.

114 *David and Solomon* p. 154.

115 *The Bible Unearthed* p. 248, 247, 223.

116   *Re-reading Sappho* Ed. Ellen Greene (University of California Press 1996) p. 1.

117   Rainey *The Annotated Waste Land* p. 108, n.221.

118   David Fuller 'Music' *T.S. Eliot in Context* ed. Jason Harding (Cambridge University Press 2011) p. 141.

119   *The Birth of Tragedy* p. 39-42.

120   *The Poems of Eliot* p. 607.[I] 31-34.

121   Examined in detail in the second book of this series, *The Primal Chorus of the Sacred Wood*.

122   Addressing Schopenhauer's *principium individuationis*. Nietzsche's 'wretched Bell Jar' may have inspired Sylvia Plath's *The Bell Jar*, one of the fundamental explorations in modern literature of human alienation, particularly that of women.

123   *The Birth of Tragedy* p. 101 (Trans. Whitehead)

124   Willis Barnstone *The Complete poems of Sappho* (Shambala Boston & London 2009) p. 123.

125   See painting *Sappho and Alcaeus* by Lawrence Alma-Tadema, 1881.

126   Hesiod Homeric Hymns and Homerica, Project Gutenberg

127   Barnstone *Sappho* p. xxix.

128   Josephine Quinn 'Alphabet Politics' *The New York Review of Books* Jan 19th 2023.

129   Barnstone *Sappho* p. xiv.

130   Gosetti-Murrayjohn p. 31 fn.25

131   *Princeton* p. 576.

132   'Geoffrey Chaucer note asking for time off work identified as his handwriting' *Guardian* 10 July 2023.

133   James George Frazer *Folk-Lore In The Old Testament. Studies In Comparative Religion: Legend And Law* Vol. 1 (MacMillan 1918) p. 374. In *Ulysses*, Leopold Bloom ponders a quasi-theological theory of the time, that Hebrew was the *Ur*-language of ancient Irish, connected through a king of Scythia who, it was theorised, was an ancestor of the Phoenicians who first occupied Spain and then ancient Ireland (U.17.724-773/ UA.577.748).

134   T.S. Eliot 'Tradition and the Individual Talent' CP2.106.

135   *Princeton* p. 976, quoting Milman Parry and including arguments from Friedrich Wolf in 1795 that writing was not available to Homer.

136   T.S. Eliot 'The Frontiers of Criticism' *The Sewanee Review*, Vol. 64, No. 4 (Oct. – Dec. 1956), p. 543.

137   Barnstone *Sappho* p. xiii.

138   Erika Rohrbach 'H.D. and Sappho: "A precious inch of Palimpsest"' in *Re-reading Sappho* Ed. Ellen Greene (University of California Press 1996) p. 184, 188, 191, 192.

139   Rohrbach p. 184.

140   Susan Gubar 'Sapphistries' *Re-reading Sappho* p. 201.

141   Ezra Pound 'The Tradition' *Literary Essays of Ezra Pound* p. 92; T.S Eliot 'War-paint and Feathers' CP2.138.

142   B. C. Southam *a Guide to The Selected poems of T.S. Eliot* 6th Ed. (Harvest 1994) p. 171. For Rainey and for 'many readers the entire passage of the "violet hour" recalls Dante'. Ricks and McCue note that Eliot 'marked the Italian in the copy his mother had given him ... 'Twas now the hour that turns back the desire of those who sail the seas and melts their heart". Rainey *The Annotated Waste Land* p. 108; *The Poems of T.S. Eliot* p. 663.

143 T.S. Eliot *Murder in the Cathedral* (Faber and Faber 1982) p. 76.

144 *Ulysses* 10.184.

145 Ovid *Metamorphoses* Trans & Ed. Charles Martin (Norton Critical Edition 2010) p. 7.

146 Thomas Allen *The History and Antiquities of London, Westminster, Southwark, and Other Parts Adjacent* Volume 3 (George Virtue, Ivy Lane 1828) p. 179.

147 Rainey 'With Automatic Hand: *The Waste Land*' *The New Cambridge Companion to The Waste Land* p. 83.

148 *Ulysses* 15.605, 15.2088-2114, 15.2168-73. The gramophone is later underlined in Eliot's 1933 notes for his lecture on James Joyce as the single word 'Gramophone'.

149 T.S. Eliot *Eeldrop and Appleplex* CP1.528

150 An echo of this imagery is seen in the 1921 petition to save Magnus Martyr and other City churches from demolition, warning that 'sentence of death has been passed upon certain City Churches (those Lamps of Faith)'. See Magnus Martyr Petition.

151 *Princeton* p. 1254

152 Michael Spitzer *The Musical Human* (Bloomsbury 2022) p. 381.

153 Diarmaid McCulloch *A History of Christianity* (Penguin books 2009) p. 180.

154 Diarmaid McCulloch *A History of Christianity* Television Series, Episode 1, 11:20+.

155 MacCulloch *A History of Christianity* p. 178.

156 Nick Page *A Nearly Infallible History of Christianity* (Hodder & Stoughton 2013) p. 77.

157 Catholic.org/encyclopaedia/

158 Pythagoras is credited with discovering the dynamics of string tuning, where the length of string is in inverse proportion to the pitch of a musical note produced; the ratio of three-two, known as the 'pure perfect fifth;' and the ratios of musical intervals, eventually facilitating the science of the measurement of sound.

159 *The Rock* p. 20.

160 William M. Barton *The Pervigilium Veneris* (Bloomsbury Academic 2020) p. 1, 32.

161 Barton *The Pervigilium Veneris* p. 65.

162 Barton *The Pervigilium Veneris* p. 32.

163 Alternative translations of the chorus include 'To-morrow shall be love for the loveless, | and for the lover to-morrow shall be love', and, 'Tomorrow let him love that never loved, | And we who have loved, let us love again'. F. W. Cornish *The Poems Of Gaius Valerius Catullus* trans. F. W. Cornish (The Loeb Classical Library, London: William Heinemann; New York: G. P. Putnam's Sons 1916) p. 349: Ruth Sheffield Dement *The Lesbiad of Catullus and Pervigilium Veneris Songs Of A Wayfarer* (The Alderbrink Press Chicago 1915) p. 9.

164 Barton *The Pervigilium Veneris* p. 1.

165 Barton *The Pervigilium Veneris*: 'the mention of Hybla ... serves more to set the poem in the proverbially fecund landscape of Latin literature', but also notes that a scholar makes a sensible link 'to the town of Hybla Geraetus on the southern slopes of Aetna, now the modern day Sicilian town of Paternò'. p. 113.

166 Barton *The Pervigilium Veneris* p. 38.

167 Barton *The Pervigilium Veneris* p. 40.

168 *The Poems of T.S. Eliot* p. 385

169 Russell *A History of Western Philosophy* Book p. 1, 13.

170 T.S. Eliot 'Catholicism and International Order' 1933 CP4.536.

171 St. Augustine *Confessions* Trans. Henry Chadwick (Oxford World Classics 2008) p. 39.

172 *Augustine: Confessions* Trans and Ed. Albert C. Outler (Library of Congress Catalog Card Number: 55-5021) Introduction.

173 London Metropolitan Archive, Magnus Martyr, A375/6 18 –.

174 Hollis *A Biography of a Poem* p. 233.

175 St. Augustine *City of God* Trans. Henry Bettenson (Penguin Books 2003) Book XVIII Ch. 1, p. 761.

176 Jason Harding 'Unravelling Eliot' *The New Cambridge Companion to T.S. Eliot* Ed. Jason Harding (Cambridge University Press 2017) p.1 3.

177 Josephus *Antiquities of the Jews*.

178 See Christopher Kelly 'Someone Else's Empire' *London Review of Books* 5th Jan 2023, reviewing Dominic Perring's *London in the Roman World* (Oxford 2023).

179 stmagnusmartyr.org.uk

180 *Thus Spoke Zarathustra* p. 79

181 *Thus Spoke Zarathustra* p. 87.

182 Friedrich Nietzsche 'Expeditions of an Untimely Man' *Twilight of the Idols* Trans. R.J. Hollingdale (Penguin books 2003) §1, p. 78.

183 Eliot borrows that compliment as a salute to Ezra Pound in the dedication of *The Waste Land*: 'For Ezra Pound | il miglior fabbro'. A central theme in the poetry of Guinzelli is the conjunction of earthly and divine desire, a theme of Eliot's poem from the outset in 'desire' [3].

184 Cleanth Brooks Essay 1939, referring to Dante's *Purgatorio*, in *Modern Poetry and the Tradition*.

185 *Ulysses* 1.708.

186 *Facsimile and Transcript* p. 47.

187 Mario Praz *The Romantic Agony* (Oxford university Press 1970) p. v, vi, 55-83.

188 *Blake's Poetry and Designs* Ed. Mary Lynn Johnson and John E. Grant (Norton Critical Edition) p. 71, 66, 71.

189 Friedrich Nietzsche *The Will to Power* Trans. R. Kevin Hill and Michael A. Scarpitti. Ed. R. Kevin Hill (Penguin Classics 2017) §1042, p. 571 (on Dionysus).

190 David Lyle Jeffrey *A Dictionary of Biblical Tradition* (William B. Eerdmanns 1992) p. 199.

191 Siobhan Lyons 'Nietzsche, Satan and the Romantics: The Devil as 'Tragic Hero' in Romanticism' in *Philosophical Approaches to the Devil* (Routledge New York 2015) p. 33.

192 *Thus Spake Zarathustra*, Part I, 8: 'The Tree on the Hill'.

193 'Dante' 1929 CP3.712. Fn. 20: 'Dante's Satan is a gigantic, bat-winged figure, with three faces of different hues, weeping bloody tears and half-encased in ice. The fresco may be the gargantuan Satan with sinners in his mouth in the Last Judgment (1398) of Taddeo di Bartolo [Taddeo Bartoli] (ca. 1362-1422)'.

194 *Facsimile and Transcript* p. 47, 145-151.

195 T.S. Eliot 'Byron' 1937 CP5.430.

196 16th century Epics of Italian Renaissance tradition, celebrating the crusader capture of Jerusalem in 1099, of the ottava rima form later favoured by Byron.

197 *The Romantic Agony* p. 60 – 71.

198 Stephen Greenblatt *The Rise and Fall of Adam and Eve* (The Bodley Head London 2017) p. 210.

199 *Shelley's Poetry and Prose* Eds. Donald H. Reiman and Neil Fraistat (Norton 2002) p. 526.

200 In 1920's London churches such as Magnus Martyr, women covered their heads with scarves.

201 http://www.anglicanlibrary.org/homilies

202 Willis Barnstone *The Complete Poems of Sappho* (Shambala Boston & London 2009) p. 95.

203 Anglicanlibrary.org/homilies/

204 Russell *History of Western Philosophy* p. 770

205 S.T. Coleridge *The Statesman's Manual* (Gale and Fenner, M. Richardson, Hatchard 1816) p.66, Appendix, ix-xi.

206 *The Statesman's Manual* Appendix xi.

207 *Princeton* p. 1255.

208 Ange Mlinko 'His Nemesis was Stupidity' *The New York Review of Books* April 7th 2002, p. 29-30.

209 Charles Baudelaire *The Flowers of Evil* Trans. James McGowan (Oxford Worlds Classics 2008) p. 351 fn.7.

210 Charles Baudelaire *The Flowers of Evil* Trans. Aaron Poochigian (Liveright 2022) p. 351, 5-7.

211 T.S. Eliot 'From Poe to Valery' 1948 CP7.298.

212 *The Romantic Agony* p. 145.

213 Robert Crawford *Eliot After The Waste Land* (Jonathan Cape 2022) p. 138.

214 T.S. Eliot Lecture VIII: 'The Nineteenth Century: Summary and Comparison' CP2.742

215 Johann Wolfgang Goethe *Faust* Part I, Trans. David Luke (Oxford university Press 2008) 742-7, p. 25.

216 T.S. Eliot 'The Possibility of a Poetic Drama' *The Sacred Wood* (Faber and Faber 1997) p. 55.

217 Walter Kauffman 'Shakespeare versus Goethe' *From Shakespeare to Existentialism* (Princeton University Press 1980) p. 35.

218 Walter Kauffman 'Goethe and the History of Ideas' *From Shakespeare to Existentialism* (Princeton University Press 1980) p. 51-2.

219 *Princeton* p. 1219.

220 Friedrich Nietzsche *Beyond Good and Evil* Eds. Rolf Peter Horstmann and Judith Norman, Trans. Judith Norman (Cambridge University Press 2002) §232 p. 124.

221 *Facsimile and Transcript* p.27.

222 Simone de Beauvoir *The Second Sex* (Vintage Classics 1997) p. 282.

223 *Ulysses* 14.1-6, UA. 14.1-6 p. 408.

224 Virginia Woolf *A Room of One's Own* (Penguin 2000) p. 30.

225 Letter to T.S. Eliot 24th January 1922. Letters 1, p. 625-6.

226 Spurr *Anglo-Catholic in Religion': T.S. Eliot and Christianity* p. 34,19.

227 Spurr *Anglo-Catholic in Religion': T.S. Eliot and Christianity* p. 38. For Eliot's comment on 'Wren's Interiors', see *Notes on the Waste Land* 264.

228 *Homily Against Peril of Idolatry* Society for Promoting Christian Knowledge (Gilbert & Rivington, London 1837) p. 23.

229 Spurr *Anglo-Catholic in Religion': T.S. Eliot and Christianity* p. 40.

230 The social and political fervour involved at the time of *The Waste Land* can be understood from an aspect of the battle of creeds in the previous century; the experience of John Henry Newman, the Tractarian forefather of Anglo-Catholicism. He was 'lost to Rome', leaving the Church of England to become a Roman Catholic. 'I was quite unprepared for the outbreak, and was startled at its violence ... I had been posted up by the marshal on the buttery-hatch of every College of my University, after the manner of discommoned pastry-cooks, and when in every part of the country and every class of society, through every organ and opportunity of opinion, in newspapers, in periodicals, at meetings, in pulpits, at dinner-tables, in coffee-rooms, in railway carriages, I was denounced as a traitor who had laid his train and was detected in the very act of firing it against the time-honoured Establishment'. *Apologia Pro Vita Sua.*

231 Letters 1 p. 587.

232 stmagnusmartyr.org.uk

233 London County Council *Proposed Demolition of Nineteen City Churches* (P.S. King and Son Ltd) 1920, p. 18.

234 T.S. Eliot, 'The Perfect Critic' 1921 CP2.267.

235 Spurr *Anglo-Catholic in Religion': T.S. Eliot and Christianity* p. 38-40.

236 See Magnus Martyr petition.

237 Friedrich Nietzsche *On the Genealogy of Morals* 2nd essay § 24, p. 75.

238 Iconoclast (n.) "breaker or destroyer of images," 1590s, from French *iconoclaste* and directly from Medieval Latin *iconoclastes*, from Late Greek *eikonoklastes*, from *eikon* (genitive *eikonos*) "image" + *klastes* "breaker" ... Originally in reference to those in the Eastern Church in 8c. and 9c. whose mobs of followers destroyed icons and other religious objects on the grounds that they were idols. Applied to 16c.-17c. Protestants in Netherlands who vandalized former Catholic churches on similar grounds. Extended sense of "one who attacks orthodox beliefs or cherished institutions" is first attested 1842. clastic (adj.): "consisting of broken pieces, breaking up into fragments" ... from Latinized form of Greek *klastos* "broken in pieces." (Etymology online).

239 *Homily Against Peril of Idolatry* p. 106.

240 papalencyclicals.net/councils/

241 Mary I.M. Bell *Before and after the Oxford Movement* London: The Catholic Literature Association, 1933.

242 Diarmaid MacCulloch *A History of Christianity* (Penguin books 2009) p. 649.

243 See appendix, 'Orthodox Views Changing'. *The Times* (London, England) Tuesday, May 09, 1922; pg.13.

244 Diarmaid MacCulloch *All Things Made New* (Penguin Books 2017) p. 216-7.

245 T.S. Eliot 'Milton II' 1947 CP7.23.

246 See appendix, 'Church of St. Magnus The Martyr'. *The Times* (London, England), Monday, Dec 04, 1922; pg. 14.

247 Barbara K. Lewalski 'Milton and Idolatry' *Studies in English Literature* 1500-1900, Vol. 43, No. 1, 'The English Renaissance' (Rice University Winter, 2003), p. 213, 214, 213.

248 See appendix, 'Ecclesiastical News', *The Times* (London, England), Thursday, Jan 04, 1923.; and that Fr. Fynes had responded to the court that 'the actual substitute [for the Holy Water basin] was a marmalade pot, because he could not afford better things'. (The Times 4th Dec. 1922).

249 Diarmaid MacCulloch *A History of Christianity* (Penguin books 2009) p. 639.

250 Eliot 'Phillip Massinger' *The Sacred Wood* p. 114.

251 T.S. Eliot 'Milton II' CP6.29.

252 Malcolm Gaskill 'At the House of Mr Frog' *London Review of Books* Vol. 43, no. 6, March 2021.

253 Stephen Tomkins *The Journey to the Mayflower* (Hodder & Stoughton 2021) p. 21.

254 John Strype *Annals of the Reformation and the Establishment of Religion and Other Various Occurrences in the Church of England during Queen Elizabeth's Happy Reign* (Oxford, Clarendon Press 1824) Vol. 1, Part 1, p. 254-5. With thanks to Magnus Martyr website research.

255 *The Rock* Prefatory Note CP5.90

256 Michael Bell 'Nietzscheanism' *A Concise Companion to Modernism* ed. David Bradshaw (Blackwell 2003) p. 63.

257 Max Stirner *The Ego and Its Own* Ed. David Leopold (Cambridge University Press 2006) p. 248.

258 Russell *A History of Western Philosophy* Book 1 p. 18.

259 CP3.513

260 Lyndall Gordon *Eliot's Early Years* (Oxford University Press 1977) p. 136.

261 T.S. Eliot 'Launcelot Andrewes' CP2.818.

262 Geoffrey Faber *Oxford Apostles* p. 341-2.

263 T.S. Eliot 'John Bramhall' CP3.146.

264 Ezra Pound, *Confucius,* New Directions Paperback, p. 33. First printed in 1928. However, Pound was working on such translations from an early stage, and is likely to have discussed such central tenets of Confucian thought with Eliot.

265 Ronald Schuchard and Jewel Spears Brooker 'Introduction' *The Complete Prose of T. S. Eliot: The Critical Edition: Apprentice Years, 1905–1918* (Baltimore: Johns Hopkins University Press and Faber & Faber Ltd 2014) p. xxxv, xxvii, xlix.

266 Lyndall Gordon *The Imperfect Life of T.S. Eliot* (Virago 2012) p. 224.

267 Louis Untekmeyer 'Disillusion vs. Dogma' *Freeman* January 1923, in *The Critical Heritage* Vol. 1. Ed. Michael Grant (Routledge London and New York) p. 144.

268 T' S. Eliot, 'Phillip Massinger' *The Sacred Wood* (Faber and Faber 1997) p. 105.

269 T. S. Eliot, 'Thoughts after Lambeth' CP4.226.

270 See book 2 in this series, *The Primal Chorus of the Sacred Wood*.

271 Hollis *A Biography of a Poem* p. 343.

272 John Henry Newman *Tract 4.*

273 Jerome Rothenberg *Technicians of the Sacred* (Anchors Books, Doubleday & Co, New York 1931) Pre-face xix.

274 Robert Crawford *Young Eliot. From St. Louis to The Waste Land* (Vintage 2016) p. 73, 98.

275 Jason Harding 'T.S. Eliot and The Egoist' *T.S. Eliot and the Concept of Tradition* Eds. Giovanni Cianci and Jason Harding (Cambridge University Press 2007) p. 94, 96-7.

276 T. S, Eliot, 'An unsigned first review of *Group Theories of Religion and the Individual* by Clement C. J. Webb' 1916 CP1.417-9: T. S, Eliot, 'Second review of *Group Theories of Religion and the Individual* by Clement C. J. Webb' 1916 CP1.432.

277 John Xiros Cooper 'T.S. Eliot's Social Criticism' *The New Cambridge Companion to T. S. Eliot* Ed. Jason Harding (Cambridge University Press 2015) p. 146.

278 T.S. Eliot 'London Letter' in *The Dial* October 1921 CP2.370.

279 T. S. Eliot 'The interpretation of Primitive Ritual' CP1.114.

280 T. S. Eliot 'Tradition and the Individual Talent' 1919 CP2.106.

281 See the next book in this series, *The Primal Chorus of the Sacred Wood*.

282 Eliot 'Euripides and Professor Murray' 1920, CP2.197.

283 Jane Harrison 'The Influence of Darwinism on the Study of Religions' *Darwin and Modern Science: Essays in Commemoration of the Centenary of the Birth of Charles Darwin and the Fiftieth Anniversary of the Publication of the Origin of the Species.* (Cambridge University Press 2009) p. 497. First published 1909.

284 Edward Tylor *Primitive Culture: Researches Into The Development Of Mythology, Philosophy, Religion Language, Art, And Custom* (London, John Murray, Albemarle Street, 1920) p. 425.

285 T.S. Eliot 'The Beating of a Drum' CP2.471. 'Darwin, *The Origin of Species* (1849); Henry Sumner Maine, *Ancient Law: Its Connection with the Early History of Society and its Relation to Modern Ideas* (1861); Edward Burnett Tylor, *Primitive Culture: Researches into the Development of Mythology, Philosophy, Religion, Language, Art, and Custom* (1871). Eliot wrote on the distinction between interpretation and fact, particularly in the social sciences, in 'The Interpretation of Primitive Ritual' CP1.106. Fn. 3, CP2.471.

286 Jane Ellen Harrison *Ancient Art and Ritual* (Oxford University Press 1948) p. 9. First printed 1913.

287 T. S. Eliot 'The interpretation of Primitive Ritual' CP1.113.

288 Harrison *Ancient Art and Ritual* Prefatory Note.

289 Martha C. Carpenter *Ritual, Myth and the Modernist Text: The Influence of Jane Ellen Harrison on Joyce, Eliot and Woolf* (Routledge 1998) p. 38-40.

290 Jessie Weston 'Preface' *From Ritual to Romance* (Dover Publications 1997).

291 Jane Harrison 'The Influence of Darwinism on the Study of Religions' p. 494.

292 Jane Harrison *Themis* xviii – xix.

293 Spurr *Anglo-Catholic in Religion* p. 41.

294 Carpentier *Ritual, Myth and the Modernist Text* p. 16, 54.

295 In his syllabus notes of 1918, under the heading 'Elizabethan Drama' and the sub-heading 'The Earliest Forms of Drama', Eliot wrote 'Popular festival and religious rite'. It is unclear whether the argument here is that the earliest Elizabethan drama emerged from a meld of festival and rite, or whether Eliot intended to argue, per Harrison, that art and religion arose from the same impulse. T.S. Eliot 'Syllabus for a Tutorial Class in Modern English Literature' CP1.754.

296 Harrison *Ancient Art and Ritual* Chapter II, 'Primitive Ritual: Pantomimic Dances', p.42.

297 Harrison, Jane. *Prolegomena to the study of the Greek Religion* (Cambridge: at the University Press 1908) p. 413.

298 Carpentier *Ritual, Myth and the Modernist Text: The Influence of Jane Ellen Harrison* p. 5.

299 Nietzsche *The Birth of Tragedy* Trans. Douglas Smith (Oxford university Press 2000) p. 22-23.

300 Crawford *Eliot after The Waste Land* p. 25.

301 K. J. Phillips 'Jane Harrison and Modernism' *Journal of Modern Literature* Vol. 17, No. 4 Spring 1991 (Indiana University Press) p. 467, 473-4.

302 Carpentier *Ritual, Myth and the Modernist Text: The Influence of Jane Ellen Harrison* p .6.

303 Jewel Spears Brooker 'Eliot's Philosophical Studies: Bergson, Frazer, Bradley' *The New Cambridge Companion to T. S. Eliot* Ed. Jason Harding (Cambridge University Press 2015) p. 176.

304 Nietzsche *The Birth of Tragedy* Trans. Douglas Smith, Intro. p. vii; Friedrich Nietzsche *On the Genealogy of Morals* Trans. Douglas Smith (Oxford University Press 1996) Preface, p. 2.

305 John Richardson *Nietzsche's New Darwinism* (Oxford university Press 2004) p. 3.

306 Ronald Schuchard and Jewel Spears Brooker 'Introduction' *The Complete Prose* Vol. 1 *Apprentice Years 1905-1918* CP1.xxxiv.

307 See appendix, *The Times* (London, England), Monday, Mar 31, 1924, reporting Father Fynes-Clinton's ongoing court struggle to protect and add to imagery in Magnus Martyr.

308 *The Poems of Eliot* p. 502, an extended examination by Ricks and McCue.

309 I.A. Richards 'Mr Eliot's poems' *New Statesman* 20th February 1926.

310 Jessie L. Weston *From Ritual to Romance* (Dover Publications 1997) p. 64.

311 T.S. Eliot *Choruses From The Rock* in *the Poems of T.S. Eliot* p. 168 VII:4-25.

312 Jessie L. Weston *From Ritual to Romance* p. 23.

313 Frazer *The Golden Bough* p. 365.

314 T.S. Eliot 'Byron' CP5.431.

315 Prefatory Note to *The Rock* CP5.90.

316 Book XXX. https://www.ccel.org/ccel/bede/

317 John Julius Norwich *The Popes A History* (Vintage 2012) p. 46. This Augustine is not the Augustine of Carthage.

318 *Facsimile and Transcript* p. 29, 41.

319 Hesiod *Theogony* 175-200.

320 Frazer *The Golden Bough* p. 389.

321 Spurr *Anglo-Catholic in Religion* p. 161, writing on *Four Quartets*. Page 160 holds a photograph of Our Lady of good Voyage in Gloucester, Massachusetts.

322 Frazer *The Golden Bough* p. 386.

323 Shakespeare *Anthony and Cleopatra* 5.2.307.

324 Pliny the Elder, *The Natural History*, Book II. *An Account Of The World And The Elements*, Chap. 6. (8.) 'Of The Nature Of The Stars; Of The Motion Of The Planets.' (www.perseus.tufts.edu)

325 Pliny the Elder *Natural History* Vol. 1 (Printed for the Wernerian Club, George Barclay Leicester Square 1847-48) Book II, Chapter XXV p. 65-6, fn. 1.

326 Herodotus, *The Histories*, Book 1, chapter 105.

327 David Lyle Jeffrey *A Dictionary of Biblical Tradition* (William B. Eerdmanns 1992) p. 60.

328   William Dever *Did God Have a Wife* p. 236.

329   *Homily Against Peril of Idolatry* p. 61.

330   Ovid *Fasti* Trans. James George Frazer (William Heinemann Ltd & Harvard University Press 1959). 1st printed 1931. *Fasti* IV. 61-4 p. 193; p.189. p. 199.

331   Barnstone *Sappho* p. xiv.

332   Ovid's *Fasti* Introduction p. xvii / xix / xxi.

333   Ovid *Fasti* p. 193.

334   Ovid *Fasti* p. 195.

335   Ovid *Fasti* p. 199.

336   *The Poems of T.S. Eliot* p. 550.

337   Angela Gosetti-Murrayjohn 'Sappho as the Tenth Muse in Hellenistic Epigram' *Arethusa* Vol. 39 No. 1 (Winter 2006) pp. 21-45, p22. A conceit first 'fashioned by Dioscorides' and later expressed, no later than 250BCE, in this epigram 'spuriously' attributed to Plato.

338   Gosetti-Murrayjohn 'Sappho as the Tenth Muse in Hellenistic Epigram' p. 32 – 34.

339   Barnstone *Sappho* p. xx, 33.

340   Eliot lived from birth with a congenital double hernia.

341   Jewel Spears Brooker *Mastery and Escape: T. S. Eliot and the Dialectic of Modernism* (University of Massachusetts Press 1994) p. 56.

342   Jane Harrison *The Religion of Ancient Greece* (Constable & Co, London 1913) p. 11.

343   *The Golden Bough* p. 302-4.

344   Ezekiel 8.

345   Harrison *Ancient Art and Ritual* p. 12.

346   Barnstone *Sappho* p. 10, 140.

347   T.S. Eliot 'London Letter: September 1921' CP2 p.369.

348   Pliny the Elder *Natural History* Book II Chapter XVIII p. 56.

349   Spurr *Anglo-Catholic in Religion* p. 131.

350   Newadvent.org.

351   Hope Mirrlees *Paris: A Poem* (Faber & Faber 2020) p. 7.

352   Frazer *The Golden Bough* p. 348, 364.

353   Nietzsche *The Gay Science* Preface to 2nd edition.

354   Pound Paris letter the Dial June 1922.

355   *Ulysses* 1:85; 3.31; 3.395; 14.248.

356   *Ulysses* 1.77-85.

357   Don Gifford with Robert J. Seidman *Ulysses Annotated* (University of California Press 2008) p. 399.

358   *Ulysses* 13.1076-1079, 13.2-8.

359   Ezra Pound 'Paris Letter' *The Dial* June 1922.

360   *Ulysses* 14.297-301, 303.

361   Hope Mirrlees *Collected Poems* Ed. Sandeep Parmar (Carcanet Press 2011) p. 46.

362   *The New Freewoman* Issue 4, August 1913. Attributed to an anonymous author of the 'F.R.A.I' (Fellow of the Royal Anthropological Institute).

363   *Ulysses Annotated* 1.85.

364   *Imaginations and Reveries* George William Russell (A.E.) (Maunsel & Co. Dublin & London 1915) p. 118-9.

365 T.S. Eliot *Lecture* Notes *for English* 1933 CP4.790-1, 785.

366 Eliot '*Ulysses*, Order, and Myth' CP2.477.

367 *The New Freewoman: An Individualist Review* No. 1, Vol. 1, 1913.

368 Mary Wollstonecraft *A Vindication of the Rights of Woman* Ed. Deidre Shauna Lynch (Norton Critical Edition 3rd ed. 2009) p. 22.

369 Sandra M. Gilbert and Susan Gubar 'Mary Shelley's Monstrous Eve" in *Mary Shelley's Frankenstein* Ed. J. Paul Hunter (Norton Critical Edition 2012) p. 330.

370 Wollstonecraft *A Vindication of the Rights of Woman* p. 29.

371 Nietzsche *The Gay Science* II § p. 66.

372 Fredrich Nietzsche *Ecce Homo* Trans. R.J. Hollingdale (Penguin Books 2004) p. 45.

373 Joseph Conrad *Heart of Darkness* (Penguin Classics 2007) p. 43.

374 *Ulysses* 3.370-380.

375 Marianne Moore *Complete Poems* (MacMillian, Penguin Books 1994) p. 62.

376 Sir James George Frazer *Folk-Lore In The Old Testament. Studies In Comparative Religion: Legend And Law* Vol. 1 (MacMillan 1918) p. 3.

377 Harrison *Themis* xxix, p. 512.

378 T.S. Eliot 'Baudelaire' CP3.162.

379 Barnstone *Sappho* p. 63.

380 Rachel Potter 'Gender and Obscenity in The Waste Land' *The Cambridge Companion to The Waste Land* ed. Gabrielle McIntire (Cambridge University Press 2015) p. 133.

381 Mark Ford 'Hyacinth Boy', reviewing *T.S. Eliot: The Making of an American Poet* by James E. Miller. London Review of Books Vol. 28 No. 18 · 21 September 2006.

382 Gail McDonald 'Gender and Sexuality' *The New Cambridge Companion to T.S. Eliot* Ed. Jason Harding (Cambridge University Press 2017) p. 164.

383 *Exchanges*, Summer 2021, T.S. Eliot Society UK, quoting *The Writer's Chapbook* edited by George Plimpton (Penguin Books, 1989).

384 markthomaskrone.wordpress.com/category/american-history/

385 *The Poems of T.S. Eliot* p. 595.

386 *Oxford Apostles* p. 85, 122, 130, 202.

387 *Oxford Apostles* p . 216-7. *Toto coelo* – diametrically opposed, literally 'all Heaven'.

388 *Oxford Apostles* p. 218.

389 Gail McDonald 'Gender and Sexuality' *The New Cambridge Companion to T.S. Eliot* Ed. Jason Harding (Cambridge University Press 2017) p. 168.

390 Spurr 'T.S. Eliot and Christianity' *The New Cambridge Companion to T.S. Eliot* p. 197. See *Letters* 3, p. 711.

391 T.S. Eliot *Clarke Lecture* I CP2.609, 623 fn.1.

392 Ovid *Fasti* p. 195. See 'April and the Muses'.

Index

Appendix: The Broken Images of Magnus Martyr from 1922

Court ordered removal of imagery including a gilded throne and picture of the Madonna from Magnus Martyr. *The Times*, Monday, Jul 31, 1922.

limits. He had no doubt that the rector of this parish was a hard-working and earnest priest, but there were certain articles here which must be removed without the least possible delay. They are :—(1) the tabernacle on the Holy Table which was proved by evidence to be used for Reservation of the Sacrament ; (2) the gilded throne, which seemed to be used entirely in the Reservation ; (3) the second Holy Table made of wood ; (4) the picture of the Madonna and Child on the re-table ; (5) the iron frame for forty-nine candles with a receptacle in which candles were kept ; (6) the holy water stoup ; (7) the vat and brush for sprinkling ; (8) the Crucifix affixed to the south wall near the font ; (9) a small Crucifix attached to the inside of the rector's pew, which pew had been proved to have been used as a confessional ; (10) the Veronica picture ; (11) the catafalque used in requiem masses ; (12) the sepulchre ; and (13) the English Missal.

Illegal Practices in Magnus Martyr. *The Times*, Letters. Wednesday, Aug 02, 1922.

" ILLEGAL PRACTICES."

No well-informed person is likely to object to Chancellor Errington's judgment in the case of St. Magnus the Martyr, especially as he dealt so courteously with its rector. As these ornaments and practices are "illegal" in St. Magnus, they are equally "illegal" in many hundreds of churches throughout the country. But a law which is not enforced, except in a sporadic manner, tends both to fall into disrepute and to awaken popular sympathy for its unlucky victims. If, however, the requirements of Parliamentary law are to be enforced against all churches of this group, then in ten years we shall have another powerful organization erected outside the Established Church ; and the problem of unity (or at least confederation) may be still further postponed, and the Parliamentary Church confronted by a strong and growing rival.—REV. J. PLOWDEN-WARDLAW, Rector of Beckenham.

Objections to Anglo-Catholic practices, *The Times* Tuesday, May 09, 1922; pg. 13.

ORTHODOX VIEWS CHANGING.

ARCHBISHOP ON THE FAITH.

A representative deputation of the clergy and laity of the Church of England waited upon the Archbishop of Canterbury yesterday to present a memorial bearing nearly 1,400 lay signatures and 500 clerical signatures, publicly protesting "against the violation of law, and neglect of moral obligations, which are now allowed to prevail among many of the clergy of the Church of England," and by which, the memorial declared, the whole basis of the Church as established by law is being undermined.

The memorialists declared that they desired only the observance of the doctrine and worship prescribed by the Book of Common Prayer, and the Articles of the Church of England, which are formally acknowledged by all clergy to be agreeable to the Word of God ; and they appealed to the authorities of the Church to maintain the rights of members of the Reformed Church of England in their most sacred interests.

Sir W. Joynson-Hicks, M.P., introducing the deputation, said they represented members of both Houses of Parliament, 44 members of the National Church Assembly, and a large number of clergy and laity. The memorial dealt with the spread of modernism and ritualism in the Church during the last 20 years. The deputation represented the great body of Church opinion which believed firmly in the old doctrines attacked by modernists and ritualists, and they appealed to the Archbishop, as head of the Church, to give them help and encouragement. They saw with grave anxiety the attitude taken up by the Cambridge Conference last year, and the new view taken by a great many Church writers and speakers as to the nature of God.

Since the Royal Commission of 1903 things have gone from bad to worse. The Roman Catholic Mass had been practised in St. Saviour's, Hoxton, and the Bishop was impotent to deal with it. At St. Magnus-the-Martyr, a presentation of the Bishop of London, there was even the service of the blackening of faces at the Communion rail on Ash Wednesday. A year ago a clergyman in the diocese of Bath and Wells, inhibited by the Bishop, left the Church of England, but, failing to get Orders in the Church of Rome, returned, and to the scandal of many Church-people, was permitted by the Bishop of London to act as curate at one of the extreme high churches in the East of London.

Bishop Ingham said the memorialists were not consciously serving any party in the Church. They came from no society—they were simply Church folk, who longed for some unity. But more vital than unity was the continuity of Faith as the Church of England had understood it for 350 years.

City Church Dispute. *The Times* Tuesday, Nov 21, 1922.

CITY CHURCH DISPUTE.

ORNAMENTS AT ST. MAGNUS THE MARTYR.

An order was made on July 29 by the Consistorial and Episcopal Court of London on the petition of certain parishioners of the united parishes of St. Magnus the Martyr, London Bridge, St. Margaret, New Fish-street, and St. Michael, Crooked-lane, that a faculty should issue for the removal from the Church of St. Magnus of certain articles or ornaments alleged to have been introduced without a faculty and to be illegal, the faculty to be suspended for a month to give the rector and churchwardens an opportunity of removing the articles. On November 7 the petitioners applied for the issue of a faculty, alleging that certain of the articles had not been removed, and that though some had been removed others of the same nature had been substituted without a faculty. A citation to all interested persons was therefore posted during the week-end by order of the vicar-general on the main door of the Church of St. Magnus, to show cause why the faculty directed to issue after the lapse of a month for the removal of the articles should not also authorize the removal of any substituted articles.

The reredos, Moses, Aaron, the New Testament, the Continuity of Scripture and the Scheme of Redemption. St. Magnus The Martyr. *The Times* (London, England), Monday, Mar 31, 1924; pg. 7.

THE RECTOR'S EVIDENCE.

The Rev. H. J. Fynes-Clinton, the rector of St. Magnus the Martyr, gave evidence in support of the petition. As to the proposed enlargement of the sanctuary, there was at present, he said, not sufficient room for the epistoler and gospeller and others to be there. The alterations in the reredos were matters of architectural beauty. Two things most prominent in the church were the pictures of Moses and Aaron as representing the Old Testament, and he desired to keep them. There was nothing there to represent the New Testament, and therefore he should like to have the figure of Our Saviour in order to show the continuity of Holy Scripture and the whole scheme of redemption. It was

St. Magnus-the-Martyr Chancellor's Judgement.

The altarpiece as an exception to superstitious abuse of imagery in churches. 'City Church's Ornaments' *The Times* (London, England), Monday, Apr 14, 1924; pg. 14.

With regard to No. 3⁻ (the reredos), the only objection taken was to the Rood figures forming the upper portion. There was a well-recognized distinction between figures forming part of a reredos and figures placed in isolated positions, and although these figures surmounted the reredos, they formed, in his opinion, an integral part of it and offered no likelihood of superstitious abuse. He therefore sanctioned this reredos.

Protestant Truth Society *The Times* Tuesday, May 19, 1925; pg. 18.
Evangelical Christianity as the Fundamnetal need of the world today.

Scriptures.   There were signs of the setting
up of a God of human reason in place of a
God of revelation.   Evangelical Christianity
was the fundamental need of the world to-day.
Mr. J. A. KENSIT said that the chief force
arrayed against English Protestantism was
Anglo-Catholicism.   One of the best illustrations of the defiant lawlessness of the Anglo-
Catholic party was seen in the case of St.
Magnus-the-Martyr, London Bridge. The
whole internal arrangements of that Wren
edifice had been transformed into a tawdry
imitation of a Romish chapel. The Bishop
of London's complicity in the matter was
perhaps the gravest scandal of all.